HOPE FOR BEREAVED

Understanding, Coping And Growing
Through Grief

A Handbook
of Helpful Articles
Written By Bereaved People
For Bereaved People and
Those Who Want to Help Them

by
Therese S. Schoeneck

Editor
Kathleen Jacques

Cover
Peggy Dupee

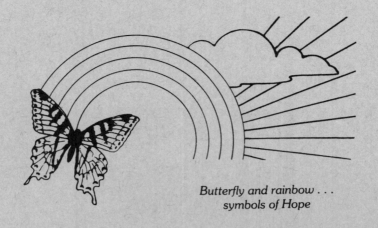

*Butterfly and rainbow . . .
symbols of Hope*

The colors of the rainbow were chosen for this book because the rainbow is an ancient symbol of HOPE. A butterfly is also a symbol of HOPE. For many people the butterfly signifies that life changes and goes on . . . going from this life to a new and better life. Just as a beautiful butterfly emerges from its cocoon, hopefully you will eventually emerge from your grief.

Quote on cover by Helen Keller

PRINTING HISTORY
First mimeographed edition September 1982
 (9 printings through September 1985)
Revised edition April 1986
Second printing March 1987
Third printing March 1988
Fourth printing June 1990
Fifth printing June 1991
Sixth printing January 1995
Printed in the United States of America

HOPE FOR BEREAVED, INC.
4500 Onondaga Boulevard
Syracuse, New York 13219

(315) 475-HOPE
475-4673
(315) 475-9675

HOW TO USE THIS BOOK

The section "When A Loved One Has Died" is written for anyone who has experienced the death of an infant, child, spouse, parent, sibling, relative or friend by illness, accident, suicide or murder. It is also offered to their relatives, friends and those professionals who wish to better understand grief and learn ways of reaching out to the bereaved. You may choose to read this entire section or specific articles as they apply. Then you may choose to read the following sections that apply to your particular bereavement. REPETITION: Since many concepts of grief are common to various experiences and feelings, you will find some duplication throughout the book. Inasmuch as some readers may want to read only the section that pertains to their current struggle, some repetition is necessary.

C O N T E N T S

I WASN'T GOING CRAZY . . .   I WAS GRIEVING

On August 21, 1977 my husband and I were sleeping peacefully at our camp. We were awakened by the ringing of the phone at 2:00 a.m. I could tell by my husband's responses that something was wrong. He turned from the phone and told me that our daughter, Mary, had been in an accident and was in Community Hospital. We threw on our clothes. As we were rushing out of camp I grabbed a book to read. I envisioned that she would have to stay in the hospital so I brought the book to read as I sat by her bed.

When we arrived at the hospital they ushered us into a room. My heart sank. I knew the news was going to be bad when they didn't bring us to her. Then the nurse told us Mary had been killed in a car accident—her neck was broken when the car hit a telephone pole. The nurse asked if we wanted to see her. I went in first. It was so hard to believe. She only had a little bandage on her head. It just looked as if she was asleep. She had on a plaid shirt, jeans and her favorite "shit kicker boots." I kissed her and told her that we loved her and I knew she would go to God. My interest in life after death plus my faith helped me as I stood in that hospital room. I reasoned that Mary might still hear me, as our hearing is the last to go, or she was in heaven; and either way she would hear me.

That fateful night began one of the most painful journeys of my life. I was not prepared for the strong feelings that slammed into me. At first I didn't believe it. I thought that it was a bad dream and I would wake up any minute. Much of the days surrounding the wake and funeral are a blur. Many people came to the wake but I only remember what two of them said. In each instance they said, "I know just how you feel." I screamed inside - "Oh no you don't!" Then they told me that they had a child die. I had worked with the first man for five years. His son had died six years before. The other couple's son had died ten years ago but we had only known them through church for five years. I remember thinking - they eat, go to work, look normal - somehow we will too - it was my first glimmer of HOPE.

I tried to be strong. With hindsight I now realize that such strength is not realistic and not helpful to you or your family. I would sob in the shower so my family wouldn't hear me. I started to swim a lot because I could cry in the lake and no one would know. Food no longer appealed to me. At first I lived on tea and Italian cookies. A week later I returned to work because I wanted to be busy - I didn't want time to think. Yet there were times that I would stop right in the middle of a sentence. I would forget what I was talking about. I would leave my desk and then forget what I was getting. It was difficult to concentrate.

In early October we went to a meeting in Denver. I slept, ate and felt so much better; I realized that I was removed from the reality of Mary's death. I wasn't expecting her to call or come through the door as I did when I was home. After we returned the reality hit. It scared me as I thought that I was getting worse - going backwards. I didn't think that I could feel any worse, but I did. When I really hit the pits I finally talked to two friends. It helped so much. I would be handling things fairly well for about three weeks and then I would start "sliding" down into the pits. After three weeks of "sliding" I would reach out for help. Talking about my feelings helped me to understand what aspect of grief was giving me trouble. This became a pattern that developed and was more acute at holidays and special family events. I hurt so much when I was in the pits that when I started to feel that I was going "down" again I would panic. Looking back it would seem that I should have realized that the "bad days" always passed and that I did feel better again. But grief wears you out. You don't think clearly. I couldn't figure out my anxious feelings and the pure panic of feeling so devastated. I remember thinking that not only had Mary died, but now I was going crazy. My family didn't need that too.

I couldn't believe the physical symptoms of grief. I lost my appetite and eventually lost 20 pounds. I had shaky legs, a knot in my stomach, sleeplessness and my throat felt like it had a carrot going sideways. I felt like the ad on television where the gorilla slams the suitcase all over his cage. It seemed that the feelings of grief were slamming me from wall to wall. I would drop exhausted until the next onslaught - the next feeling slammed into me. No matter what I was doing - working, driving, cleaning - Mary seemed to "sit over my left eye." I could think or work on other things but I also thought about Mary and her death. I eventually shared with my sister-in-law Carol and faithful friend Peggy that I didn't like the person I had become. I couldn't understand. I wasn't being a witch to my family or friends; if anything I was being nicer because I had became more aware of how important my family and friends were to me. Later, when I learned that a low self-esteem goes with the territory of grief, I felt my self-esteem rise.

In the years since Mary's death I have learned so much about grief and about life. I now know that I wasn't going crazy. I was experiencing the range of strong emotions that accompany the death of a loved one. I learned to "lean into my pain." I hated that advice because I didn't like to hurt, but I realized I had no choice. If I didn't lean into my pain I would become bitter and cold. It is called *grief work* and the term is so true. It was the hardest work that I have ever done.

After Mary's death I wanted so much to talk with others who had survived the death of their child. I would have gone hundreds of miles to be with people who had a similar experience. I hoped that maybe they had a magic formula to take the pain away or at least some ideas for coping. Our first Thanksgiving and Christmas had been so painful, even though as a family we had many caring people in our lives. Fifteen months after Mary's death, as Christmas was approaching, I suggested to my boss and friend, Fr. Joe Phillips, Director of Family Life Education, that I thought it would be helpful to hold a meeting for bereaved parents to talk about ways of coping with the holidays. During the meeting someone asked if we could meet the next month. That was the beginning of our HOPE FOR BEREAVED PARENT(S) monthly support group meetings. I was fortunate to work at Family Life Education (a department of the Diocese of Syracuse) and therefore was able to use the meeting rooms, office equipment and mailing permit.

I held the first meeting in order to help other bereaved parents. I never realized how much it would help me. Since I was one of the coordinators I had to be prepared to speak on a different topic each month. In order to do this I had to face my own feelings about anger, depression, expectations, etc. I also read a lot to gain more understanding. In talking and listening to other parents I learned that so many of my feelings were normal. It is really true that in helping others we ourselves are helped.

I never envisioned all the various support groups that would be formed or the many services that we would be able to offer. We would never be able to accomplish all this without our beautiful, dedicated volunteers. About four months after our first meeting, Donna Kalb offered to help. Her son had died four years before. Seeing how well she was doing gave me great hope that someday I would do as well. Donna's volunteering set the tone for the encouragement of other bereaved people to join us and for the shared decision making that holds true today. Currently over 200 volunteers help in so many ways: completing monthly mailings;

typing; processing labels; coordinating groups; writing articles; coordinating publicity; collating; recording; wrapping and mailing handbooks; providing telephone help; providing hospitality; sending condolence notes; doing fund-raising; providing community education, etc. Due to the greatly expanded requests for our services, in May, 1985 Christine Beattie became coordinator. The Rosamond Gifford Charitable Corporation funded this much-needed position.

This handbook started out as articles to be included with our monthly meeting notice. In June, 1982 I was asked to speak on grief at the annual fall meeting of the National Association of Diocesan Family Life Directors in San Diego. That prompted putting articles together and developing materials on how to start support groups. It has all been most rewarding.

It is possible to survive grief . . . to eventually even grow from it. I have come to treasure my memories with Mary and have become determined to build more memories with my family and friends. The bereaved volunteers have become my treasured friends.

I hope that the following pages will help you to understand your grief, to work on your grief and to grow through your grief. Hold onto HOPE that eventually you will find that life is worth living.

✳ ✳

"A CURE FOR SORROW"

There is an old Chinese tale about the woman whose only son died. In her grief, she went to the holy man and said, "What prayers, what magical incantations do you have to bring my son back to life?" Instead of sending her away or reasoning with her, he said to her, "Fetch me a mustard seed from a home that has never known sorrow. We will use it to drive the sorrow out of your life." The woman set off at once in search of that magical mustard seed. She came first to a splendid mansion, knocked at the door, and said, "I am looking for a home that has never known sorrow. Is this such a place? It is very important to me." They told her, "You've certainly come to the wrong place," and began to describe all the tragic things that had recently befallen them. The woman said to herself, "Who is better able to help these poor, unfortunate people than I, who have had a misfortune of my own?" She stayed to comfort them, then went on in her search for a home that had never known sorrow. But wherever she turned, in hovels and in palaces, she found one tale after another of sadness and misfortune. Ultimately, she became so involved in ministering to other people's grief that she forgot about her quest for the magical mustard seed, never realizing that it had in fact driven the sorrow out of her life.

WHEN A LOVED ONE HAS DIED

GRIEF DESCRIBED
THERE IS HELP
HOW DO I COPE?
QUESTIONS

EXPERIENCES OF GRIEF

Grief is a normal and natural reaction to the death of a loved one. Most of us are not prepared for the long journey of grief which is sometimes devastating, frightening, and often lonely. We may think, do, and say things that are very unlike us. There seems to be no respite, no end to the intense feelings that we experience.

Grief has been likened to a raw open wound. With great care it eventually will heal but there will always be a scar. Life will never be the same but eventually you will get better.

The experiences of grief have been compared to enduring a fierce storm at sea. The waves are peaked and close together ∿∿∿∿. Eventually the sea becomes calmer 〰〰〰 , but occasionally the storm regroups, strengthening without any warning. For several hours, days, or weeks, you may not feel grief; then suddenly you meet someone, or see something, or hear something, and grief resumes. It seems as if you are taking one step forward and two back.

Grief has its common and its unique sides. Although it is a universal experience, no two people grieve the same, even in the same family. Like a snowflake or a fingerprint, each person's grief has characteristics all its own.

It is important to understand some of the following concepts about grief:

GRIEF WORK The expression "grief work" is very true. It may be the hardest work that you will ever perform. It is draining.

CONTROL We CANNOT control the feelings that arise within us. These feelings come from deep inside, but we can choose what to do with them. We can accept or reject them. To deny only prolongs our grief. Remember, what we do determines whether we remain in our grief or survive. Feelings are not bad or wrong. They should be recognized and faced honestly.

CHOICES About grief: there are no choices, you MUST go through it. The expression of grief is essential for good emotional and physical health even though it is painful and difficult. There are no easy answers or short cuts, no way under, over, or around your grief. Although grief may hurt desperately, you must go through it.

MAJOR DECISIONS It is strongly suggested not to make major decisions (such as moving, money matters, etc.) unless absolutely necessary during the early stages of grief when judgment is cloudy. The conventional wisdom, "Never act in haste" was never more applicable.

LISTENER(S) Find someone who will listen. Talking is therapy.

GRIEF HAS NO TIMETABLE Grief often takes much longer than the bereaved or the people in their lives expect. It helps to take one hour, one day at a time.

REMEMBER People have a natural inclination to recover. Eventually you'll look back and realize; you weren't going crazy . . . you were grieving.

BE PATIENT WITH YOURSELF.   RECOVERING FROM GRIEF TAKES TIME.

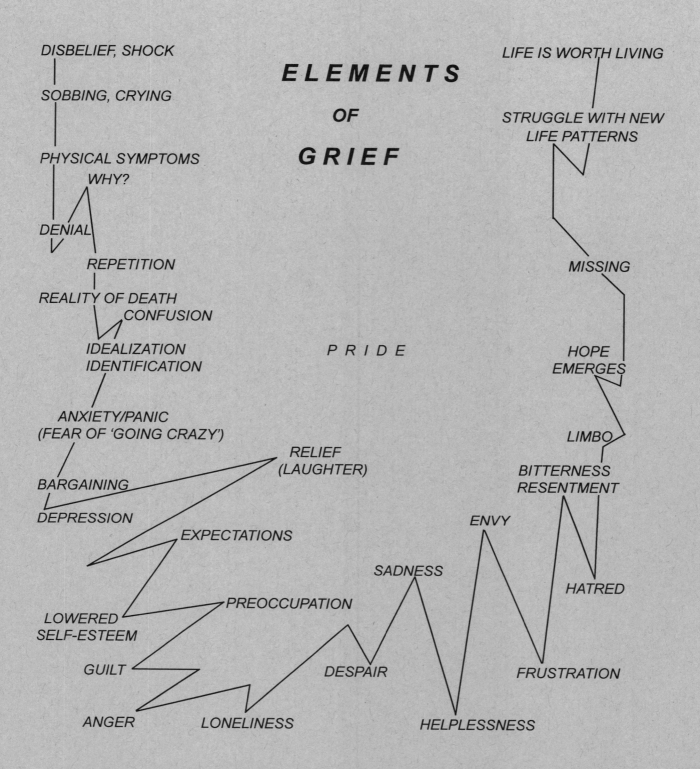

ELEMENTS

OF

GRIEF

DISBELIEF, SHOCK

SOBBING, CRYING

PHYSICAL SYMPTOMS
WHY?

DENIAL

REPETITION

REALITY OF DEATH
CONFUSION

IDEALIZATION
IDENTIFICATION

ANXIETY/PANIC
(FEAR OF 'GOING CRAZY')

BARGAINING

DEPRESSION

RELIEF
(LAUGHTER)

EXPECTATIONS

LOWERED
SELF-ESTEEM

PREOCCUPATION

GUILT

ANGER

LONELINESS

DESPAIR

SADNESS

HELPLESSNESS

PRIDE

ENVY

FRUSTRATION

HATRED

BITTERNESS
RESENTMENT

LIMBO

HOPE
EMERGES

MISSING

STRUGGLE WITH NEW
LIFE PATTERNS

LIFE IS WORTH LIVING

It is important to understand the various elements of grief. The graph gives the picture of grief, but it may be misleading. Everyone does not necessarily go through every element, nor do they go through them in any set order. Each person has his or her own timetable and his or her own style of grief. You may struggle with several feelings at the same time. The depth and duration of each experience is different for everyone. You may experience a feeling briefly, intermittently or struggle with it daily. Understanding the various phases helps you to cope. Knowing that others have gone through this pain and have eventually been able to reinvest themselves in life gives one a sense of HOPE.

DISBELIEF: "It can't be true." You keep thinking that any minute you will wake up from a nightmare. Sometimes you can't cry at first because you don't really believe it happened. Often people will comment on how well you are doing. Inside you know that the reason you appear to be doing so well is that you just don't believe it.

SHOCK: Shock is nature's way of softening the blow. It serves as a cushion - giving you time to absorb the fact of your loss. You hear the words, but do not comprehend the full impact. Emotions seem frozen. You feel disoriented, restless, numb, bewildered, stunned and unable to think. It takes everything just to function. You go through the motions like a robot and feel as if you are an observer watching this happen to someone else.

SOBBING / CRYING: Sobbing means to weep aloud with short, gasping breaths. Sobbing is an outlet for the deep strong emotions that accompany the death of a loved one. Some people cry often and cry a lot. Others push down their tears, but this may lead to psychological or physical problems. It is helpful to cry - to release all that pent-up emotion. Cry alone or with others - but take time to cry. The book WHEN GOING TO PIECES HOLDS YOU TOGETHER, says it very well. The advice "don't cry" is ill advised. Accept the grief - don't try to be brave and fight it. At first, you need to take time to grieve daily. Looking at pictures/mementos, playing special music, may aid in releasing pent-up tears. Men can and should cry. Crying is a good model for children. When adults cry, children learn that it is "okay" to cry and to express their feelings. Children learn to share their feelings instead of suppressing them and struggling alone.

PHYSICAL SYMPTOMS: You may experience some of the following: lack or increase of appetite; sleeplessness or oversleeping; knot or emptiness in pit of stomach; tightness in throat; shaky legs; headaches; stomach aches; sighing to get your breath; trembling; chills; fatigue; chest pains; general achiness; difficulty swallowing and/or speaking; digestive disorders (indigestion, nausea, diarrhea); feeling weak or faint; tension; slower in speech or movement; temporary paralysis of limb or sight. It helps to understand some of these symptoms may be a part of grief and emerge any time. It is advisable to have a physical checkup to make sure that there is not another cause for your physical ailments. Take care of yourself by establishing a simple routine (good nutrition, adequate rest and time for relaxation). Exercise aids sleep and may lighten depression.

DENIAL: The phone will ring, the door opens, or you will see someone, and at first you think that it is your loved one. You may subconsciously be searching for your loved one when out in a crowd. It takes time to believe what happened. Even though you know the fact of death, you continue not to really believe it. Many habits continue, such as setting the table for the same number, expecting your loved one to come home at the regular time, buying his/her favorite food, watching a TV program and saying: "I've got to tell him/her what happened." This shows our unconscious denial of death. Denial provides a buffer zone from the reality of what has happened.

WHY?: Often we keep asking "WHY?" "Why did he/she have to die?" We don't necessarily expect an answer, but the question "WHY" seems to need to be asked repeatedly in an effort to make sense of the loss. The question may be unanswered, but it is important to ask the question until we can take the step of letting the question go. Rabbi Kushner states in his book WHEN BAD THINGS HAPPEN TO GOOD PEOPLE that often the "why" is not a question, but a cry of pain.

REPETITION: You may find that you are saying almost the same things to the same people. The same thoughts keep running through your head. In saying the words and hearing ourselves over and over again, it helps us to believe what has happened. It is important to find friends who will listen, especially someone who has experienced a similar sorrow.

REALITY OF DEATH: "It's true." "It really happened." This is a frightening time. We feel that we are getting worse. Often this happens after people who have been so helpful have returned to their own busy lives. It seems as if we are going backwards. Actually, this reality has to "hit." The best advice is to "lean into the pain." As much as we don't want to hurt, we must.

CONFUSION: "I can't think." "I forget what I am saying halfway through a sentence." The simplest decisions seem impossible. It is difficult to concentrate and follow through on things. You feel disorganized and error-prone. Bereaved often feel impatient and want to do something, but feel unclear as to what to do. Sometimes motivation to do something may be very low and basic survival needs may not even be met. Confusion abounds because you are using all your emotional energy to grieve and there is very little left over for anything else. The weariness due to grief may affect thinking and concentration.

IDEALIZATION: At first, you may only focus on the best qualities - seeing your loved one as perfect. It is a very normal reaction, but it is important to be aware of others in the family. They may compare themselves to the "perfect" loved one and feel that they are not as loved - that it would be better if they had died instead.

IDENTIFICATION: Many people seek to identify with their loved one who has died by wearing their clothes, taking up a sport they liked, planning to follow in their footsteps, etc. It is a way of "staying close."

ANXIETY / PANIC: (Fear of "Going Crazy"): At first you may fear being alone. You worry about the future and may be afraid that something else will happen to another loved one. You often panic at the approach of special dates (birthday, holidays, anniversary of the death). Usually they are not as difficult as the days prior to the special days. This is due to our unbelievable panic and apprehension. You may feel as if you are "GOING CRAZY." It may seem as if you are losing control of yourself. Usually we don't tell anyone that we think we are "going crazy." Sometimes bereaved have thoughts of suicide as the only way to escape the physical and emotional pain. We panic at the prospect of "always feeling like this." We feel that we should be doing better and panic when we don't. Our situation may seem hopeless and our thinking becomes jumbled. Panic is normal. If panic seems intolerable, you need to do something about it. Talking about our feelings, getting busy with something, sobbing, screaming, exercise - all may help to release the "panicky" feelings. Emotional and physical fatigue contribute to our panic. Good nutrition and rest are vital.

BARGAINING: You want "things to be as they were." You may hope that just wishing will bring back the person. You may try to bargain with God that "things will be different;" that you will try to be a better person if only the loved one can be alive again.

DEPRESSION: It is a feeling of being in the "pits." You hurt so much. Sometimes you just don't care about anything. You just sit. Mornings are terrible. So is the time and the day of the week that your loved one died. It's an effort just to get out of bed, to shop, or fix a simple meal. Talk things over with a friend who cares and will listen. This helps a person to avoid becoming seriously depressed. Talking to others in a support group of bereaved people who know what you are going through also helps a great deal.

SEVERE DEPRESSION: It is a feeling of deep, overwhelming sadness and hopelessness that lasts for longer than two weeks. Other symptoms may be: loss of appetite; insomnia; inability to enjoy anything; anxious or restless behavior; apathy; preoccupation with thoughts of suicide; wishing to be dead; loss of interest in sex; difficulty in concentration and making decisions; poor memory; irritability; feelings of worthlessness; inability to cry even if one desperately needs and wants to; intense guilt and withdrawal from relatives and friends. It is important for bereaved people not to become alarmed, because everyone experiences some or all of these symptoms at some time. If six or more of these symptoms are severe and continue over an extended period of time (so that pain and problems outweigh pleasure much of the time), then it would be advisable to get professional help.

RELIEF (Laughter): This phase comes and goes. Often after the reality "hits," or after a particularly troublesome time, you feel better and may even think that the difficult times are over. There is a sense of great relief at no longer feeling down. Appreciate the relief . . .the grief will return soon enough. It is helpful to recall the fun times. Wholesome fun and laughter are beneficial. It is not being disloyal to our loved one to enjoy life. In fact, plan things to which you can look forward. Having a sense of humor is often mentioned by bereaved as being helpful.

EXPECTATIONS: We often expect too much of ourselves. We want to handle the grief better and more quickly than is humanly possible. Submerging our feelings is very detrimental because we still have to face these feelings eventually. The expectations of others, "You must be over your grief by now," only add to our burden. Often we will expect that after the holidays, or after some special day, we will feel "much better." This kind of expectation only hinders the grief process. It is more helpful not to have a timetable of how we should feel, or when we will get better. Taking one day at a time, or half a day, or one hour at a time is more realistic.

LOWERED SELF-ESTEEM: A bereaved person's confidence is often undermined. In a study on self-esteem using a scale of 100, it was found that an average person's self-esteem was in the 70's and generally a bereaved person's was in the teens. Understanding the impact of grief on your self-esteem may help you find ways of coping.

PREOCCUPATION: Your loved one who has died may be in your thoughts constantly. You may think of nothing but the loss. You may even dream of your loved one, or be preoccupied with his/her image. Even at work, church, doing the dishes — in fact, no matter what you are doing — you may find that part of your thoughts are always about your loved one. The intensity of this preoccupation usually lessens with time.

GUILT: Many people are tortured by "if onlys," and "what ifs." "If only I had called;" "If only we hadn't let him/her take the car that night;" or "If only I had taken time to listen and visit." We tend to blame ourselves for something we did or didn't do that may have contributed to the death, or for things that we wish we had done for our loved one. Feelings of guilt are normal, though often not realistic. It is best not to push down the guilt. Talk about it until you can let it go. Hopefully, in time, you will realize that you did the best you could under the circumstances. None of us are perfect. The past is behind us. All we can do with guilt is to learn from it for the other people in our lives. When the death is by suicide, it is especially important to remember we can't control the behavior of another person.

ANGER: Anger may be directed at ourselves; others (including family members, spouse, doctors, nurses, person who caused accident); the person who died; God; or we may experience a general irritability. We may feel angry toward people who push us to accept our loss too soon, or who pretend that nothing happened. Anger is normal. Pushing down anger is harmful and may cause things like ulcers, high blood pressure, or depression. Unacknowledged anger may be directed at innocent people and unrelated events. It will come out one way or another. It is often difficult to admit being angry. Erroneously we may think, "nice people don't get angry." It is important to recognize our anger. It is helpful to find ways to express our anger, such as screaming in a private place, walking, swimming, aerobic classes, keeping a journal, tennis, golf- even installing a punching bag in our home. Talking about our anger also helps us to define, understand, and learn how to handle it. To suppress anger can lead to deeper than normal depression and bitterness. It is important to acknowledge our anger and to take steps to handle it.

LONELINESS: After the initial help, relatives' and friends' lives return to normal and we are often left to deal with our grief alone. Co-workers, friends, neighbors and sometimes even family may avoid us or change the subject. Some friends withdraw, because they are hurting, and do not know how to help us. We often become isolated in our grief. The widowed often say, "I not only lost my spouse, but my friends as well." In reality, few people are able to help or to understand. Support groups can be helpful. Some aspects of grief cannot be totally shared, even in the same family. It is difficult for husbands and wives to help each other. As Harriett Schiff, author of THE BEREAVED PARENT, states: "It is difficult to lean on someone who is already doubled over in pain." Especially at first when we are hurting so much, we realize that we are not much fun for others to be around. When others have all their loved ones alive, it makes us feel even lonelier. We may feel intense loneliness due to the absence of our loved one, because we are unable to share thoughts and feelings, to touch, to be understood. We feel empty without our loved one.

DESPAIR: "How can I go on?" You may come to the point where the agony seems intolerable. You can't bear it - you think that you won't be able to survive. Your hopes and dreams are dashed. It may seem as if there would be little difference if you lived or died. You may have suicidal thoughts. Feelings of desperation, despondency, pessimism and loss of all hope seem to surround you. If you are a smoker you may smoke more than ever due to nervousness, or to an attitude that you don't care if you ever take care of yourself again. Sometimes it is blackest before the burden of grief begins to lift. Talk to someone who has made it through grief.

SADNESS: We miss our loved one and feel deprived of his/her presence. We may feel unhappy, inconsolable, distressed, sorrowful, dejected and heartbroken. These feelings seem to pervade our life.

HELPLESSNESS: "What am I going to do?" We feel helpless about our feelings --- our grief. It seems as if we are unable to help ourselves to cope, or to get better. We do not seem to be capable of aiding other family members. We may feel self-pity. Although we realize that we had no control over what happened, we feel a sense of powerlessness at not being able to prevent it.

ENVY: You may feel jealous of people who still have their loved ones to enjoy. With a child's death, dreams for their future are gone. This pertains to college, job, wedding, grandchildren - things you would have shared together. When a spouse dies, you envy others watching their children and grandchildren grow up and enjoying retirement together.

FRUSTRATION: Many frustrations are a part of our grief. "Why am I feeling so upset for so long?" We become disappointed with ourselves that we are not coping as well as we think we should. So many impulses, thoughts, feelings and actions that had become habits are stopped in mid-course. We are left with these unfulfilled emotions, desires and thoughts buzzing about in our heads or sitting in our stomachs.

RESENTMENT / BITTERNESS / HATRED: Bereaved people often feel resentful about the death and their changed circumstances. Sometimes there is a (sub)conscious hostility toward others whose families are still intact. Some bereaved feel hatred toward those responsible for the death. These bitter feelings should be recognized and worked on, or the bitterness could last for many years. Hatred and bitterness drain you of energy and may be destructive to your health and relationships. When these feelings are left unattended, healing becomes blocked.

LIMBO: Eventually we may reach an in-between point between the reality of death and the point where life seems worthwhile again. We may feel a little better at last, but be uncertain of what to do next. It may take much longer than we would like before our zest for living returns. We often live behind a facade - masking our feelings and saying that "we are fine."

HOPE EMERGES: You realize that your grief is softening. At first the pain was with you constantly. Now the pain of grief is briefer and comes less frequently. The good days outbalance the bad days. You feel encouraged that you will get better. Things like shopping (which had been so painful before), painting the living room, looking forward to events, etc., all become a part of your life again. Once again you are effective at work and home, able to make decisions and handle problems. Generally you are able to sleep and eat as you did before. You are able to care about others. You begin to realize that you are moving forward and can once again enjoy life. You smile and laugh again and are rewarded with the smiles of family, friends and strangers.

MISSING: You will always miss your loved one. Special family events, such as holidays, birthdays, weddings, anniversaries, even a song or a special TV program, will trigger the feeling of longing for your loved one. Seeing other families enjoying special events "that might have been for you" also deepens your feeling of yearning. You can't help but wish your loved one were alive. You miss countless things that were special about your relationship . . . a hug, a kiss, a smile, a phone call, or hearing them say "I Love You," or "Thank You." For some people, when there was a special relationship, the missing can be more acute. If relatives live out of town, they may find coming home for a visit especially difficult. Their feelings of missing, anger, guilt, etc., may be intensified. The reality of the death is more believable at home where their loved one is undeniably missing.

STRUGGLE WITH NEW LIFE PATTERNS: You realize that you have a choice. You can rebuild a new life. It will be different without your loved one, but life can be enjoyed again. It is important to seek meaning in living. Learn how to make happiness happen in your life. It is estimated that over 70% of marriages where a child has died become endangered and end in separation or divorce. It is important to be aware of such statistics and to renew the marriage. You need to reinvest in work, activities and friends. New friends can be found among other bereaved. You may find it necessary or helpful to move, find a job, do volunteer work, join a support group, etc. Be open to renewing familiar patterns and friendships, but be ready to try new ways of living.

LIFE IS WORTH LIVING: Eventually we are able to think and talk about our loved one with happiness and a sense of peace. We have learned to accept the death and can see options and possibilities for the future. We may experience renewed meaning in life. There is the possibility of emotional, spiritual and personal growth. Often we become a different person - stronger, more involved, wiser, more compassionate, concerned, understanding and aware. Our loved ones have entered a beautiful new life without pain and problems. We will be together someday. Meanwhile, they would want us to live, love and appreciate this life and the people in our life to the fullest.

PRIDE: This feeling was not listed on the original graph and yet, for many of us, it greatly affected how we handled our grief. It is placed in the middle of the graph to show how it can negatively color so many other experiences of grief. For many of us, we are too "proud" to ask for or accept help. When asked how we are feeling we say "fine" when in reality we are falling apart inside. We are apt to think "I can do it by myself," not realizing how unprepared we are for the death of a loved one. Sharing such deep grief does help us to cope and understand. The word "proud" means to hold one's self high, to turn one's head. Bereaved so often do this to overcompensate for how really low they feel. We are stubborn about letting anyone know how we feel. This makes it difficult for others to give us the help we so desperately need. We should consider if our grief is being complicated by our PRIDE, and if so work on ourselves to ask for and accept help.

****

THE BUTTERFLY

Out of the tragedy of the Nazi concentration camps comes a beautiful story. In the children's camps, boys and girls began to scratch out butterflies on the walls in reaction to their dismal prospects of surviving. These drawings became a network of communication among the children. Those who understood and drew these wonderful creatures belonged to the club of the butterfly. The butterfly therefore symbolized youth, life, and HOPE.

EXPECTATIONS

There is very little written about expectations in the life of the grieving person. Many times the unrealistic expectations of ourselves and of others can greatly hinder the eventual readjustment for the bereaved. In wishing to "handle it better," we often keep expecting more from ourselves than is possible at this time. When we don't feel better, or act better, and yet think that we should, we become disappointed in ourselves. We have just expected too much of ourselves.

A timetable for grief may be part of the expectation. If I read that one stage took a certain length of time and I wasn't there yet, I would panic that I wasn't "where I should be."

Often family and friends unwittingly place expectations on us. "It has been 3 weeks," "3 months" or "8 months" and "you must be better now" "you must be back to normal." These expressed or even implied, unrealistic expectations by or of others become a pressure on the bereaved.

After the shock and denial, the very pain-filled reality hits. This grief is unbearable heartache and sorrow. Unbearable, yet we have no choice. We must go through it. Complicating this stage is the fact that most people expect that by now you're recovering, when in reality you are not. Many find talking about their feelings helps. Generally, thinking them out is not enough, since usually grief feelings can't be intellectualized away or thought away. A common experience of many grieving people is that the people we expect to be most supportive often move away from us just when we need them most. This bewildering phenomenon can be attributed in part to a general lack of knowledge of what grief is, leading to unrealistic expectations being placed on the bereaved person. Sometimes it is helpful to communicate about our loss with someone new, since some old friends often just want us to return to our old selves again, which is unrealistic on their part.

After the holidays or anniversary of the death, grieving people may expect that everything will be much better. The New Year is often a time of resolutions - of intending to change some habit or attitude. It is not helpful to expect to be much better. When things do not get better, we become discouraged. It may be more helpful to consider January 1 as the day after December 31. Without such unrealistic expectations of the New Year, or of the time after the anniversary, it may gradually become a time of healing and growth; not because we expected it, but because we did not have unrealistic expectations. It is important not to have a timetable for grief.

IT WILL NEVER BE THE SAME . . .

Unrealistically we hope that things will somehow be the same . . . that our life - our family - will get back to "normal." As time goes on, we realize that "it will never be the same." We will always miss our loved one who has died. At special holidays and family gatherings, there is always one person missing. Some family members and friends assume that we are back to normal. They just do not understand.

BUT
E...V...E...N..T...U...A...L...L...Y
LIFE SHOULD GET BETTER

At first, we are in shock — it is difficult to think clearly — to imagine that we will ever be able to function. When the reality "hits," we usually feel more devastated. It just seems that life will forever be like this. Some bereaved do stay at this phase. Most bereaved, with time and a great deal of effort, do "get better." They recognize that life will never be the same, but the people in their lives become more treasured than ever. Many bereaved grow from their experience of grief -they reach out to others in need. EVENTUALLY, life picks up and goes on. The pain subsides. We can laugh, make plans, work, enjoy things, relax, pray . . . in other words, become involved in life again. It doesn't happen overnight. It may take years, but hold on to HO P E and keep trying.

A MOTHER LOOKS BACK

For me, grief took much longer than I expected. Lack of sleep and overactivity took their toll. I learned that I should be much gentler with myself, lower my EXPECTA-TIONS and throw out my subconscious timetable. I would recognize that pride often kept me from getting the help or support that I needed. Frequently, I check to see that I have "balance" in my life. If there had been a support group when Mary died, I would have been in the front row. The support group meetings and friendships that I have formed with other bereaved people have been invaluable to me in my understanding, acceptance and in my reinvestment in life. Reading also helped me to understand grief and why I felt as I did. For many of us our faith that our loved one is in heaven and that we will all be together again has kept us going through the rough times, and offers hope in the future. Lean into your pain - don't put it on a shelf. You can't go around it, over it, or under it. You must go through it. I have learned to . . .

TAKE
ONE DAY,
ONE HOUR
AT A TIME

ON DEALING WITH DEATH
by Rev. Kenneth Czillinger

1. Generally it takes 18-24 months just to STABILIZE after the death of a family member. It can take much longer when the death was a violent one. Recognize the length of the mourning process. Beware of developing unrealistic expectations of yourself.

2. Your worst times usually are not at the moment a tragic event takes place. Then you're in a state of shock or numbness. Often you slide "into the pits" 4-7 months after the event. Strangely, when you're in the pits and tempted to despair, this may be the time when most people expect you to be over your loss.

3. When people ask you how you're doing, don't always say, "fine." Let some people know how terrible you feel.

4. Talking with a true friend or with others who've been there and survived can be very helpful. Those who've been there speak your language. Only they can say, "I know, I understand." You are not alone.

5. Often depression is a cover for anger. Learn to uncork your bottle and find appropriate ways to release your bottled-up anger. What you're going through seems so unfair and unjust.

6. Take time to lament, to experience being a victim. It may be necessary to spend some time feeling sorry for yourself. "Pity parties" sometimes are necessary and can be therapeutic.

7. It's all right to cry, to question, to be weak. Beware of allowing yourself to be "put on a pedestal" by others who tell you what an inspiration you are because of your strength and your ability to cope so well. If they only knew!

8. Remember you may be a rookie at the grief experience you're going through. This may be the first death of someone close. You're new at this, and you don't know what to do or how to act. You need help.

9. Reach out and try to help others in some small ways at least. This little step forward may help prevent you from dwelling on yourself.

10. Many times of crisis ultimately can become times of opportunity. Mysteriously, your faith in yourself, in others and in God can be deepened through crisis. Seek out persons who can serve as symbols of hope to you.

Rev. Kenneth Czillinger, of Cincinnati, Ohio, has been involved in bereavement work since 1972. Permission to reprint granted by Rev. Czillinger.

"WHEN WILL I GET BETTER?
by Mickey Vorobel

The question "When will I get better?" is asked by many people who have had a loved one die. Unknowingly, you have just displayed progress in the healing process. Remember that there is no "timetable" on how long it will take for you to actually feel better. I think one of the important factors to bear in mind is that you are NO LONGER the same person you were before your loved one died.

It sometimes feels as though you are born all over again, only this time as an adult with a broken heart. Well-meaning families and friends at times expect too much of us, only because they have never experienced the agony of the death of a loved one. Bear in mind that for every step we take forward, we take two steps backward; but when we take that one forward, it is a major accomplishment.

I guess one of the first signs of my getting better was when I read back through some of my feelings that I wrote down well over a year and a half ago. It has always been my goal to write a book about my son's suicide. When I read some of the notes, I was shocked and surprised at how I felt; each page was filled with pain, anger, bitterness, my own suicide thoughts and I always ended each page with, When will I get better?"

No earth-shattering answers will come to any of us during the grief process. Somehow we develop a strength on our own of learning to cope and deal with it. You cannot go around it, under it, or over it, as I tried so many times - YOU must go through it to survive.

Ironically, we have no choice when our loved one dies; it is out of our control, but we do have a choice in healing ourselves. It's the hardest task we will ever have to perform.

Getting better came to me by being active in our Bereaved Parents Group. In the early stages of my healing process, I could only attend the meetings and sit and listen. I was too overwhelmed with pain, anger and guilt to say anything. By becoming involved and listening to others, I had a sense of feeling that "I was getting better." Just being around other parents reduced the intensity of my pain; I began to see a light at the end of my tunnel of nightmares.

Don't be afraid to keep a private diary. Write down your thoughts and feelings, and in time to come you too will be amazed when you look back. It is difficult to remember how you felt each week, but when you have it in writing, believe me, you will find that you are getting better.

Mickey Vorobel has been an active participant in the Bereaved Parent and Survivors support groups both in Binghamton and Syracuse. She founded the Support Group for Survivors in Binghamton.

"WILL THINGS EVER BE THE WAY THEY WERE?"
by Mark Scrivani

In one of the old "Leave it to Beaver" television episodes, Beaver anticipates with great joy and excitement seeing one of his old buddies that he hasn't seen for five years. Now a young teenager, he can't wait to play "Cowboy and Indians." He had the whole weekend planned with a full agenda, doing all the things he and his friend used to do. When he sees his pal they start right in playing the games of their youth. Their intense fun lasts only a short while, and Beaver quickly begins to realize that he's becoming bored. By the end of the weekend, the whole adventure has been a great disappointment. In the final segment, Beaver says to his father, "Gee Dad, I guess doing all the things I did as a kid just aren't that much fun anymore."

We all have a need to return to, and maintain, normalcy, particularly after a major loss such as the death of a loved one. The return to a "normal" lifestyle is important, but it is also important to keep what will be "normal" in perspective. One of the wonders of life is the constant change that takes place. I believe that nothing is the same from one day to the next. The changes are usually imperceptible and often insignificant enough that we believe we are in a routine. It is only when a great change occurs that we devote our energies to dealing with the loss and the grieving process.

Let us examine ourselves for a moment. I am not the same person I was a generation, a year, a week, or even an hour ago. Neither are you. We are constantly changing beings, and nature gives us the incredible power to constantly adapt to these changes, both small and large. Of course, the larger the change, the longer the amount of time we need to adapt. There is no greater change in our lives than the death of a loved one, and our mourning process must act accordingly. A paramount aspect of change and loss is that we do grow from it. Difficult? Yes. Painful? Without question. I remind you that when children grow physically, they occasionally experience physical pain. We call this process "growing pains." It is vital to keep in mind that growing pains also exist emotionally, psychologically, and spiritually when we grieve. There is no escape from the pain, but to avoid the pain would cheat us from further growth.

We tend to hold on to the past, particularly when we are dealing with the loss of a loved one. But "holding on" implies a stunting of ourselves. Perhaps we can allow ourselves to "let go" and thereby "live with" the past. We can then allow ourselves to learn, cherish, appreciate and grow from the legacy our loved ones left behind. In this way, we can keep the loved one alive and vital in such a way that no monument, altar or untouched room could possibly provide in and of itself.

It is good to remember how it was, but know that the life of yesterday can never be the life of today, even if our loved ones who died were able to return. I do not deny that for many of you, life was more pleasant when the deceased person was alive. Yet, even if we had the power to turn back the hands of time, we ourselves would be veritable strangers to that time. Remember, time is our friend, not our enemy. Time can provide us with the opportunity to grow, to remember, to improve ourselves, to know what we have gained from the short time we spent with our loved ones. Time continues, it does not stop or go back. Time forces us to walk through our grief. Even when we experience our "relapses," our emotional roller coaster during mourning, time helps us to know that in reality we are growing.

There is increasing proof that life after life does indeed exist. Death is not the opposite of life, but a transition to a new, more spectacular life. Nature provides us with a clue to this "secret" when we observe the caterpillar spin its winter cocoon, and become a springtime butterfly. And when we are finally reunited with our loved ones, it is not a reunion at all - because they were always with us, and we were always with them.

Mark Scrivani is the coordinator of "Hope For Youth" support group. He has experienced the death of a brother and his father. Mark is the author of several books on grief for children. To purchase his books, see the order form in the back of this book. Mark is a therapist in private practice.

It's OK To Be Selfish During Grief
by Rev. Richard B. Gilbert

Healthy grieving is selfish grieving. It is the self (*my* life, *my* context, *my* feelings, *my* dreams, *my* relationships, *my* expectations, *my* needs) that has been most hurt by this significant death.

When you allow yourself to own your own needs and claim them, you can begin to have a healthy, whole sense of grieving that not only better addresses your journey but also can better equip the others who depend on you in life.

"A MESSAGE FROM MARY"

This cartoon was given to me by our daughter, Mary, the spring before she died. She knew I liked the saying, "Take time to smell the flowers." I placed it on the freezer door with a magnet. A year or so after Mary died, it caught my attention. I have had copies made and often remind myself of its message for me.

TAKE TIME TO:

Relax - laugh - have fun.
Enjoy our family and friends.
Appreciate the world we live in.
Go for a walk.
Slow down a bit.
Try to LIVE LIFE to the fullest.

Therese Schoeneck

"A word of advice, sir-take time to smell the flowers along the way!"

ELEMENTS OF A STABBED / BROKEN HEART
by Rev. Kenneth Czillinger

1. You miss what you received. Separation causes a tremendous void or hole in your life. Part of you dies.

2. Emptiness - loneliness - quiet - a sense of being incomplete - all change the meaning of your home.

3. Words cannot express the pain caused by the loss of affection and touch in your life.

4. You feel cheated. Hopes - dreams - plans have been crushed.

5. You are haunted by if's - if onlys - regrets - painful memories.

6. You may not know the whole truth about the causes of death or the circumstances surrounding the death.

7. You experience being tormented by "videotape replays" of an inappropriate or unhappy death.

8. You have had a bad experience with persons - systems you expected to support you (i.e., life squad, hospital, doctor, nurse, clergy, funeral director).

9. Fear of whether you can go on living disturbs you.

10. You feel rejected, deserted, abandoned, useless, not needed anymore.

11. It takes time for the fullness of the reality to sink in. You never again will see your loved one(s) here on earth. The absence, the letting go, the good-bye is permanent.

12. You experience psychic numbness, a sense of being unprepared for the death, that you're in the midst of a nightmare or on some "fantasyland" trip.

13. You are overwhelmed by questions and doubts; about yourself, about your future, about others, about God - Church - Temple - Faith.

14. You definitely are the victim of a horrible tragedy. You have a right to lament.

15. Anger, guilt and depression are three emotions you experience a lot. Learn to "uncork your bottle" and appropriately release these and other emotions.

16. You worry about being a burden to others. You don't want to trouble people, to bother them, to upset their lives.

17. Wherever you go, whatever you do, you find no peace.

18. Hurtful comments from others add to your grief.

19. Even though you "hurt like hell", you have to play a role as actor/actress and not show your hurt.

20. You are tempted to avoid - run from the truth about the death or dying process.

21. Unfortunately, you carry additional crosses besides the death.

22. It is hard to tell people later on who did not know about the death.

23. You fail to share your grief because you've been "put on a pedestal" by others and you choose to try and live up to the image of being an inspiration.

ELEMENTS OF HEALING

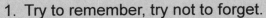

1. Try to remember, try not to forget.
2. Good memories (*I remember when*...stories) are important.
3. Time can result in either healing or infection.
4. You need support from both inside and outside your family.
5. Faith - Prayer - Community of Faith; where would you turn without them?
6. Learning about the experience of others gives insight into your own story.
7. Assume whatever you are going through is normal.
8. Share the pain of your darkness.
9. Be sensitive to the fact that people grieve differently.
10. Sharing with those who have been there has a special meaning.
11. Feel free to protest the "why" of death.
12. Take time and space for yourself and work through your guilt over doing so.
13. Take time to laugh and to cry.
14. Take the initiative and make things happen for yourself; work, activity, exercise.
15. Life will never be like it was. You will need to create a new life, make new choices, develop new friendships.
16. Reach out and help others. Beware of dwelling on yourself.
17. Confront guilt by realizing you did the best you could. ("All things considered, with no rehearsal for what you went through, you did the best you could".)
18. Be grateful if you experience a happy death.
19. You must let go of your loved one(s).
20. Through dreams, visions and other means, it is possible to experience the comforting and reassuring presence of your loved one(s). Don't be afraid to ask God for some sign of your loved one(s) presence.
21. There is nothing wrong with talking to the dead.
22. Persons who have been down the road before you can be symbols of hope.
23. Your experience of death may cause others to make significant changes for the better in their lives and relationships.

Rev. Kenneth Czillinger discusses his "Elements" in an eight cassette album from N. C. R. cassettes entitled "A TIME TO GRIEVE," available at most religious book stores. He is well known nationally for his work with bereaved people.

Permission to reprint granted by Rev. Czillinger.

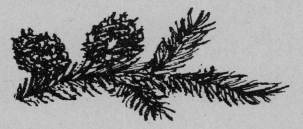

JULY 4TH - NOT ALWAYS A CELEBRATION
by Pat Fatti

The Fourth of July is an American holiday to which everyone looks forward. Families and friends gather together for picnics, cookouts, fireworks, parades, swimming, boating and the beginning of summer vacations. It is a wonderful day.

The Fourth of July has a different ring for our family. We still plan on being together, but one of our children will be terribly missed and thought about as we gather on that day. It was July 4th, 1980 that we witnessed that terrible boat accident on Skaneateles Lake. On that day, our long-time friends, Ruth, Dick, and their daughter Susan, were spending the holiday with us at our summer house on the lake. Our three daughters and a son (our oldest son was interning in Connecticut) were there with their friends and other family members. The weather was beautiful and everyone was having a nice day swimming, water-skiing, eating, playing games and just visiting. We planned to display fireworks that evening.

About 7:30 p.m. our Lisa (10) and Susan (12), who were wearing their life jackets, received permission from their fathers to use the rowboat. There was not much activity on the lake. Our daughter Mary Pat and her boyfriend were in the motorboat, pulling her older brother Frank on water skis. Another daughter Carol, her boyfriend and other relatives were on shore, watching. Ruth and I were in the back yard playing badminton. We were looking for Susan and Lisa to play, not knowing they were in the boat.

Suddenly we heard this loud noise, and went running. Another motorboat pulling a skier ran over the girls' rowboat and the girls were in the water. Mary Pat and her boyfriend went to the overturned boat and jumped into the water. Mary Pat started screaming - I thought it was Lisa. Another boat went to help and they took Susan to shore. Mary Pat and her friend brought Lisa to us and our neighbor jumped into the boat and started CPR; but when I saw her, I knew she was gone from us. She had severe cuts and she had lost a lot of blood. My husband (who had suffered a heart attack the year before) and I went to the house and he almost passed out. There were people and emergency trucks all over, and a minister came to talk with us. An ambulance quickly took Susan to the hospital with her mom and dad. We waited half an hour for another ambulance. An emergency truck took my husband Frank and daughter Carol to another hospital.

My daughter Mary Pat, a cousin, a friend and I went to the hospital to be with Lisa. There we saw Lisa, all wrapped up in sheets with just her beautiful face showing. I told her I loved her and then prayed. The doctor told me she died instantly from the severe blow. At the time it just didn't register - she is dead/final. I didn't feel like I was part of the whole scene - I was watching from the sideline. A nurse called our priest and he met us at the hospital where Frank was undergoing tests. Our daughter Carol was there. I told them about Lisa, and we all cried together. I didn't cry much; I was numb. Father said a prayer for us. After a bit, Frank was released from the hospital and friends took us home.

So many people were crushed by this accident. We had to call our son in Connecticut. Then we learned that Susan was also dead, and I called my dear friend Ruth to tell her I was so sorry. Our friendship goes back a long way. Ruth and I had become friends while working together right after high school. I was in their wedding and they were godparents for our second son. Susan was the youngest of their four children. After hearing the news, many of our close friends came to be with us.

I have an anger inside, of which I am not always aware. My husband believes I am angry with him for letting this accident happen. Fathers sometimes have the terrible feeling they should have protected their child from this kind of happening. I don't know who I am angry with - maybe God, or myself for not being able to accept this tragedy. I keep trying but then deny I am angry; however, my anger comes out at times. It has been very hard on the family. Each family member grieves differently, and as parents it is very hard to help any of them because you are trying to help yourself.

I believe I have a message for people to hear. Several times I tried to write this article, but it is very painful to recall the story. My friends have been burdened with the repetition of my thoughts and feelings because I have a need to express them over and over. At first, I could not believe it had happened; I tried to close it out, but every morning it was there again.

I did talk to my friend Ruth every day for at least three months and then at least three times a week just to discuss our thoughts and feelings. Six months later I went to a Hope For Bereaved Support Group Meeting with a friend. Without those friends who listened to me, and my strong faith in God, I could not have gotten through that time. You do go on for the family because they need you, but I hurt so badly that I just wanted to be with Lisa. She was my baby, and now I pray to her. I am so happy I had her for almost 11 years. She was so special.

Even now, I go to the Hope For Bereaved Parents meetings, because I feel I can help the people who attend and are newly bereaved. Sharing your thoughts and feelings with another grieving person does help. Sometimes we cry, and that helps too. It is a cleansing feeling. I have made many good friends at HOPE FOR BEREAVED. I go there to answer the 475-HOPE helpline and do some typing and publicity for the bereaved groups. Many of the people at HOPE have experienced the death of a loved one. They are all very caring people who want to help. The monthly meetings are open to anyone who needs to talk, or to just sit and listen. At the meetings you receive important help that will enable you to work through the grieving process.

If you are recently bereaved, you may think that you will not be able to survive the death of your loved one. I know that I couldn't imagine life without Lisa or that we would ever be happy again. It took a great deal of time, plus lots of grief work. Time, faith, friends and many efforts made by us helped to soften our grief. Hold on to HOPE that you, too, will get better.

Pat and Frank Fatti are volunteers at HOPE FOR BEREAVED.

PRIDE AND THE GRIEF PROCESS
by Eunice Brown

I am not a person who easily asks for help. I am basically a "helper" and I tend to expect people to see my needs. About a year after our son's death I called a friend and asked her if she would like to go to lunch. To my surprise she said she couldn't possibly go to lunch because so-and-so was getting married on her soap opera and she couldn't miss it! I considered her a good friend, who had tried to take my grief away. She tried to make me happy and she tried to make me laugh, but she wanted it to happen all at once and didn't know I just needed her to be there for me and to say "yes" when I asked her (in my way) for help. My mistake was not telling her I was having a bad day and needed her friendship right then. I simply said, "Okay," and thought to myself - "How dare she put a soap opera above my needs!"

I had to realize that people are not mind readers. It's painful when old friends just don't seem to understand, all the time; so we look for other areas and some new friends who do understand. I found my needs met through those new friends, but I still consider the "old friends," friends. I have grown a great deal in my long journey through grief. I think it has made me a better person. I hope others think so, too.

26

CANCER . . . A LONG TIME GRIEVING
by Eunice Brown

There Are Three Things Which Are Real:
God, Human Folly And Laughter
The First Two Are Beyond Our Comprehension
So We Must Do What We Can With The Third.
            The Ramanyana

In October of 1978 when our oldest son was diagnosed as having cancer, I remember my first reactions - I was angry and I cried. Then, as we sat in the waiting room at the hospital in Minneapolis, I immediately began to feel a surge of hope - people were being cured of cancer every day - and I was certain Keith would be one of the lucky ones.

He had a massive germ cell tumor which had wrapped itself around one kidney. The doctors decided on chemotherapy to shrink the tumor to operable size. For the next six months he entered the hospital every month for four days of chemo. The treatment was devastating to his body. He lost his hair, his appetite, weight; it made him sick to his stomach and caused sores in his mouth, to say nothing of what it did to his self-esteem. Being an actor, his looks were very important to him. I remember the first time I saw him after the treatments, and I hoped the shock did not show on my face. Through it all, he pursued his acting career, either on stage or behind the scenes directing. He maintained his sense of humor and his zest for life throughout his illness.

In April of 1979, he was operated on once again to remove the tumor-the kidney had to be removed also. In June of 1979, having gained back his weight and looking the picture of health, he married the wonderful girl who stuck by him and helped him back to health. It was the happiest wedding we had ever attended. As Cheryl's wedding gift to Keith, she sang "You Needed Me." There weren't too many dry eyes - but they were tears of joy and life went on. It was a happy time for all of us - we felt we had been given a gift, as we did when he was born.

In March of 1980, eleven months after the surgery, in his regular checkup the doctor discovered the tumor had again appeared. Being so many miles away was difficult for us. Most of the time I felt there wasn't much I could do but pray, and that was difficult because I was angry at God. It was at this point that I lost the hope that I had in the beginning; the hope that he would be cured. We visited on the phone. They came home for the holidays, and we spent eight days with them during the summer when he was feeling pretty well. He was back on chemotherapy every month, and he became well-known to the nurses and staff at the Metropolitan Medical Center. He delighted in teasing anyone whenever he could. He was in the hospital over New Years, and they celebrated by putting goldfish in an IV bag!

In September of 1981, he became very ill and was put in intensive care. This was the point when I went through my denial stage. He rallied and was somewhat better, but never left the hospital. Early in November the phone call came. By the time we arrived, he had been told he was dying. The chemotherapy had lost its effectiveness, and the tumor was growing rapidly. As we spent those many hours by his bedside, I wished I could trade places with him. I marveled at his attitude, his calmness, his conversation about his childhood, his planning of his funeral - he wanted nothing "maudlin, egotistical, or trendy." He also wanted a celebration of his life, not his death. He asked his many friends (who would come at all hours, whenever their schedules permitted) to do all the things he loved to do, singing, dancing, comedy routines; and he wanted Cheryl to sing "You Needed Me." I wondered if he was being "the actor" even in his dying. Eventually, I knew he wasn't, that he really accepted, was able to let go of life, and was at peace.

I, like all parents, want to pay tribute to my son, but I cannot forget the time our relationship was not the best. As he was dying, I had an opportunity to ask his forgiveness for that time in his life when I was not supportive of him -that time I felt I was not a good mother. Weak as he was, he took my face in his hands and said, "Mom, you've always been a good mother." It's not easy to ask a child to forgive you; pride gets in the way.

On November 10, 1981, at 6 A.M. Keith lost his long and difficult battle to conquer cancer. He weighed under 85 pounds. He was 30 years old. After the horrible empty feeling in the pit of my stomach had subsided, that same feeling, anger, surfaced again. I was not angry with the doctors and hospital personnel. I know they did all they could do. They were all kind, caring people and they cried with us. Many of them attended his funeral. They had come to think of him not as a patient but as a friend. Our pastor called us from Liverpool before we left the hospital. He has always been supportive through our grief. My anger was more general, over the fact that a cure had not been found. Keith had few political heroes - one of the few was Hubert Humphrey. It is ironic that he is buried in the same cemetery, and even though it was his wish to be buried in Minneapolis, I am angry because I cannot visit his grave.

The first year was difficult; I cried a great deal, I screamed when no one was in the house with me, I pounded my fists on the wall, (I don't recommend this, I really hurt my hands) and I ran (not literally). No matter how bad the weather was, I left the house and went someplace every day. I was fortunate to have some good friends I could lean on, especially one; she was always there when I needed her. We moved to a quieter neighborhood, and it was a good move for us. Dick and I attended several Hope For Bereaved Parents Support Group meetings. What has been most helpful for me is volunteering - once a month has become twice a week - helping in whatever way I can. To help someone else has helped me, and being with others who have experienced the loss of someone close, even if we don't talk about it all the time, is very therapeutic. There is a special bond that I have never felt with other friends. We can gripe at or with each other and there is always understanding. We will never get over the death of our son, but we have gotten better - time has healed. When I look around and see the beautiful friendships I have made, a little of that question WHY? (that all grieving people ask) is answered for me. It is almost five years, and I may still get a little teary-eyed when I hear the song "You Needed Me," but I know its okay - it brings back the sad memories but also the happy ones.

Keith is kept alive for us by the favorite stories told by his wife, brothers and sisters, and even though he never got a chance to share his talents with the world, knowing him as I do, I'm sure he's entertaining Someone and Someone's enjoying it!

THANK YOU, BROTHER

I knew a young man, he was a friend to all
He seemed to walk the way, that others only dream
He showed me how to laugh, his smiles always near
I know you're out there somewhere, and I want you to hear
I got a message from you, 'Bout liven' free
Doesn't take a smart man, only one who can see
Years went by before I knew you, there's only one thing to do
I'm gonna live to the fullest, Remember who taught me, too
I have no regrets about you, Loving you was easy to do
You taught me to laugh and I never knew why
I know before that, I could only cry
I want to thank you brother, I want to thank you from my heart.

-- An excerpt from a song written by "D.J." Brown in 1981

Eunice and Dick Brown are active volunteers at HOPE FOR BEREAVED

WHICH CHAPTER IN DR. SPOCK??
TO BEREAVED GRANDPARENTS
By MARGARET GERNER, MSW

I am powerlessness.   I am helplessness.   I am frustration.

I sit here with her, and cry with her: She cries for her daughter, and I cry for mine. I can't help her. I can't reach inside and take her broken heart. I must watch her suffer day after day, and see her desolation.

I listen to her tell me over and over how she misses Emily, how she wants her back. I can't bring Emily back for her. I can't buy her an even better Emily than she had, like I could buy her an even better toy when she was a child. I can't kiss the hurt and make it go away. I can't even kiss a small part of it away. There's no Band-Aid large enough to cover her bleeding heart.

There was a time I could listen to her talk about a fickle boyfriend and tell her it would be okay, and know in my heart that in two weeks she wouldn't even think of him. Can I tell her it'll be okay in two weeks when I know it will never be okay, that she will carry this pain of "what might have been" in her deepest heart for the rest of her life?

I see this young woman, my child, who was once carefree and fun-loving and bubbling with life, slumped in a chair with her eyes full of agony. Where is my power now? Where is my mother's bag of tricks that will make it all better? Why can't I join her in the aloneness of her grief? As tight as my arms wrap around her, I can't reach that aloneness.

Where are the magic words that will give her comfort? What chapter in Dr. Spock tells me how to do this? He has told me everything else I've needed to know. Where are the answers? I should have them: I am the mother.

What can I give her to make her better? A cold, wet washcloth will ease the swelling of her crying eyes, but it won't stop the reason for her tears. What treat will bring joy back to her? What prize will bring that "happy child" smile back again?

I know that someday she'll find happiness again, that her life will have meaning again. I can hold out hope for her someday, but what about now? This minute? This hour? This day?

I can give her my love and my prayers and my care and my concern. I could give her my life. But even that won't help.

Reprinted with permission from Margaret Gerner, St. Louis Chapter, The Compassionate Friends

---

"Suffering itself does not do us in or sabotage the will to live. Usually we sabotage ourselves by foolishly trying to live our lives in isolation. Without the comfort and love of other human beings, none of us is very strong. Aligned with others who accept us and support us, we can survive most anything."

Anne Kaiser Stearns
LIVING THROUGH PERSONAL CRISIS

THE BUTTERFLY: A Symbol of Hope
A Symbol of New Life
by Eunice Brown

The butterfly lays a tiny dewdrop of an egg on a juicy milkweed leaf. Inside the egg is her baby. When the baby hatches, however, she is not a beautiful butterfly like her mother. She is a caterpillar who eats and chews on the milkweed leaf for two weeks. The caterpillar's skin doesn't grow with her, so she has to take it off. She spins a little thread, clings to it, puffs air under her old skin until it splits. She stretches and twists, until she emerges dressed in a new and larger skin. She eats, grows, and changes her skin three times.

Then she hides in a dark, cool place and spins a little button, hooking herself there. Once again she crawls from her old skin, but this time takes off her caterpillar feet, head and horns. Underneath is a cocoon, hanging by a black thread. She hangs for days in stillness; no longer a caterpillar, but a chrysalis, preparing her secret. Then one day a head can be seen - a foot comes out. She struggles and struggles. She must pump something from her body into her wings to strengthen them. After a long time she emerges, fanning her wings slowly to dry them. Then she rests for hours. This beautiful butterfly has never flown. She had done nothing but a "caterpillar crawl". Finally she soars into the air as though she has been flying forever.

We might be tempted to help release the butterfly from her cocoon. It is human nature to want to assist; but if we do, she will fall to the ground and die. By the struggle to free herself, she strengthens her wings enough to survive and fly.

Grief is certainly like this process. We feel ugly, we change, we hide, we sometimes spin a cocoon around ourselves, and we struggle. Like the butterfly, we need to free ourselves. It takes a long time. There is a difference, however; others may help us as we struggle. We need not do it all alone as the butterfly does; but the ultimate responsibility is ours. We have to grieve, hurt, cry, be angry, and struggle to free ourselves from the cocoon of grief. And one day we do emerge - a beautiful butterfly - a stronger person, a more compassionate person, a more understanding person.

BY CHOOSING TO CONFRONT GRIEF WE CAN OVERCOME OUR LOSS
by ADOLFO QUEZADA

MY OLD FRIEND GRIEF is back. He comes to visit me once in a while just to remind me that I am still a broken man. Surely there has been much healing since my son died six years ago, and surely I have adjusted to a world without him by now. But the truth is, *we never completely heal, we never totally adjust to the loss of a major love.*

Such is the nature of loss that no matter how much time has passed, and no matter how much life has been experienced, the heart of the bereaved will never be the same. It is as though a part of us also dies with the person we lose through death, or other forms of permanent separation. We will be all right, but we will never be the same.

And so my old friend Grief drops in to say hello. Sometimes he enters through the door of my memory. I'll hear a certain song or smell a certain fragrance, or I'll look at a certain picture and I'll remember how it used to be. Sometimes it brings a smile to my face, sometimes a tear.

Some may say that such remembering is not healthy, that we ought not to dwell on thoughts that make us sad. Yet, the opposite is true. Grief revisited is grief acknowledged, and grief confronted is grief resolved.

But if grief is resolved, why do we still feel a sense of loss come anniversaries and holidays, and even when we least expect it? Why do we feel a lump in the throat, even six years after the loss? It is because healing does not mean forgetting, and because moving on with life does not mean that we don't take a part of our lost loved one with us.

Of course, the intensity of the pain decreases over time if we allow Grief to visit us from time to time. But if the intensity remains, or if our life is still dysfunctional years after our loss, we may be stuck and in need of professional help to get unstuck.

Sometimes my old friend Grief sneaks up on me. I'll feel an unexplained but profound sadness that clings to me for days. Then I'll recognize the grief and cry a little, and then I can go on. It's as though the ones we loved and lost are determined not to be forgotten.

My old friend Grief doesn't get in the way of my living. He just wants to come along and chat sometimes. In fact, Grief has taught me a few things about living that I would not have learned on my own. Old Grief has taught me, over the years, that if I try to deny the reality of a major loss in my life I end up having to deny life altogether. He has taught me that although the pain of loss is great, I must confront it and experience it fully or risk emotional paralysis.

Old Grief has also taught me that I can survive great losses, and that although my world is very different after a major loss, it is still my world and I must live in it. He has taught me that when I am pruned by the losses that come, when I let go I can flourish again in season and bring forth the good fruit that comes, not in spite of my loss, but because of it.

My old friend Grief has taught me that the loss of a loved one does not mean the loss of love, for love is stronger than separation and longer than the permanence of death.

My old friend Grief may leave me for a while, but he'll be back again to remind me to confront my new reality, and to gain through loss and pain.

"I will turn their mourning into joy, I will comfort them, and give them gladness over sorrow." (Jeremiah 31:13, The New Oxford Annotated Bible.)

This article appeared in the Tucson, Arizona, Daily Star. Adolfo Quezada, M.A., M.Ed., is a Tucson counselor and author.

SUGGESTIONS FOR HELPING YOURSELF THROUGH GRIEF

This title is not meant to indicate that others in our lives do not help us through grief. We do need the help of relatives and friends, and may need the help of professional counseling. At the same time, it is important for us to make the effort to help ourselves. Remember that grief takes a lot of energy. Treat yourself with the same care and affection that you would offer to a good friend in the same situation. Most of us are aware of "LOVE YOUR NEIGHBOR" - we forget the part- "AS YOU LOVE YOURSELF." Not all suggestions will be helpful to everyone. Grief has its unique sides. Choose the ideas that appeal to you.

BE PATIENT WITH YOURSELF

- Go gently. Don't rush too much. Your body, mind and heart need energy to mend.
- Don't take on new responsibilities right away. Don't over extend yourself. Keep decision making to a minimum. Don't compare yourself to other bereaved. It may seem that you aren't adjusting as well as they; in reality you don't know what's behind their public facade.
- Throw away notions of a fixed period of mourning: one year and then you're "over it." This is fiction. Grief takes time, whatever time it takes.

ASK FOR AND ACCEPT HELP

- Don't be afraid to ask for help from those close to you when you need it. So much hurt and pain go unheeded during grief because we don't want to bother anyone else with our problems. Wouldn't you want someone close to you to ask for help if they needed it? Our family and friends can't read our minds. Some relatives and friends will not be able to handle your grief. It is very important to find someone who cares, and understands with whom you may talk freely. Seek out an understanding friend, another bereaved person or a support group member.
- Accept help and support when offered. It's okay to need comforting. Often people wait to be told when you're ready to talk or if you need anything. Tell them.
- Pray to the person who has died.
- If you are troubled and need help, contact your local twenty-four hour hotline.
- Join a self-help group. They offer support, understanding, friendship and HOPE.
- Give yourself some time to sort out your thoughts but don't build a wall around yourself in fear of being hurt again. It is important to love and enjoy the people in your life instead of distancing yourself from them.
- If grief is intense and prolonged, it may harm your physical and mental well being. If it is necessary, seek out a competent counselor. Check to see if your health insurance covers the charges. It is important to take care of yourself.
- Feel what you feel. You don't choose your emotions, they choose you.
- It's okay to cry. Crying makes you feel better.
- It's okay to be angry. You may be angry with yourself, God, the person who died, others, or just angry in general. Don't push it down. Let it out (hit a pillow or punching bag, scream, swim, chop wood, exercise, etc.).
- Thinking you are going crazy is a very normal reaction. Most grieving people experience this. You are not losing your mind, only reacting to the death.
- Depression is common to those in grief. Be careful not to totally withdraw yourself from others. If your depression becomes severe or you're considering suicide, get professional help immediately.
- The emotions of a survivor are often raw. It is important to let these feelings out. If you don't, they will come out some other time, some other way. That is certain. You won't suffer nearly as much from "getting too upset" as you will from being brave and keeping your honest emotions all locked up inside. Share your "falling to pieces" with supportive loved ones, as often as you feel the need.
- You may have psychosomatic complaints, physical problems brought on by an emotional reaction. The physical problems are real; take steps to remedy them.

LEAN INTO THE PAIN

- Lean into the pain. It can not be outrun. You can't go around it, over it or under it; you must go through it and feel the full force of the pain to survive. Be careful not to get stuck at some phase. Keep working on your grief.
- Save time to grieve and time to face the grief. Don't throw yourself into your work or other activities that leave you no time for grieving.
- In a time of severe grief be extremely careful in the use of either alcohol or prescription drugs. Tranquilizers don't end the pain; they only mask it. This may lead to further withdrawal, loneliness and even addiction. Grief work is done best when you are awake, not drugged into sleepiness.
- If grief is unresolved, seek the help of a counselor or clergy who understands grief.
- Be determined to work through your grief.

BE GOOD TO YOURSELF

- Keep a journal. It is a good way to understand what you are feeling and thinking. Hopefully, when you reread it later you will see that you are getting better.
- Try to get adequate rest. Go to bed earlier. Avoid caffeine in coffee, tea and colas.
- Good nutrition is important.
- If Sundays, holidays, etc., are especially difficult times, schedule activities that you find particularly comforting into these time periods.
- Read recommended books on grief. It helps you to understand what you are going through. You may find suggestions for coping.
- Moderate exercise helps (walking, tennis, swimming, aerobics, etc.). It offers an opportunity to work off frustration and may aid sleep.
- Begin to build a pleasant time with family and friends. Don't feel guilty if you have a good time. Your loved one would want you to be happy. They would want you to live this life to the fullest and to the best of your ability.
- Do things a little differently, yet try not to make a lot of changes. This sounds like a contradiction, but it is not.
- Plan things to which you can look forward - a trip, visit, lunch with a special friend. Start today to build memories for tomorrow.
- Find quotes or posters that are helpful to you and hang where you can see them.
- Become involved in the needs of others. Helping others will build your self-confidence and enhance your self-worth. Join either a volunteer or support group, i.e. phoning; attending meetings; typing; collating newsletters. It does much to ease the pain.
- Be good to yourself: take a hot relaxing bath; enjoy the outdoors; take time for yourself (movie, theater, dinner out, read a novel, take a walk).
- Put balance in your life: pray, rest, work, read, relax.
- When you feel ready, aim at regaining a healthy, balanced life by broadening your interests. Take time for activities that can bring some purpose into your life. Think about doing something you've always wanted to do: taking a class, learning tennis, volunteer work, joining church groups, becoming involved in community projects or hobby clubs. Learn and do something new as well as rediscover old interests, activities and friends.
- Remember: Take your life one moment, one hour, one day at a time.

REMEMBER-GRIEF TAKES TIME

- Do not have unrealistic expectations of yourself. Grief takes TIME. It comes and goes.
- Remember, you will get better. Hold on to HOPE. Some days you just seem to exist, but better days will be back. Gradually, you will develop a renewed sense of purpose.

WHERE I FOUND HELP
by Mary Ballard

After my son David died, my emotions were all awry. I had always cried easily before, but now I had trouble keeping a dry eye. I avoided meeting new people because I was afraid that someone would ask me how many children I had; but if anyone asked me about David's death, I gave a detailed description. I felt lost, but couldn't admit it. I felt so weak, but fought to show strength. I couldn't sleep through the night and I didn't want to eat. I felt such despair and I felt such guilt.

At the time of David's funeral and burial someone at the funeral home mentioned that there was a support group that helps people when their loved one has died. A few weeks later, when I was so heavily burdened with my grief, I called the funeral home to find a telephone number where I could get more information. I didn't have any idea who I was calling when dialed the 475-HOPE line. I just wanted to find someone to help me. A volunteer for Hope For Bereaved answered my call. She gave me the information I requested and the date and time of the next meeting. Her very open and friendly manner encouraged me to go to that meeting.

The second Wednesday in November, 1984 I arrived alone at the Family Life Education Center where the meetings were held. I hated going places alone and I felt so self-conscious, but when I entered the building a friendly face soon greeted me and asked if she could help me. Coincidentally, it was the same person I had talked to on the phone.

She remembered talking to me. She welcomed me and told me a little about all the groups that meet each month. There was even a group for survivors of suicide (until that point, I hadn't told her that David had died by suicide). I was amazed -I couldn't believe that there were enough people whose loved one had died by suicide to make up their own group.

I remember those first meetings, but I remember them as if I wasn't there and had been told about them. There was a man named Joe* who talked about a particular subject during the first half of the meeting, and during the second half a very attractive lady* led a group discussion. You were encouraged to talk if you wanted to, but you were never made to feel that you had to. I had no idea what to expect before that evening and was pleased how comfortable I felt. I spoke up sometimes; I didn't want to draw attention to myself, but sometimes I felt the need to speak. And when I did, people listened. Some people in the group might comment on what I had to say, or Father Joe might say uh-huh, uh-huh and ask another question or make a comment that really made me think. The way everyone acted reminded me of something I heard a long time ago: Feelings are neither right or wrong; they just are. I heard some really different thoughts and feelings from people in the group, yet no one was judging another. Everything and everyone was accepted. And with that open attitude of others, it was easier for me to start becoming open with myself.

I remember one particular meeting; the topic was guilt. I cried through the whole meeting. I was so embarrassed, but no one acted like I was doing anything wrong. I learned at that meeting that one of the reasons it is so hard for survivors of suicide to work through their grief is because of the sense of guilt that is so common to those who are left behind. I felt I should have been able to stop him!! That is a very common feeling and I was relieved to find that I wasn't the only one who felt that way.

There is another meeting that stands out in my mind. The topic was "You're Not Going Crazy ...You're Grieving!" I was dumfounded that the feelings and thoughts that I had were common to all. As one person would comment on a specific symptom, whether it be concerning appetite (too much or too little), sleeplessness, memory loss, or what have you, the rest of us just sat there and nodded our heads - "Me, too!" I was delighted to learn that what I was feeling was normal - normal, that is, for what I was going through.

I later found out that "Joe" is Father Joe Phillips, who was moderator of HOPE FOR SURVIVORS, and the "attractive lady" is Christine Beattie, coordinator HOPE FOR SURVIVORS.

Every month there was a different topic, and every month there were new revelations. Some meetings meant more to me than others. But even if one particular meeting didn't excite me I was anxious to come back to the next one, for it might - and usually did. But each meeting helped me at a time when I needed help so badly.

HOPE FOR BEREAVED - Hope For Survivors - helped me to get in touch with my feelings, helped me to understand things that I thought I would never feel, things that could never happen to me. They helped me to understand their suggestions for working through grief, and their suggestions worked. They had to, because they all are based on tried and true experiences.

As I said, I had never attended a support group before, but I am so glad that I did. And although I am so very sorry to see new members each month because that means someone else has died, I am so very happy that they have come so we can try to help them work through their grief, just as they all helped me.

Mary Ballard is an active volunteer and a member of HOPE FOR SURVIVORS: Those Whom Suicide Leaves Behind.

WE'RE ONLY HUMAN!
by Judy Sittner

When our daughter Jill died in September, 1987, I suddenly became afraid of everything - afraid to sleep, afraid to go into her room, even afraid to love the other members of my family. I was even more afraid of myself; unable to judge what was the "right" thing to do, afraid of making mistakes, uncertain how I might behave or feel the next day or the next hour. How was I ever going to be able to cope with life, and my job in a gift shop?

Although I had found working to be very therapeutic, now with the holidays coming I wasn't so sure. Not only was I facing the first Thanksgiving and Christmas without our daughter, I was going to be faced with all the glitz that is "Christmas" for retail stores. How would I react to the customers, the music, the decorations? How would people react to me?

I decided to write a letter to my coworkers to express my concerns. I had wondered if they would be uncomfortable or feel awkward working with me now, not knowing how to act, what to say or not to say. I told them that at times I was uncomfortable myself, especially about not being able to predict at any time what things might upset me. But I wanted them to remember that as much as my heart was aching, I was still approachable, that I could still laugh at a funny story, joke about the "mad rush" of the season, share the serenity of a starlit night, and cherish the warmth of a fond embrace.

The response to my letter was very positive. It gave all of us at work a chance to clear the air, and it gave me the courage to finally talk to my family and friends about my feelings. Through this, I received a special awareness - the ability to accept the fact that it's okay not to be perfect or in perfect control all the time. And as much as I can feel the pain of the loss, I can allow myself to feel the delights that living still has to offer, which are still out there. We just have to hang on to HOPE and give ourselves TIME. After all, we're only human!

Judy Sittner attended HOPE FOR BEREAVED Parents' Support Group until she moved to Rochester. It is heartwarming to see in print how someone has turned a difficult situation or painful time into one of growth and support.

LEANING INTO YOUR PAIN: WHAT A "LOUSY" PLACE TO BE
by Dr. Terry O'Brien

The pain that results from the death of a loved one can be excruciating. This pain takes on both physical and emotional manifestations. You might feel physically numb or exhausted; a tightness in your stomach, chest or throat; hollow, light-headed or shaky within; dizzy, nauseous, constipated or prone to diarrhea. Emotional feelings such as nervousness, fear, anxiety, anger, rage, guilt, depression, desperation, helplessness and hopelessness may emerge in clusters at varying intervals like a powerful overwhelming wave or a wet, dark blanket. The physical and emotional dimensions of grief come in great intensity like a powerful unexpected cramp. Leaning into this pain runs against our grain. Our instinctive tendencies move us to avoid the pain with all its unpleasantness. Leaning into the pain seems foolhardy and even masochistic. Who wants to be in such an uncomfortable and lousy place as grief? Certainly few people choose such pain but many find themselves victimized by the death of a loved one.

The pain of grief grips each of us differently. Like a fingerprint, each person's journey with grief will vary somewhat. But the general reality is this: one cannot go around, under or over grief. One must go through grief by leaning into the pain to work it out. It sounds dreadful! It feels terrible! But unless one goes through its fires, one has difficulty in future relationships. The unfinished business - those feelings, thoughts, intentions and behaviors that were never transacted or broached with the dead loved one - clogs us up. If this blockage stays, one tends to get sick. For many the blockage doesn't totally restrict their interacting with others, but it certainly does affect these relationships. For a person to flow interpersonally, exchanging his precious gifts of self with another, the damned up reservoirs of past grief need to be eroded and opened up. Thus the term "grief work" is very apropos. Work it is! It's very hard and personally draining but only by attending to such pain can we move on to future close relationships in a healthy manner and place the deceased loved one in a proper perspective.

After one loses an arm or leg, for whatever reason, the time for physical and emotional rehabilitation is considerable. Sadly, little time, thought and energy is given to our rehabilitation after the death of a loved one. People move on, denying, avoiding and rationalizing. This ultimately prolongs one's grief even though its intensity seems to diminish, and it renders one less competent interpersonally because of what is locked or blocked in our inner reservoirs of pain. Some argue that at least they are not conscious of hurting; but they are nonetheless limited because they have denied an important reality -- their pain given the death of a loved one. Our own fears of dying and by extension the deaths of those closest to us are so difficult to fathom and digest. They are put out of our conscious awareness. Such is the human tendency to recoil from life's pain.

But how is one to lean into the pain, to more effectively work through grief? Grief work is in essence a thorough and on-going review process. It is very repetitive. It takes a long time. It is never fully or finally accomplished, but the intensity of the pain does lessen and the frequency of the pain becomes more intermittent. Certain occasions, dates, seasons, songs; people or places may trigger our grief anew, but with time and earnest attention our fears turn into nods and even smiles as we remember our loved ones.

Keeping a daily or at least a regular journal noting your thoughts, feelings, intentions, behaviors and dreams is another way of regularly expressing grief. Writing gets at one's inner experience and puts it out onto paper. This is a healthy means of self-expression. Another helpful method of working on grief is to write a letter to the dead loved one. In this letter express your feelings, whatever was not said or done or intended that may be of concern. If you are working with a therapist or talking to a good friend or family person, have them read the letter and possibly R.S.V.P. as your dead loved one might. To R.S.V.P. a person must know much about the deceased and be competent and comfortable with this technique.

Leaning into the pain by reflecting upon the meaning and the significance of "linking objects" - these objects which are retained, held onto, or preserved which hold intact our connection with our dead loved ones - is another important vehicle for grieving. Linking objects such as a room maintained just as it was, a special chair kept in the same place which no one else uses, a baseball mitt, a musical instrument, a hat, or the dead person's closet left intact, etc., can become like shrines which keep our grief stuck. Slowly we begin to change and let go of our "linking objects." This reflects that we are working through our grief and beginning to let go of our beloved as they were then and moving toward accepting them as they are now. This is a gradual process of letting go which is a key component of grieving. Linking objects are not easily discarded. Most often the bereaved rearranges a room, lets others use the special chair, packs and moves the clothing, gives away some possessions while putting aside a few special things. The key is flexibility and gradual change. The shrine-like nature of the object diminishes. We remember and treasure but these memories are not frozen in time or prone to consistently render one breathless. We still tear up, we begin to smile but our predominant feeling becomes a deeper understanding, acceptance and appreciation for the beloved. This is another indication that the grief process is moving ahead.

Two other important ways of working through grief are affirmation and visualization. A bereaved person's self-esteem tends to lessen considerably during one's grief. So often she/he will say to her or himself "I can't" or "I'll never be able," etc. Such statements tend to be negative. Self-talk such as this limits one and can become self-fulfilling. "I can't" becomes "won't" which then becomes "don't". Negative vicious cycles confirm such self-talk which keeps one's self-esteem low and the person mired in self-defeating grief. Self-talk needs to become more positive. Instead of focusing on one's liabilities, center on one's possibilities - what one "can do." If you attend to what you "can do," you "will do." Sometimes this seems so difficult! To aid in this regard use creative visualization. Get into a relaxed posture and breathe deeply for a few minutes. As you exhale, let go of your conscious thoughts and concerns. Let your deep breathing begin to relax you. Feel lighter and more relaxed. Now envision yourself doing those things you can do (or want to do) or being the way you would like to be. See yourself being and doing those positive, more creative and self-affirming behaviors which will enable you to cope more effectively. Let this visualization serve you as your game plan. Work at actualizing your visualized ways of being. As you do this, your self-esteem will begin to increase and you will be working most effectively on your grief.

A final suggestion for coping with the pain of your grief is to clearly delineate in writing or conversation what you miss and do not miss concerning your loved one. Early in grief the focus is almost totally on what one misses about a loved one. Later on in the grief process one is usually more ready to look at what one does not miss about a deceased loved one. Sometimes there is a hesitancy to acknowledge what one does not miss. Coming to terms with ambivalent feelings is an important aspect of grief. The questions "what you miss" and "what you do not miss" about a loved one hone in on the humanness of relationships and the mix of feelings a bereaved person experiences; love, disappointment, respect, anger, appreciation, guilt, resentment, etc. These are just some of the emotions one may feel toward a dead loved one. Acknowledging, accepting and acting upon these emotions appropriately is a vital task in the grieving process.

The aforementioned methods of coping with grief are specific suggestions for how one can lean into the pain. Granted, it is a "lousy" place to be. But not to be there, to deny or avoid one's pain invalidates your reality. Not to grieve the death of a loved one prevents one from getting on with life again. Only by leaning into the pain can one regain a perspective on life and move on, not permanently depleted, and in the long haul enhanced because your metal was processed in one of life's most trying furnaces. Let us move on as we resolve to continue journeying along life's way.

Terrance O'Brien, Ph.D., is a marriage and family therapist in private practice, special consultant/trainer for HOPE FOR BEREAVED and a local/national presenter of workshops.

COPING AS A FAMILY

Communication is the key to coping and growing as a family through grief. It is important to be together to talk, cry, rage, or even sit in silence. At the same time there should be respect for each member's way of handling their grief. Some family members will grieve privately, others openly, and others a combination of these two styles. In many ways each family member must grieve alone. Here are some suggestions to help with family grief.

- Continue to give attention and time to your present family members when you are together. Let them know that you love them.
- Maintain balance of attention between deceased family member and surviving family members.
- Try to be sensitive to each others' feelings. Feelings are often difficult to verbalize. Listen to what is meant as well as what is said.
- Hugs, a hand on the arm or back give comfort and a sense of closeness.
- It may be helpful to set aside time to be "alone together" as a family or to even hold a family meeting. Encourage but don't pressure family members to talk and express grief in their own way. Be a good listener.
- Plan family projects or trips.
- Make a "family diary" in which each family member may contribute a writing or drawing. You may want to make a collage together.
- Be careful not to give each other the silent treatment. Make sure the person who has died continues to be part of family conversations.
- Respect the life stages of various family members; an adolescent might gravitate towards peers in coping with grief. Everyone has a unique way of grieving which can at times be at cross purposes among family members. Accept each person's method of coping.
- Discuss the loved one's former role in the family which now necessitates changes in family duties and new roles for the survivors in the family. Be careful not to expect a family member to replace or to be the same as the member who died (expecting a young boy whose father died to be "the man of the house" or a son whose sibling died to be like that sibling in schoolwork, sports, etc.). Discuss what will be missed and irreplaceable.
- If depression, withdrawal, grief or family problems are getting out of control, seek professional help.
- Recognize that anniversaries, birthdays and special holidays will be difficult for the family and each member of the family. Discuss together how to observe these occasions. Should there be a variation on traditional celebrations? Do any family members have particular concerns, suggestions?
- Consult family members on the disposition of the deceased loved one's possessions, including their room. Take your time and tread carefully where these precious mementoes are concerned. If possible, put off making major decisions about moving, giving away possessions, etc.
- Studies show that a bereaved persons self-esteem is extremely low. Survivors should work on their image of themselves and help each family member to think and feel good about themselves.
- Remember it is difficult to help your family if you are falling apart. Working on your own grief will eventually enable you to help your family to cope with their grief.
- As a family or individual pray to your loved one who has died to help the family cope with their grief.
- If you can learn to share your grief as a family hopefully you will grow as a family.

SUDDEN DEATH - vs. - THE EXPECTED

The sudden, swift-moving death blow is by far the hardest for most to handle. We aren't ready. We are left up in the air in the midst of life. We have so many nagging after-thoughts, wishes and desires, now never to be spoken. Our minds can recognize that the sudden death experience may certainly keep our loved one from the suffering, which we really didn't want. But we feel the relationship ruptured within us, and rarely can this heal as naturally or as quickly as in the lingering illness process.

Always there is dispute comparing the sudden death versus a long, lasting illness. Truly, neither is better than the other! Each has its own particular struggle and its own type of compensation. When dealing with the awful, painful, day-to-day suffering of a loved one, sudden death seems so much easier. But we must remember, with a sudden death there is no last, lingering touch, no planning together, no seeking advice and working out family matters, no visits from family and friends. There is no gradual adjustment and releasing that is natural as you watch a body change, abilities fade, suffering deplete the life-force.

When we are dealing with sudden death, we have more to think through alone. We have to forgive and release. From within ourselves we have to make well that which has occurred, without the interaction of the one that has gone. The process depends so much upon our own self, and usually we are confused and hurt and can't function really well. We seem to go in circles repeating over and over; last words, last actions, the story of the occurrence. We seem to be trying to make it acceptable to our own mind. I think of it as trying to untangle a large knot. The knot is our hopes, our dreams, and our plans for the future that became scrambled with the death event.

I remember as a child swinging high in the air; a sudden slip and then the jolting sensation of hitting the ground. Shocked, stunned, with the air knocked out of me, I remember the feeling of trying to reorient myself. This is not unlike the feelings of sudden loss. Your picture of family, friends, your personal reality, are jolted by the blow and trauma of unexpected death. The blank feeling of non-reality sweeps in and out. The emphasis centers around catching one's breath just as from the fall from the swing. The head spits out the situation with "This does not compute!" It is now that the basic self-discipline, consideration and concern for others, endurance and freedom of expression that are deeply ingrained in each personality, can serve us. Those traits we call character, deep and underlying our personal approach to life, are revealed. The mind kicks in and out . . . sometimes sharp and alert, supplying all the data we need; sometimes failing us completely. Names won't come; memory fails; our logic refuses to function. As the computer spits and sputters, trying to get caught up with the events of the moment, the basic qualities of personality express.

For everyone, it is important that we deal with the experience in such a way that healing may occur in our lives. Our system innately knows how to heal and adjust. It has done so many times in several different turns of events. Our inner strength can soar; we can heal and hope and live once again. How we handle the experience of pain and loss either moves us toward healing or blocks the ability to rebuild and repair.

Reprinted with permission from A New Age Handbook On Death And Dying by Carol W. Parrish-Harra, Devorss & Company Publishers, 1982.

HOW TO HELP GRIEVING PEOPLE

Relatives, friends and neighbors are supportive at the time of a death, during the wake and funeral. Food, flowers and their presence are among the many thoughtful expressions. After the funeral, many grieving people wonder what happened to their friends. They need their support and caring even more when the reality begins to hit and the long process of grief begins. Their help is essential, since immediate family members have their hands full of grief and may find it difficult to give support to one another, or may not live nearby. Your help and understanding can make a significant difference in the healing of your friend's grief. Unresolved grief can lead to physical or mental illness, suicide or premature death. A grieving person needs friends who are willing to: LISTEN; cry with them; sit with them; reminisce; care; have creative ideas for coping; be honest; help them feel loved and needed; believe that they will make it through their grief. Ways of helping grieving people are as limitless as your imagination.

1. All that is necessary is a squeeze of the hand, a kiss, a hug, your presence. If you want to say something, say "I'm sorry" or "I care."

2. Offer to help with practical matters; i.e., errands, fixing food, caring for children. Say, "I'm going to the store. Do you need bread, milk, etc.? I'll get them." It is not helpful to say, "Call me if there is anything I can do."

3. Don't be afraid to cry openly if you were close to the deceased. Often the bereaved find themselves comforting you, but at the same time they understand your tears and don't feel so alone in their grief.

4. It is not necessary to ask questions about how the death happened. Let the bereaved tell you as much as they want, when they are ready. A helpful question might be, "Would you like to talk? I'll listen".

5. Don't say, "I know just how you feel." You don't.

6. The bereaved may ask "WHY?" It is often a cry of pain rather than a question. It is not necessary to answer, but if you do, you may reply, "I don't know why."

7. Don't use platitudes like "Life is for the living," or "It's God's will." Explanations rarely console. It's better to say nothing.

8. Recognize that the bereaved may be angry. They may be angry at God, the person who died, the clergy, doctors, rescue teams, other family members, etc. Encourage them to acknowledge their anger and to find healthy ways of handling it.

9. Be available to LISTEN frequently. Most bereaved want to talk about the person who has died. Encourage them to talk about the deceased. Do not change the conversation or avoid mentioning the person's name.

10. Read about the various phases of grief so you can understand and help the bereaved to understand.

11. Be PATIENT. Don't say, "You will get over it in time." Mourning may take a long time. The bereaved need you to stand by them for as long as necessary. Encourage them to be patient with themselves as there is no timetable for grief.

12. Accept whatever feelings are expressed. Do not say, "You shouldn't feel like that." This attitude puts pressure on the bereaved to push down their feelings. Encourage them to express their feelings - cry, hit a pillow, scream, etc.

13. Be aware that a bereaved person's self-esteem may be very low.

14. When someone feels guilty and is filled with "if onlys," it is not helpful to say, "Don't feel guilty." This only adds to their negative view of themselves. They would handle it better if they could. One response could be, "I don't think that you are guilty. You did the best you could at the time, but don't push down your feelings of guilt. You are welcome to talk about it with me as often as you need, until you can let it go."

15. Depression is often part of grief. It is a scary feeling. To be able to talk things over with an understanding friend or loved one is one factor that may help prevent a person from becoming severely depressed.

16. Give special attention to the children in the family. DO NOT tell them not to cry or not to upset the adults.

17. Suggest that the bereaved person keep a journal.

18. The bereaved may appear to be getting worse. Be aware this is often due to the reality of the death hitting them.

19. Be aware of physical reactions to the death (lack of appetite, sleeplessness, headaches, inability to concentrate). These affect the person's coping ability, energy and recovery.

20. Be aware of the use of drugs and alcohol. Medication should only be taken under the supervision of a physician. Often these only delay the grief response.

21. Sometimes the pain of bereavement is so intense that thoughts of suicide occur. Don't be shocked by this. Instead, try to be a truly confiding friend.

22. Don't say, "It has been 4 months, 6 months, 1 year, etc. You must be over it by now." Life will never be the same.

23. Encourage counseling if grief is getting out of hand.

24. Suggest that grieving people take part in support groups. Sharing similar experiences helps. Offer to attend a support group meeting with them. The meetings are not morbid. They offer understanding, friendship, suggestions for coping and HOPE.

25. Suggest that the bereaved postpone major decisions such as moving, giving everything away, etc. Later they may regret their hasty decisions. It is best for the bereaved to keep decision-making to a minimum.

26. Suggest exercise to help work off bottled-up tension and anger, to relax and to aid sleep. Offer to join them for tennis, exercise classes, swimming, a walk, etc.

27. Practice unconditional love. Feelings of rage, anger and frustration are not pleasant to observe or listen to; but it is necessary for the bereaved to recognize and work on these feelings in order to work through the grief, rather than become stuck.

28. Help the bereaved to avoid unrealistic expectations as to how they "should" feel and when they will be better. It is helpful when appropriate to say, "I don't know how you do as well as you do."

29. Don't avoid the bereaved. This adds to their loss. As the widowed often say, "I not only lost my spouse, but my friends as well."

30. Be aware that weekends, holidays and evenings may be more difficult.

31. Consider sending a note at the time of their loved one's birthday, anniversary, death or other special days.

32. Practice continuing acts of thoughtfulness-a note, visit, plant, helpful book on grief, plate of cookies, phone call, invitation for lunch, dinner, coffee. Take the initiative in calling the bereaved.

GRIEF: OUTSIDE LOOKING IN
by Peggy Dupee

My purpose in writing this article is two-fold: First, to help friends of grieving people get through the barrier; and second, to let those grieving know what your close friend is going through at the same time.

Several years ago my friend experienced the death of her young daughter in an auto accident. The months that followed were horrid. She had tremendous grief to live with and I had to stand by and watch her suffer.

Outwardly she looked fine, but I could see the dull ache in her eyes - after all, we had been friends for a long time and I could read her moods. After several weeks of asking "How are you?" and hearing her reply "OK!" or "Fine," I began to feel left out. It bothered me because up to this point we had shared both the joys and disappointments of our lives. Now she wasn't sharing her grief and she wasn't even looking at me any more. I didn't like what was happening, yet I was afraid to say anything for fear that it would add to her sorrow. I began to be unhappy and after some soul searching I figured out why I felt that way. You see, I was grieving too - for my friend and the death of her daughter and also for what I thought was the loss of our relationship. I was lonely and sad and left out. First, I told myself that these thoughts and feelings were selfish and how could I begin to compare our losses. Then, I thought to myself that while the grief was certainly different and the degree of mine could not begin to be the horrendous burden of her grief, nonetheless, I too was grieving.

Through the years we had shared so much, even sandwiches; now I wanted to help her by sharing her grief and she was shutting me out. She was so wrapped up in her grief that she no longer could see another person's frustration. This wasn't the woman who had always been so concerned about people and their feelings (we used to say she was so sweet - it was sickening!!)

I made a conscious decision to do something about my feelings, so the next time I asked "How are you?" and she replied "Fine," I looked at her and said "Bull——." She was startled, but she did begin to be honest about her feelings. Next, I pointed out to her that she didn't look at me anymore and I asked her if I had dandruff, because she always looked at my shoulders, not into my eyes. We laughed, and she began to look at me again. The next step was to be available to listen when she wanted to talk about her daughter, her feelings, her fears, etc. She did call on me many, many times when she needed to talk. While this took vast amounts of my time and emotional energy, at last I felt like I was doing something to help my friend through this crisis. My own grief over the loss of a close friendship began to be set aside as the relationship began to thrive again.

You have to be willing to risk a lot to be honest with a friend - they may not want your help. You also must be prepared to be emotionally drained at times and maybe have a sore ear from listening for hours on end. But if you value the friendship it is worth all the effort, and when your friend laughs again it's wonderful to be a part of that moment.

To those of you who are grieving - let your friends into your grief. They cannot understand how terrible it is for you, but they can empathize with you, and it will help you through the process if you can be honest with them while they listen to you. Remember, they too may be grieving the loss of your friendship.

I've read many books and articles on grief and they have helped me to understand some of the impact death can have on a person. One thing seems to be lacking in all these writings, and that is the impact it has on those of us who are on the outside looking in.

After some time had passed my friend began writing. She would ask me to proof read for her. I remember one occasion she asked me to proof read an article containing some suggestions on how to help a friend through grief. As I read, I became angry because innocently she had suggested that being there and listening wasn't difficult for a friend. Well I knew otherwise, and I flew into her office and reacted with "It's NOT easy'.!" We discussed it and she changed the wording of that sentence.

Three years after her daughter's death, my friend gave me a plaque with the following poem on it:

"At times I need to talk to someone who'll understand
A someone who'll just listen, or lend a helping hand
In you I've always trusted my deepest thoughts and fears
We've weathered it together the happiness, the tears
I often pause to wonder whatever would I do
Had I lived this life and never had a loving friend like you"
author "Sue"

I read it often because it hangs over my kitchen sink - it's there to remind me how important I was to her and also that our friendship was definitely worth my efforts.

Peggy Dupee is an understanding friend to all of us and a volunteer at HOPE FOR BEREAVED

GRIEF: INSIDE LOOKING OUT
by Therese Schoeneck

The above is a very important article and I am glad that Peggy shared her thoughts. Right from the beginning I can remember not wanting to "dump" any of my grief on anyone else. At the wake I felt so sorry for the people trying to console us. I put myself in their shoes and thought - How difficult! - and tried to comfort them. As a family we were all hurting so much that I did not want to add to the pain of any of them. I thought that this was too painful to share; I had to somehow struggle through by myself. Even though I hurt I did not want to cause others to hurt if I could help it.

About 6 weeks after Mary died, Peggy and I attended a conference in Denver. I had really lost my appetite so all I wanted to do was "share" sandwiches. When we returned, Peggy wrote me a note explaining how difficult it was to see me in pain, and yet I was shutting her out. She said, "I wish you would share your grief with me as we shared sandwiches." That note opened my eyes and I started really telling Peggy how I felt. I will always be grateful to Peggy for her offer and thankful that I accepted. As I write this 9 1/2 years later I can't imagine being as happy, as at peace as I am now, without all her help.

What I meant regarding it is "easy" to help a grieving friend is that it is not complicated. A friend does not have to take courses on grief education, do extensive reading on grief or be a trained counselor. Helping a grieving friend may be draining and can be very time consuming. We are apt to repeat ourselves and our feelings may be strong. We are often devastated, confused, depressed, angry, and may feel guilty - to name a few of our reactions. But we do need people to reach out to us, to show their concern. As bereaved we need to accept the offers of our family and friends. I thank God that Peggy didn't give up on me and that I finally accepted her very valuable help.

OFFERING AND ACCEPTING HELP CAN MAKE A DIFFERENCE!

WHAT YOU/YOUR CHURCH/SYNAGOGUE CAN DO TO HELP GRIEVING PEOPLE

DO NOT AVOID THE BEREAVED - REACH OUT TO THEM - IN WORDS AND ACTIONS

Form a bereavement "team" of people who wish to reach out to the bereaved.
THINGS TO DO IMMEDIATELY:
Visit the bereaved family within a short time after a call from clergy/rabbi *if appropriate*
Extend your (and church/synagogue members') sympathy
Offer your help:
— answer the phone
— prepare meals
— usher in callers
— pick up the house
Organize food donations
Provide child care
Arrange for cars and drivers to:
— meet travelers at airport
— run errands
— drive at funeral
Offer your home for out-of-towners to stay overnight
Offer help with care of invalid, or ailing family members
Offer to help with funeral/liturgy services
Offer to occupy the house during calling hours or funeral

CONTINUE TO VISIT AND REACH OUT TO THE BEREAVED. DON'T JUST SEND THINGS BUT ALSO GO YOURSELF TO LISTEN AND SAY YOU CARE, ESPECIALLY AFTER THE FUNERAL, ALL DURING THE FIRST YEAR, HOLIDAYS, SPECIAL DAYS AND BEYOND.

Be aware of things NOT to say:
It was God's will.
You can have other children.
He/she'd be leaving anyway for college/marriage, etc.
(*to boy*) Now, you are the man of the house.
He/she had a good life.
He/she is out of pain.
I know someone who had two family members die (do not minimize their loss).
I know how you feel.
You must be over it by now.
At least you have other children.
(*to children*) Don't cry. It will upset your mother. Be brave for your parent(s).

IF YOU WANT TO SAY SOMETHING, SIMPLY SAY: "I'M SORRY" OR "I CARE" OR "I LOVE YOU." ALL THAT IS REALLY NECESSARY IS A SQUEEZE OF THE HAND, A KISS, A HUG, OR YOUR PRESENCE.

Other ways to help later:

FOR THE CHURCH OR SYNAGOGUE

Establish and maintain a library of helpful books on grief.

Announce support group meetings in Church/Synagogue bulletins; post brochures.

Give a Homily/Sermon on grief (to help bereaved, to prepare others, to help others understand).

Be aware of appropriate agencies, counselors and/or support groups/services for the bereaved.

Establish a list of telephone friends.

Contact local agencies/support groups to obtain a panel to speak on what it's like to be a bereaved person and ways to help.

Show a film such as "Living When A Loved One Dies" by Earl Grollman to congregation or special organization within your church.

Study HOPE FOR BEREAVED Handbook* or other books on grief for deeper understanding.

For further ideas see article "HOW TO HELP GRIEVING PEOPLE".

FOR THE INDIVIDUAL:

Visit the bereaved - bring a helpful book (Hope For Bereaved Handbook* has many practical suggestions).

Bring or send pertinent brochures to bereaved.

Offer to attend support group with them or possibly find someone in area who attends so they can ride together.

Gently draw bereaved into quiet outside activity.

Be especially aware of loneliness of widowed. Invite to appropriate church/synagogue events or to your home.

Offer friendship, help and HOPE.

The Handbook may be ordered from HOPE FOR BEREAVED, Inc. (see inside front cover for address and phone number to obtain current prices).

Design a Needs List to include in church bulletin. Below is a sample.

BEREAVED - When there is a death in our church/synagogue, we would like to be able to offer assistance from the caring people of our community. Many families do not need the help, and we certainly want to respect their wishes. There are others who would benefit from having someone in our church/synagogue come forth to help with some of the following:

— House sit - during the wake and/or funeral

— Baby sit - sit with babies, elderly or home-bound during the wake and/or funeral

— Help plan Liturgy or service

— Pick up out-of-town relatives at airport, etc.

— House out-of-town relatives

— Arrange for use of church/synagogue hall after funeral

— Help prepare food after funeral

— Run errands

— Organize food donations

— Follow-up letter   NAME:

— Follow-up visit   ADDRESS:

— Maintain grief library   PHONE NO:

— Other

SUGGESTIONS FOR CLERGY
FOR HELPING THEIR GRIEVING PARISHIONERS

Death takes a heavy toll. Even though we believe our loved one is in heaven, the grief we experience is often frightening and even devastating. We are not prepared for such pain and intense feelings of grief. Parents do not expect to outlive their children. For the widowed, their whole life changes drastically. At times their loneliness seems unbearable. The death of a parent or sibling is so painful. The cause of death also may add to the grief . . . prolonged illness, sudden death, murder or suicide.

Usually the first people we turn to are the clergy. We are seeking comfort and help in coping. In many cases, subconsciously we want our clergy to be like Superman - to spin the world back as Superman did when Lois Lane died in the earthquake. We want them to take away the pain....to somehow intercede with God so that the death of our loved one is just a nightmare, not a reality. This wish is unrealistic and only lasts a short while. What we basically need and want is for our clergy to be truly compassionate, to be concerned for us, and to be present when possible.

It may be a difficult part of your ministry, but for the bereaved it may be a critical turning point in their faith. With understanding, care and help, the bereaved may experience emotional, spiritual and personal growth. Without this help they may turn from the church with bitterness and disappointment.

In general, people tend to avoid the bereaved due to feeling uncomfortable and not knowing what to say or do. The following suggestions are offered by the many bereaved people who have been helped and encouraged by their clergy:

Study Grief: It is important to understand the various Experiences of Grief in order to be helpful to the bereaved (see graph page 10).

It Helps To Listen: Many bereaved ramble, repeat and cry in their shock and confusion. Listening with patience, empathy and compassion shows that you care.

Be Comfortable With Silence: Silence on your part shows that you don't have all the answers. It gives the bereaved time to think and express their feelings.

Why????: The bereaved often ask why. We aren't looking for answers. It is a cry of pain. It is better not to try to answer the 'why' because usually there is no satisfactory answer. It is more helpful to LISTEN. If we ask for a specific answer, one response might be -"I don't know."

Be There: Just your concern, your actual presence is helpful. We realize that you are busy. It means a great deal to us that you make the effort to be with us.

Hugs - Not Words: A hug, a hand on our arm or shoulder, or just being near us is comforting. If you want to say something, say "I'm sorry," or "I wish I could take some of your pain away."

Explanations Rarely Console: Avoid clichés such as "It's God's will"; "He's out of pain"; "She lived a good life"; "Now you have an angel in heaven"; "God needed a flower in His garden"; "You're young - you can have other babies"; "At least you have other children." Although these ideas may bring comfort to some bereaved, they bring negative reactions to most of us.

46

Share Your Feelings: If you show hurt, bewilderment, anger, etc., it actually helps the family. We in turn can then express our feelings rather than suppress them. We know that you care because you show that you hurt, too.

Be Accepting: We may blame you, God, or the world for the death. We may make some "off-the-wall" comments or express our grief in other negative ways. Understand that we may be experiencing the worst emotional pain of our lives.

Be Careful Of Expectations: Help us to understand that the pain that accompanies grief is normal and not to expect ourselves to be strong. Even with great faith in God, there is real pain from grief.

AT THE TIME OF DEATH

Go To The Family as soon as possible after being notified of the death. It is important to be sensitive to the different types of death. When death is by SUICIDE the family may need your caring even more. They need to understand that God doesn't judge a person just on his last act, but on his entire life. The person who died was not turning away from God or his family, but trying to escape from his deep, inner pain.

Help The Family with decisions and funeral arrangements. Involve the family in planning the funeral service. MAKE THE FUNERAL SERVICE PERSONAL. Refer to the deceased by name. At the wake or other feasible place obtain stories, preferences, habits, outlooks and values of the deceased so as to color the eulogy/homily in a personal manner. Investigate the possibility of a resurrection choir to sing at the funeral. Acknowledge the pain of grief as well as God's love. Offer the family HOPE - that they will be together again with their loved one.

ON-GOING CONCERN

Reach Out: Form a bereavement team. It helps if you or your bereavement team, church minister or deacon make a personal visit or telephone the family from time to time. It is important to be particularity sensitive around the holidays, birthdays, and anniversary of the death.

Suggest Support Groups: Self-help groups (others who have experienced the death of a loved one) offer suggestions for coping, practical help, support, friendship and HOPE. Your personal encouragement may be the key factor for the bereaved in trying a support group. REALIZE that *grief takes a long time* - even years.

All Saints Day Liturgy: Send a personal invitation, if possible, (if not, put it in the bulletin) to all those who were bereaved within the past year. By means of the bulletin and posters invite others who also may be grieving. Hold a reception afterward, serving refreshments and possibly having a speaker on grief.

> *Be Present, Listen And Offer HOPE* -Your people will understand that God cares when they experience your caring; that God listens when you listen; that there is HOPE in God when you show that there is HOPE.

SUGGESTIONS FOR MEDICAL PERSONNEL
FOR HELPING GRIEVING PEOPLE

Death of a loved one is devastating for the family and may also be for the medical personnel, especially if they have become attached to the patient and family. The death of a patient seems to go against the whole concept of healing. Often you are with the patient at the moment of death. You may be the person who has to tell the family the sad news. It is never easy; but, by your compassion and genuine concern, you can be a great comfort to the newly bereaved. The following suggestions are offered by experienced nurses and bereaved people.

PREPARATION:

- Look honestly at your own feelings and possible fears about death and grief. Realize that death and grief are a part of life. If you are uncomfortable, it only adds to the family's distress.
- Attend bereavement workshops; read about and discuss grief in order to become aware of what the bereaved are experiencing and how you can help them.
- Set up procedures for coping with the patient's death and the grieving family.

BEFORE THE DEATH:

- Explain to the family how their loved one will look (general appearance, tubes, needles, machines, etc.). If possible allow the family to be present during treatment, to be involved in the patient's care as long as they don't disrupt critical medical procedures.
- Be available to answer their questions honestly and clearly.
- Frequently reassure the family that everything possible is being done. Be visible. Your competent and caring manner is comforting to the family.
- Realize that the family may need to talk about their feelings, to cry frequently. Arrange for a pastoral care team member, social worker or a trained, caring volunteer to be available to listen.
- You may need to repeat information because the family may be in denial or shock which hinders comprehension. One technique - ask family or patient to repeat what he has heard you say.

AT THE TIME OF DEATH:

- If possible, arrange for family members to be with the patient at the time of death (if they so choose). Try to be "there - with them" (if also desired).
- Give them as much time as they need to be with their loved one (alone if they prefer) after the death.
- If you are responsible for telling the family that their loved one has died and you are not comfortable doing so, send or take along someone who is. Tell the family in a clear, short statement, using the words "died" or "dead."
- Encourage the family to see the body as soon as possible after the death, allowing time to make the patient look as good as possible before the family enters the room. If the body has been mutilated, that part may be covered so that the family can at least see part of the body. Seeing the body confirms that their loved one really is dead.
- Reassure the family that everything possible was done to save/help the one who died.
- After telling the family, do whatever you can to comfort them. Don't rush away. You might put your hand on their arm, around their shoulder or just remain nearby. It is not necessary to talk. Offer your caring presence. Touching, holding or hugging gives great comfort to most people. Involve others in comforting the family. Try to strike a balance between being available, yet not imposing on their privacy. Give them time to pray.
- Be a good LISTENER. Don't force conversation or change the subject. Refer to the person who died by name. Invite the family to assist with post mortem care or part of it if they wish.

- Provide an atmosphere where the bereaved are encouraged to express their feelings: to cry: to ventilate their anger. Some hospitals provide a "screaming room."
- It helps the bereaved when the caregivers grieve openly with the family. When you cry, show frustration, anger, etc. within reason you model for the family that it is okay (even good) to do so.
- Realize the family may need to talk about the deceased and the details of the death.
- Some families may appreciate a follow-up visit at a later time in order to clear up any unanswered questions. Encourage this - it is beneficial to both you and the family.
- Try to suggest what needs to be done next, while giving the bereaved an opportunity to make small decisions.
- Don't be surprised if the family takes their anger or frustration out on you. Realize that their anger may not really be directed at you personally. Either way, it needs to be expressed and discussed.
- Don't be quick to offer medication to the bereaved. Grief is painful, yet it must be faced. The grieving process should not be postponed.
- Don't give rationalizations or clichés. Don't say, "I know how you feel." You might say "I wish I could take some of your pain away."
- If possible, visit the funeral home, attend the funeral, or send a note to the family. This means so much to the family. It shows that you really care.
- If the survivor arrives at the hospital alone, ask for the name and number of someone to call to be with them.
- Asking about organ transplants is extremely sensitive, yet so important. Decide upon an appropriate approach. Consult your local organ donation center for ideas.
- Don't avoid the bereaved because you're uncomfortable. They need you to reach out to them - to obviously care about them.

SUBSEQUENT ILLNESS DUE TO GRIEF: Grief can have profound effects on the grieving person's health. Some studies show that grieving people spend more time in hospitals than non-grieving people. Some research points to the bereaveds' susceptibility to cancer. Grief may lead to depression and anxiety. It can produce changes in the respiratory, nervous, GI and hormonal systems and may alter heart and immune system functions that affect survival. It is important to realize that many of your patients may be hospitalized because of the effects grief has on their health.

SUPPORT FOR MEDICAL STAFF:
- Include other support persons in working with the family: e.g. clergy, social workers, hospice personnel, physicians, nurses, therapists and pastoral care team members. Hold interdisciplinary staff meetings which can be valuable for all who work with the dying and bereaved.
- Establish death and grief education for students in nursing and medical schools and for hospital personnel.
- Provide formal or informal counseling, support meetings or help for those who work with the dying and their bereaved families.
- Stress is a normal part of life. Burnout is not. Read, take steps/courses to alleviate stress associated with bereavement.
- Support each other as you work with the dying and their bereaved families.
- Bring grief resources within the hospital and community to the attention of the staff.

SPECIAL CONCERNS:
- When your family member or friend dies: read about grief, join a support group, find someone with whom you may share your grief. Be patient with yourself. Grief takes time!
- If a child has died, don't tell the parents that they can have another child or at least they have other children. Children are not interchangeable.
- If an infant dies, suggest that the parents: hold the dead infant for awhile; take pictures of the infant; name the child. Provide some on-the-spot counseling.

WHAT TEACHERS AND SCHOOL PERSONNEL CAN DO TO HELP GRIEVING STUDENTS

Children are usually completely unprepared for the grief that they experience when a loved one dies. Often their adult family members and friends have their 'hands full' with their own grief and do not realize that the children need understanding and comforting, too. Teachers may find it difficult to help a grieving student. Classmates don't know what to say or do. This leaves the bereaved child to struggle with the unknown, painful feelings of grief by him/herself. It is difficult for adults to express their grief. Children are usually even more limited than adults in expressing themselves. When a classmate dies, the entire student body may be affected in varying degrees. Since a student spends six or more hours in school each day, it is critical that their "school family" learn ways of reaching out and helping their bereaved student/classmate. To ignore or minimize their grief is to deny the child a much needed avenue for understanding and help. Our focus in this article will be on grief due to death, but the suggestions will apply to any grief - separation, divorce, moving, breakup of a friendship, unemployment, etc.

Grow In Your Understanding:

In order to be helpful to bereaved students it is important that teachers and other school personnel understand what it is like to be bereaved and ways of coping.
- Look honestly at your own feelings about death and grief. Do you ignore, suppress or acknowledge them?
- Read some of the many helpful books on bereavement and helping a grieving child.
- Attend workshops on grief; sponsor an in-service day on grief.

Grief Is A Part Of Life:

Take advantage of the many teachable moments to discuss death and grief before it occurs. Children should be taught that death and grief are a part of life, just as being born, sleeping, eating, etc.
- Develop special units on death and grief.
- Watch for earlier mourning experiences: e.g., death of a pet.
- Tell or read stories in class that will increase the students' awareness of death and grief.
- Use basic words - "die" and "dead." Avoid phrases such as "passed away," "gone to sleep," "on a trip" and "someone lost a relative." 'Lost' implies hope for return.
- Discuss appropriate television shows.

What Can I Do To Help?

Teachers: Be aware that the bereaved student may experience:
- Shock, crying, denial, anger, guilt, fear, withdrawal, depression, aggressiveness, anxiety, panic, regression and physical complaints.
- Shortened attention span.
- Behavior problems and problems with school work.
- Repressed feelings that come out in other ways or at a much later time.

It is important to:
- Interact with the bereaved student instead of avoiding him/her.
- Use the name of the person who died.
- Be patient, understanding and accepting of student's feelings.
- Nurture a student's self-esteem.
- Encourage students to express their grief in a healthy way.
- Provide a place for the student to go if they need to be alone.

Realize that grief may take a long time - even years.

Be aware that students grieve not only for parents, siblings and friends, but also for a favorite uncle, grandparents, pets.

Be responsive to a child's questions. Let answers be honest, simple and direct. If you don't understand something, let the student know that, too.

Grief hurts desperately even when it's not expressed. Help the bereaved student and classmates to realize that grief is a normal and natural reaction to loss.

If a student seeks you out to talk, take the time to really listen. Gently encourage the student to talk, but don't force conversation. Please don't change the subject - allow some expression of grief.

Realize that some bereaved students may be suicidal. They need people to listen to them, to care about them, believe them and get them help. (See article on Suicide, pp. 71 & 72)

It is okay to cry, be sad or angry. Express your grief. In fact, it models to the student that it is okay to feel this way.

If appropriate and allowed, put a hand on their shoulder or arm. A hug when you know the student well is even better.

It helps if the whole class shares their classmate's grief. (Caution; some children are uncomfortable being singled out.) The class learns about grief and the bereaved student doesn't feel so alone.

If possible, meet with a few of the bereaved student's friends to help them cope and to suggest ways that they may be of support to their friend.

Form a peer group within the school and/or facilitate the students' awareness of the Hope For Youth support group (date, time, rides).

Have grief resources well marked in the school library. Even highlight these resources in a book display occasionally.

Stay in touch with the parents.

Children's Comprehension: Listed below are some guidelines as to children's comprehension. These stages may overlap due to a variety of factors and are given as a loose framework. Children understand at their own stage of development.

- Children *up to age four* have little understanding of the meaning of death.
- Between the ages of *four and seven* death is seen as temporary or reversible. A child has a feeling for loss but has difficulty in grasping the concept of death.
- Some children *five to ten* view death as irreversible, yet perceive the deceased as retaining certain biological functions.
- Other children *six and over* view death as permanent.
- A child of *eleven to twelve* has a deep feeling of loss and knows what death is
- Adolescents *fourteen to sixteen*, according to clinical studies, may have more intense grief than any other age group, although may refrain from expressing it.

School Administration: At the time of death:

- Set up procedure for coping with the death immediately, for the next few days, and as needed.
- Hold special faculty meeting so that information regarding the death and plans for helping the students may be discussed.
- Tell facts to discourage rumors.
- Encourage teachers - especially homeroom teachers or a teacher who is best able - to share the facts of the death with the class.
- Encourage classroom discussion (offer guidelines).
- Have trained people available to listen to students and teachers.
- Encourage poems, letters, drawings, essays about death/grief (possibly print in school paper).
- Hold a voluntary assembly (if appropriate). Be understanding, but it is important not to glorify death.
- Do something to acknowledge the death; e.g., plant a tree.

- Acknowledge concern to the bereaved family.
- Consider procedure for student participation in funeral and related events. This is done on a voluntary basis in cooperation with family and school personnel.
- Refer to Teenage Suicide Handbook* for detailed suggestions applicable to any death.

In the future:
- Form a Newcomers' Club or "buddy system."
- Train peer counselors.
- Form personal growth groups.

Psychologist Iris Bolton of The Link Counseling Center in Atlanta feels that coping skills should be taught as part of the school curriculum beginning in kindergarten. "There are four things we've got to teach our kids in order to survive. We've got to develop an individual's self-esteem so that each person has an internalized, intrinsic value because of who he or she *is*, not because of what he or she *does*. We've got to teach communication skills so that each person can learn to express their feelings. And we've got to teach what I call 'positive failure.' In a culture that promotes being 'number one' in all that we do, it's important for kids to know that the *effort* is positive, that they can enjoy and grow from what they do regardless of the outcome. And finally we've got to help individuals learn to handle grief. Many suicides are triggered by some sort of loss - a parent, a good grade, even a prom date - we've got to help people learn to deal with losses and even grow from them."

What Do I Say?

All that is necessary is a squeeze of the hand, a hug, your "being there." If you want to say something, say "I'm sorry" or "I wish that I could take your pain away."

It is not helpful to say: *I know just how you feel: You must be over it by now: Don't cry, you'll upset your . . .:   Be brave for your parent(s): I know someone who had two family members die (don't minimize their loss): It was God's will: He/she lived a good life: He/she is out of pain: Now you're the man or woman of the house: Boys don't cry.*

Special Resource
- *Teenage Suicide-Prevention Intervention Response (A handbook for Schools), COSAD and Four Winds Hospital 1984. Every school should have this handbook. It not only discusses prevention but offers a step-by-step plan for the days after a sudden adolescent death. Professional & Curriculum resource list included. Write Four Winds Hospital, Katonah, NY 10536

LET'S TALK ABOUT DEATH!

I would tell my children there's a baby on the way. We would talk about names for boys or girls; we would talk about whether we should paint the bedroom pink or blue - or if you're not sure, yellow. It's the most normal thing in the world.

If we can talk about death the same way, then I think we would live differently.

- Elisabeth Kubler-Ross, M.D.

I WOULD LIKE TO GO TO A HOPE FOR BEREAVED MEETING, BUT . . .
by Donna Kalb

"We can't take your pain away but we can share it."

I would like to share with you my experience of attending a "Hope For Bereaved" meeting. I was not prepared for the grief and pain which followed the death of my son. While I had the support of my family and friends, I had the desperate need to talk to another bereaved person, someone who truly understood my feelings. I had heard of the "Hope For Bereaved" support groups from friends and from the newspaper. I knew that I wanted to attend a meeting but I was somewhat hesitant about attending for the first time. I had many questions: Would there be all couples? Is it a large gathering? Would I have to present myself or tell my story? Would I feel left out? What is the atmosphere like? Would I cry? Would I be opening my wounds again? Is it only for newly bereaved? These were just a few of my concerns.

Gathering up every ounce of courage I had, I attended my first "Hope For Bereaved" meeting. As I walked toward the entrance I noticed a sign on the door announcing the various meetings, which assured me that this was the right place and time. Upon entering I was greeted by a friendly volunteer. I was introduced to other bereaved people. Before the meeting starts there is an opportunity to talk with these bereaved people. I find that I am not alone in my grief and that my feelings are common among the bereaved.

We begin the meeting by saying the "Serenity Prayer." As I look around the room I see that there are about 30 people. There are couples, and men and women attending alone. The group is open to any bereaved person regardless of age or religion. Some members bring supporting friends or relatives. Later I find out that some of the people are newly bereaved - while for others their loved ones had died several years ago. There are people whose loved ones have died after a prolonged illness, a sudden accident, murder or by suicide. Each one with a unique grief, and yet bound together by a common thread.

A warm welcome is extended to all and the topic for the evening is announced. There is a special topic for every meeting. Some of the topics are: the stages of grief, explaining grief to children, coping with the holidays, helping yourself through grief. We are told that we are welcome to ask questions, make suggestions or just listen. The two group leaders and counselor share some of their thoughts and ideas on the subject and then ask for any response from the group. I find that some people choose to participate, while others seem to listen. I am relieved to find out that I do not have to tell my story and feel comfortable just sitting and listening. Midway, we break for coffee. This time provides an opportunity for informal conversation. This is a very significant and meaningful part of the meeting. Added sharing is done on a one-to-one basis.

The break lasts for around 15 minutes. Sometimes the groups break up into three or four smaller discussion groups for half an hour. Some people are more comfortable asking questions or sharing helpful ideas in these smaller groups. I find that I can relate to so many of the thoughts that are expressed. Feelings that were so foreign to me are felt by most bereaved people. I did not feel probed or pushed. During the course of the evening there may be tears and there is laughter. It is an atmosphere of warmth and love. There is a feeling that people genuinely care and want to help. Some people travel from various parts of Central New York to attend the gathering. The meeting ends at 9:00 with a prayer.

As I leave, the feeling I have most is one of HOPE. It has been an uplifting experience. I know that the group does not have all the answers but that it offers support and encouragement. I know that it will be helpful for me to continue to come back over a period of time. Eventually I might decide to continue to attend in order to help others in their grief, or I may decide that I do not need the support any longer. Meanwhile, I am glad that I have made the effort to understand my grief, to learn ways of coping, and to hopefully reinvest myself in my life. In helping myself I have also helped my family and friends.

Donna Kalb is one of the original members of Hope For Bereaved Support Groups. She is associate director of Hope For Bereaved.

HAVE YOU EVER WANTED TO ATTEND A MEETING BUT . . .
you thought you would be really uncomfortable?

The following comments may give you that extra measure of courage you need to attend a meeting.

Q. *"Was the meeting helpful?" Please explain.*

"Realizing there are others who have experienced the very same sadness reinforces one's hope. Support is greater than that received from friends who cannot empathize."

"Yes. I found that I was not 'the only one,' that I was not different (unbalanced), that grieving for a child is a great challenge that others find difficult to meet, also."

"Yes. I realize that what I was going through was a normal process and that time does heal, although you never forget. Good to see and talk with other people who `made it.'"

"Very, especially through the initial months. Specifically it helped to talk about the experience with others. To see that other people had lived through a similar experience was great encouragement. The people at the meeting spoke the same `language of grief' which tied my tongue when I tried to speak with people who did not understand the grief experience."

"Very much - to talk and get all my anger out without people thinking I'm crazy when I rant and rave."

"Yes. At times when I feel like running away from the grief it helped to hear and be with people who can really understand my situation. I felt no pressure to talk. Thank you, so much."

RANDOM THOUGHTS

IT'S OK TO FEEL ROTTEN Often the newly bereaved, after returning to work or just accomplishing the everyday chores of caring for their family, are assumed well on their way to recovery from their loss. In asking about a bereaved person I have so often heard "he/she is doing great." This statement reminded me again of just how important it is to give the newly bereaved permission to feel "rotten." So often a bereaved person is told to "keep a stiff upper lip." They try to mask their despair, to follow the advice so as not to burden their friends and relatives. We want people to feel better, to do better, to get better, but some days it's hard to feel up. It's helpful to say to a bereaved person IT'S OK TO FEEL ROTTEN.

THAT DAY . . . THAT HOUR The hour of your loved one's death becomes etched in your mind, so does the day of the week. For some time afterwards you may subconsciously dread that day, grow anxious as that hour approaches. Wednesday, (for example) the fourteenth at 4:30 p.m. may stab you with fear. It seems that this awareness of the time of death gives you a vivid reminder of your loss, triggering new bouts of sorrow and pain. It comes as a relief when the next month the fourteenth falls on a Saturday. Gradually we become less aware of the particular day and time. You may never forget about THAT time but it's weekly passing fades from significance. The routines of your life intervene eventually to dilute the impact of the specific time of death.

WORRY Before our daughter Mary died I had never been an extreme worrier. After her death, at times I would worry in a big way. If one of my family members was a little late I would be concerned, but if they were very late I would truly panic. As bereaved, we are so afraid that another loved one will die. If one of our loved ones was struggling with a problem I would worry out of proportion. A very wise friend told me that her mother used to say, "If you are going to worry don't bother to pray, and if you are going to pray then don't worry!" I understood but at first it was difficult to apply. I would worry and pray. Occasionally I still do this, but I try to catch myself and concentrate on praying, not worrying. I realized that my worry did not help the situation or me at all. Excessive worry can lead to stress, stomach problems, tension, headaches - in fact, many health problems. Now when I catch myself on the worry merry-go-round, I stop myself. I check to see if there is anything I can say or do to alleviate the problem. If not, I ask myself "Is worrying going to help?" I realize that worrying isn't going to help. I pray for the person or problem - in fact I give "worry" to our daughter in heaven and ask her to "take over." Life is too short to spend it worrying. There are enough problems in life without making worry a way of life.

TIME Several months after our daughter died we were with a very good friend whose help and ideas I highly esteemed. I was looking forward to his advice. I was so sure he would have the answer to this terrible grief that hurt so much. Many of his relatives had died, so he would offer real help. All he said was, "Time will heal." That wasn't the answer I expected. I had hoped for a neat formula and I wanted to hear that the hurting would stop soon. Looking back, I can see the wisdom. Time can soften our grief, but it is WHAT WE DO WITH THAT TIME that makes a DIFFERENCE. If we lean into the pain, talk about how we feel, read, attend a support group, find a purpose in life, we will help ourselves. It doesn't happen as soon as we wish, but when we look back and compare from year to year we realize that we are coping and eventually finding that life is worth living.

MISSING   I will always miss you, Mary. As time has gone by we have been able to pick up our lives and go on, enjoy life and each other. I am proud of us that we have worked so hard on our grief and are feeling much better, but there are still times that I feel sad - that I'd like to talk with you - laugh with you - dream with you. When I look back I am grateful that we are better, but it is so long since we hugged, kissed, talked. I feel that you are with us, looking over us, caring about us. But I wish we could do our loving and caring in person. I always will miss you !!! (*Written eight years after our daughter's death.*)

DRIVING AND GRIEVING DON'T MIX Most of us who are bereaved have found ourselves driving and realize that our thoughts are not on what we are doing. We can't even remember how we arrived at the point when we refocused on our driving. Especially during the first year, we are confused, numb and have lost our concentration. This confusion and lack of concentration can reoccur at other painful times, too. We go through the motions of driving a car without realizing what we are doing. This is dangerous for us and for others. Sometimes we may have been keeping in our tears at work or in front of the family. When we are finally alone in the car and the tears and thoughts flow, it is better to pull over to the side of the road or into a parking lot to do our thinking and crying. Better yet, not to drive away until we are thinking clearly. We need time in each day to think about and to work on our grief, but not while we are driving. Be aware that driving while acutely bereaved is dangerous!!!

PICTURES   It is not uncommon for you to avoid looking at snapshots of your loved one who has died. It may be too painful for a very long time. Looking at smiling faces in happier times can trigger new rounds of intense mourning. In time you will delight in those photographs, once the images aren't so poignant with loss.

CEMETERY Some people find solace in visiting the cemetery, others cannot face the prospect and go infrequently, if at all. We are all different, no one approach is "proper." We must all follow our hearts in how we deal with cemetery visits. Such visits should not become a pressure within the family. Whatever you feel compelled to do will be appropriate for you.

BIRTHS It may be difficult to feel joy at the birth of a friend or relative's baby soon after the death of your loved one. Our normal reactions of wonder and excitement may be on hold for a period. You might see this lack of enthusiasm as evidence that you have permanently lost your capacity for joy and happiness. You might feel guilty or ashamed by your reactions. You go through the motions of congratulations but the birth may actually accentuate your loss. The cycle of life may seem cruel and arbitrary. Eventually your ability to feel the goodness of life will return and so too, your normal responses. Meanwhile, accept your attitude as the natural response to life overshadowed by grief. This is not, of course, an attitude that will be universally experienced, but should you feel this way be aware that it is not at all uncommon.

REMINDERS . . . MANNERISMS Suddenly you hear a familiar laugh, see a familiar gesture. You see some idiosyncratic habit performed by someone else that you had assumed was unique to your loved one who has died. What a jolt you feel. So close but so far away still. You might wish to avoid this person with the similar mannerism so as to avoid the painful reminder of your loss, but it is often a family member. The person isn't intentionally adding to your grief and you don't really resent them, just the pain of recognition. In time you may welcome that mannerism or gesture as an echo of someone else that you love too.

I STILL CANT BEAR TO . . . It can't be repeated too many times: THERE IS NO TIMETABLE FOR GRIEF. There are no rules, no right or wrong ways to grieve. Therefore it is normal for you to have individual responses to certain aspects of a loved one's death. One person may not be able to bear the sight of their loved one's possessions, the memories are too poignant. Someone else may feel that parting with these things is too final a step, they are not ready to completely let go. Some people feel that the placing of a headstone at the grave is too final a step, too raw a reminder. They need more time. Many widows and widowers choose not to remove their wedding bands. Some parents cannot turn their child's room towards any other purpose. Eventually the bereaved may be able to cope with these symbolic last steps, but there should be no pressure to do so. You must do what you can, you must allow yourself these private bits of contact with your loved one, regardless of how much time it takes.

LIFE LIFE WAS GIVEN BY GOD... in a great big box with a wonderful ribbon on it . . . What we expect in there is joy, peace, contentment, and an abundance of love.

But we also find in that life, pain, despair and loneliness. They are all part of the same box called life. It's not until you dive into it and experience all of it that you will really know life. We learn from pain just as much as we learn from joy.

Leo Buscaglia, Author

CHOICES When you have experienced the death of a loved one, you eventually look at life from a more aware vantage point. The following is paraphrased from an excellent book on Children and Death by Dr. Elisabeth Kubler-Ross:

All of us go through windstorms. With the help of a friend we are usually able to come out of it - ever so slowly - richer in understanding and wiser about the hardships of life. "Should you shield the canyons from the windstorms, you would never see the beauty of their carvings." This doesn't mean that you should not acknowledge the pain, anguish, sadness and loneliness after the death of a loved one, but you must also know that after every Winter, Spring follows; and out of your pain... if you choose so...comes a great amount of compassion, increased understanding, wisdom, and love for others who are in pain. Out of every tragedy can come a blessing or a curse, compassion or bitterness...the choice is yours!

THOUGHTS FROM SIMON* Many people feel that their grief has been given to them to help someone else. You see, you can do either of two things with grief. You can either let it make you bitter and twisted so that nobody wants to know you, or, with the help of a church or of a loving community and society, grief can make you a better person - a strong person. I believe, you see, that if folks have worked through their bereavement and found that there is a future, then we are the folk who must go down into the valley of the darkness and lead others to the light. In my experience, in the first few months of bereavement there seems to be no end to the valley of the shadows. It seems to be totally black. But if you can meet somebody who has been through the same valley and come out on the other side and is physically and mentally intact, and able to cope with life, and enjoy life, then I think we're beginning to get somewhere.

*Excerpt from an address given to THE COMPASSIONATE FRIENDS by Rev. Simon Stephens, founder of the original organization in England and author of "Death Comes Home." THE COMPASSIONATE FRIENDS is an international self-help organization for bereaved parents.

DEPRESSION COLORS EVERYTHING GRAY

Everyone experiences depression from time to time. It may range from mild to severe. It tells us that we are human and that something is troubling us. Depression alerts us to events in our life that are giving us difficulty. Bereaved people have reason to feel down. Some feel more depressed than others. Often the inability to adequately mourn the death of a loved one leaves a person vulnerable to depression. It is important to recognize the symptoms of depression, learn ways of coping and know when to seek professional help. Depression can be handled. The goal of such management is a renewed interest in life and general sense of well being.

Depression is a common problem today. According to the National Institute of Mental Health, 20% of all Americans, 40 million people, have significant symptoms of depression at some time in their lives. Countless others go untreated and therefore unreported. This may mean that the actual incidence of depression may be 40%. If untreated, it can go on for years and can disrupt work, family relations and social life. Everyone involved suffers. One medical authority estimates that two-thirds of the people visiting doctors for physical complaints have psychological problems.

Description/Symptoms

Depression is an emotional state associated with loss. It is a feeling of sadness that may lead to apathy and withdrawal. It has been described as "the last chapter of what's the use?" Author Maggie Scarf states that "a person who is depressed has a life-ache, the pain just overwhelms everything else."

The key symptom of severe depression is a feeling of deep, pervasive sadness and hopelessness that lasts for longer than two weeks. Other typical symptoms may be: loss of appetite; insomnia; inability to enjoy anything; anxious or restless behavior; apathy; preoccupation with thoughts of suicide, or wishing to be dead; loss of interest in sex: difficulty in concentrating and making decisions; poor memory; irritability; feelings of worthlessness: inability to cry even if one desperately needs and wants to; intense guilt; and withdrawal from friends and relatives. It is important for bereaved people not to become alarmed, because everyone experiences some or all of these symptoms at some time. If several of these symptoms are severe and continue over an extended period of time (so that pain and problems outweigh pleasure most or all of the time), then it would be advisable to get professional help.

Other signs of depression may be: headaches; backaches; crying spells, if marked increase in frequency and duration; unusual self-criticism; pessimism; discouragement; neglect of appearance; gastrointestinal problems; fatigue; greatly altered motivation for work, family responsibilities, and relationships; less laughter. The definition of depression is "the act of pressing down." The physical appearance is depressed, for example: little eye contact; shoulders slumped; head hung forward; lifeless voice; slow body movements; pale; obvious lethargy. Severe depression can be immobilizing. A person may feel so bad that "they can't stand it." A depressed person lives in a world with little emotional satisfaction either in self, in activities, or in other people. The depressed withdraw from people because being around others who are enjoying themselves make the depressed feel more isolated and unhappy.

Symptoms such as sleeping too much, overeating, excessive sex drive, irrational anger, smiling depression, alcohol and drug abuse are all ways a person might attempt to mask or overcome an underlying depression. A number of somatic complaints for which there is no apparent cause may be due to depression instead of physical illness.

Change is one of the main causes of stress and consequent depression, especially sudden or disagreeable change. Change can turn lives upside down and for the bereaved change is a fact of life. Too many or too drastic changes often result in depression. Refusal to accept their own limitations or to accept the human condition are causes of depression.

Losses that one suffers in the present can trigger the memories of past losses along with their painful and troublesome emotions. Such emotional turmoil may lead to depression. Loss often precipitates angry feelings. If these feelings are not expressed openly, then they are turned inward and may become a factor of depression.

Reversing the force and momentum of depression is possible. It takes hard work and sometimes the help of a professional . . . but it is possible to alleviate depression. According to Dr. Aaron J. Beck, working to change one's depressing and usually erroneous thoughts can lead to relief. Thoughts tend to govern moods. Straightening out one's thoughts often helps one's mood. Depression can be managed.

The SELF-ESTEEM of a person in grief can be very low. At a workshop on bereavement, studies showed that based on a scale of 100 an average person's self-esteem is measured to be in the seventies, whereas a grieving person's self-esteem is in the teens. This low self-esteem can be accompanied by feelings of worthlessness and dislike for oneself. These developments need to be identified and steps taken to rebuild one's self-esteem. Given this loss of self-esteem it becomes understandable that the bereaved are so vulnerable to symptoms of depression. Dealing with depression is a first step in rebuilding your self-esteem. They go hand in hand.

IF YOU LOVE SOMEBODY, SHOW THEM

According to Virginia Satir, internationally known therapist, HUGGING is good medicine. It transfers energy and gives the person hugged an emotional boost. "You need 4 HUGS a day for survival, 8 HUGS for maintenance and 12 HUGS for growth."

IF YOU LOVE SOMEBODY, TELL THEM

SUGGESTIONS FOR COPING WITH DEPRESSION

1. Recognize that the major responsibility for alleviating your depression lies with YOU. It is important to acknowledge it and be open to accepting help.
2. Read about depression in order to recognize the symptoms, causes, types and treatments.
3. Realize that depression serves a purpose. It is best to face it and work through it, rather than avoid it.
4. Talk things over with an understanding friend or loved one. It is one factor that may help you avoid severe depression.
5. See a physician for a complete checkup and discussion of your symptoms.
6. Redirect energy in more constructive channels so there is more pleasure in your life. Pleasure is a source of energy. Take a break for a favorite activity, an evening out, a trip, etc.
7. Exercise helps you to relax, work off bottled-up tension and sleep better.
8. Work on your sorrow. Lean into your pain. Realize and accept the death. Allow yourself to experience the many feelings you get, such as anger, guilt, etc. Express your feelings - let out anger by hitting a pillow, swimming, screaming, hitting a punching bag, crying.
9. Become involved with people; do volunteer work, help others.
10. Try to look at life more positively. Try not to expect that bad things will happen. Make efforts that good will happen.
11. Avoid extra stress or big changes if possible.
12. Practice deep breathing, which stimulates physical energy.
13. Remember that good nutrition is important for mental and physical health.
14. Seek professional help if depression is severe or persistent. It will not be as debilitating or as enduring as it would be if ignored or suffered alone.
15. Examine your feelings to figure out what's specifically troubling you and what can be done.
16. Write down negative thoughts and sort through them for the ones that you might be able to solve. Dealing with problems one at a time helps.
17. Consider yoga and meditation.
18. Depression has its roots in hopelessness. Hold on to hope - grief and depression management take time.
19. Acceptance of the loss and resultant depression makes it less painful.
20. If you feel guilty, seek forgiveness. Find alternatives to self punishment.
21. Attempt thinking pleasant thoughts for one minute. This may take practice but it is a helpful habit to cultivate.
22. For someone in depression it is important to remember that alcohol is a depressant.
23. Replenish self-esteem. Try harder to like yourself. Treat yourself as you would a good friend. Be patient encouraging, forgiving. Pamper and be gentle with yourself.
24. Do something you do well, such as hobbies or special activities. Little accomplishments help you to rediscover your self-confidence.
25. Remember, you have a choice. Depression can be managed. It doesn't have to ruin lives.

GUILT . . . IF ONLY . . . WHAT IF??

Often bereaved people keep thinking "if only" and "what if" What if I had called the doctor sooner; what if we hadn't let him/her take the car that night; if only I'd said how much I loved him/her... "If onlys" can be a vicious circle. In THE BEREAVED PARENT author Harriet Schiff suggests that if we were intended to function with perfect hindsight our eyeballs would be in the back of our heads. Hindsight is not helpful since things cannot be undone.

When a loved one dies, feelings of guilt are normal, though often not realistic. We may tend to blame ourselves for something we did or didn't do that may have contributed to the death, or for things that we wish we did or didn't say or do. This is fairly common. Some bereaved, however, become tortured by their feelings of guilt and it colors their whole life. Guilt is a strong emotion which is often magnified because the bereaved are in an extremely vulnerable state. The guilt is often experienced when the bereaved try to answer the unanswerable: "Why did my loved one have to die?"

One dictionary definition describes guilt as the act or state of having done a wrong; a feeling of self-reproach resulting from the belief that one has done something wrong. It indicates that guilt has something to do with sin and blame. To be guilty for something bad is to be accountable, to be responsible for it.

Most bereaved people feel some degree of guilt. None of us can live close to another person and love deeply without hurting that person. We all do and say things we later regret. We know these things hurt our loved one. When a loved one has died we are reminded of those hurts and failings, real or imagined, of words we regret saying, incidents we'd like to forget, actions we'd like to take back. We consider every possible action that we could have taken or not taken to prevent the death.

Guilt can be real or excessive. Both feelings are authentic to the bereaved. Real guilt results from the conscious, destructive things we do to one another. It is remorse over lost opportunities within a relationship. We wish we could make up for our past mistakes. Usually it isn't until after our loved one has died that we become aware of all the lost opportunities, of all the things we neglected to do.

Excessive guilt is shouldering responsibility for the death and blaming ourselves out of all proportion. We take responsibility for matters that we are really not responsible for, at least not to such an extent. Such excessive guilt unrealistically assumes that if we hadn't done this, or had done that, our loved one would not have died. This would be assuming an unreal power and control over life and death which we just don't possess. The implication is that we see ourselves, often subconsciously, as powerful enough to have saved the life of the deceased. It would be better if we put the emphasis on the fact that we probably did the best we could under the circumstances. Rabbi Kushner in his book WHEN BAD THINGS HAPPEN TO GOOD PEOPLE suggests that "An appropriate sense of guilt makes people try to be better. But an excessive sense of guilt, tendency to blame ourselves for things which are clearly not our fault, robs us of our self-esteem and perhaps of our capacity to grow and act." If guilt is excessive or prolonged we may need some professional help in working through it.

Guilt is usually not satisfied by explanations. Often we feel helpless with our guilt because there is little that we can do to correct the situation. A direct personal relationship is desired to take away the guilt but that is impossible because our loved one is dead. However, we may still ask forgiveness of our loved one who has died. We can take an empty chair and pretend our loved one is sitting there. Then we can have a one-way conversation expressing our regrets or guilt and asking for forgiveness. This is helpful for anything we want to say to our loved one. Even though there is no response, the asking is important. Consider that in the same circumstances we would forgive them. When we feel guilty justifiably and we are unable to be forgiven directly by the deceased, we may find some relief by talking with a trusted friend about our feelings of guilt. It is important to find a friend who will listen and be accepting of our feelings, without being judgmental.

If we are truly sorry, we may at least feel God's forgiveness. In LIVING WHEN A LOVED ONE HAS DIED, author Earl Grollman, quotes a wise clergyman who said, "I believe that God forgives you. The question is: Will you forgive yourself?" Someone else tells of a compassionate friend who said, "How many times have you asked God to forgive you?" "Hundreds and hundreds" was the reply. The friend said, "Too bad you wasted so much time. God forgave you the first time you asked." When you accept forgiveness (God's), you are choosing to forgive and love yourself and to let go of your guilt. Religion and psychology stress that forgiveness is important for inner health.

Feelings of guilt, which are common in all grief, are often of major concern among survivors whose loved ones have died by suicide. "Could I have prevented it?" "Is it my fault?" "How did I fail?" Most survivors tell that their grief was complicated by extreme feelings of guilt. For some the guilt never goes away. Either they let it ruin their lives or they allow it to diminish to the point where they can handle it. When death is by suicide, it is especially important to remember we can't control the behavior of another person.

If, as a bereaved person, you feel guilty, it is important to recognize that you are feeling guilty. Ignoring or suppressing guilt only adds to its intensity. When well-meaning friends tell you that you shouldn't feel guilty they really are not being helpful. Our feelings are not wrong; they help us to understand how an event is affecting us.

It is important for you to accept your guilt, however illogical, to understand it and to deal with it. Its unhealthy and even damaging to stay with guilty feelings. It may take great effort but it is worth such effort because guilt that is unrecognized or unresolved for a long period may lead to psychosomatic illnesses and to years of unhappiness. Remember, we can't change the past. There is so much pain in grief that it is not helpful to continue to blame and accuse ourselves. Work on your guilt and hold on to HOPE.

SUGGESTIONS FOR HANDLING GUILT

- If you feel guilty it is helpful to admit it to yourself. It is important to be truthful about why you feel guilty.

- Ask yourself what things specifically are bothering you the most. Talk over your feelings of guilt with a trusted friend or professional who will listen, care and not judge. Guilt should not be glossed over nor pushed down. TALK about your guilt until YOU can let it go.

- Remember that you are human. No one is perfect. There is so much that we tried to do. There are things we did not do. Accepting our imperfections aids us in working out our guilt. Realize that living is a balance of good and bad. Try not to blame yourself for things that you did not know you were mishandling.

- Remember there is not always an answer to "why" and you do not have to find some-body (yourself) or something to blame. Ask yourself if you want to live with guilt for the rest of your life. Realize that sometimes you are powerless and that you can't control everything that happens.

- Forgive yourself; ask for the forgiveness of your loved one and of God. If your faith is shaken, try to put your religious beliefs back together and find comfort in your religion.

- If appropriate use the "empty chair" dialogue. This technique offers you the opportunity to focus on your guilt, to admit it, to understand it and deal with it.

- If guilt is hindering your recovery seek professional counseling. Don't be afraid or embar-rassed to talk about your feelings of guilt with those who have been trained to help.

- You can learn from your guilt for the other people in your life. If appropriate, adopt a new lifestyle for the future. From past mistakes you may be able to change for the better.

- Consider that your loved one would not want you to continue to suffer from guilt and grief. Try to concentrate on the special times that you had with your loved one.

- Try writing about your thoughts and feelings of guilt.

- Become determined to live life to the best of your ability. When you are able, find some purpose or meaning in your life by helping others. Volunteer - in helping others you help yourself.

- Some things are beyond our handling, coping or correcting. Perfect parenting/ partner-ship/friendship is a role beyond realistic capability. It is helpful to realize you did the best you were able to do under the circumstances. You had no training and by trial and error you did the best you could, A persons best may vary from day to day depending on life's other pressures and involvements.

- Remember, many bereaved people initially feel guilty but their guilt does lessen with effort on their part and with the perspective of time.

HELPING THE BEREAVED WITH THEIR GUILT

It is not helpful to try to talk someone out of guilt with statements such as "Don't be silly. You did everything you could" or "You shouldn't feel that way." This may lead to more guilt. Consciously or unconsciously, the bereaved may feel they are not handling their own guilt well and thus feel guilty over feeling guilty. It is better to accept their expression of guilt. The following are helpful responses: *"Its only human to feel guilty." "We have to learn to accept and live with the fact that there probably always will be some regrets." "I think you did the best you could. From what I understand though, it is helpful to talk about your feelings of guilt until YOU can let them go. I will be here to listen to you as often as you need."*

Family members and friends can best help the bereaved with their guilt by listening and understanding. Realize that although the guilt may not be logical, it is natural and very real to the bereaved. It helps to empathize with their feelings and to reinforce the good things they did for the deceased. Time, plus the understanding of friends, usually softens the guilt.

FEELINGS OF GUILT ARE NATURAL

AUTHOR'S NOTES

After our daughter Mary died it seemed every emotion of grief slammed into me. At first I did feel guilty. I wished I had said "I love you" more often. I kept thinking of things I had said and done that I wanted to take back or of things I hadn't said or done that I wished I had. Then it occurred to me that Mary understood. She probably could think of things she did or didn't say or do, too. I could be understanding of Mary. I should also be understanding of myself. Both of us did the best we could. It didn't make sense to me to become stuck in guilt. I still was struggling with the other experiences of grief. Therefore, I focused on the happy memories - on the things that went well - and chalked up the mistakes to being human.

For many bereaved, guilt is a major stumbling block to recovery. Deep guilt prevents us from working on and resolving our grief. It is so important that this guilt is not pushed down or ignored. Talk about it, work on it, accept it, read about it, get professional help if necessary but don't remain in guilt. Our loved ones would not want us to feel guilty. We can't change the past but we do have a choice to work on our guilt and hold on to HOPE. Instead of remaining with past guilt let's live today as well as possible so that we minimize our feelings of guilt in the future. This would be a tribute to our loved one and a positive step for ourselves and the people in our lives.

DO NICE PEOPLE GET ANGRY?

THEY SURE DO!! Angry feelings are a normal and healthy response to the death of a loved one. They are a sign that we have loved very deeply. Emotions such as anger are not right or wrong, they simply are. Anger is a part of us just as love and joy are. Life at time hurts and that hurt generates anger. We often see anger as the enemy, so we continue to deny it and the pressure continues to build. Many of us were inaccurately taught as children that it is not "nice" to be angry, whereas it is best to recognize and express this anger rather than to deny or repress it.

REPRESSED If we don't deal with our anger, if we don't allow ourselves natural responses and outlets, then we accumulate the anger. We may forget about it in our brain but it accumulates in our guts. We slowly fill up like a reservoir. When we reach our capacity, we begin to spill over internally by turning our anger against ourselves as depression, apathy, guilt, withdrawal or low self-esteem. We may turn to excessive alcohol or drug abuse, smoking or eating. Anger may spill outwardly against other targets - our family, friends or coworkers. If we keep our anger inside or just below the surface we may experience constant tension.

Unexpressed anger does not dissipate. It merely hides until it emerges in another form. Unrecognized anger may be suppressed for years. So much energy is required to keep the lid on. It is very tiring. Anger and hate drain you of energy.

It is important to identify your anger and allow yourself to experience it, because those who bottle up their rage often develop psychosomatic symptoms as well as experience a lack of energy. They have chronic headaches, earaches, eye aches, sinus trouble, acne, arthritis, backaches, ulcers, colitis, constipation, high blood pressure and more.

Anger may be directed at OURSELVES. We are cross at ourselves that we are not handling our grief better or that we somehow were not able to prevent the death. Anger directed at ourselves is dangerous. Anger can be likened to a hurricane. When it is directed at us it can emotionally rip us to pieces.

It may also be directed at GOD. He can handle our anger. We get angry with people we love and never would wish to hurt. We tell them how we feel. We don't expect them to reject us for our words or to change something which might not be able to be changed. We want them to give us a hearing and to care about how we feel. Our purpose is to develop understanding and to clear the air. When we tell God how we feel, we feel better for His knowing just what we think on an issue. We might as well tell Him, because He knows what we think anyway.

After her sister died, our 14 year old daughter was angry and especially angry at God. She later told me that when she came home from school she threw things around her room (I didn't notice; it always looked like that). In church she would pray to her sister and not to God. Later she wrote to a friend whose brother died about her angry feelings towards God. She concluded that the serenity prayer helped her so much that she couldn't stay mad at God. She displayed good mental health. She was honest about her anger at God and she did something with her anger.

Our anger may be directed at OTHERS; the ambulance crew, the funeral director, a nurse, another family member or other "intact" families who have not had a loved one die. It is important to recognize such anger. We are not really that angry at them. Often it is displaced anger.

For some people their anger may be directed at the DECEASED. It is understandable that our loved one might receive some of our anger. You may feel as outraged as an abandoned child. You may feel "how could you die and leave me?". Since that seems unreasonable the very thought is suppressed. It is healthy to express such anger but be sure that you are with someone who is understanding and accepting of your need to verbalize the full impact of your anger.

A more difficult type of anger to recognize is the GENERAL just plain being angry. You are not angry at anyone but angry that your loved one has died. You may be angry because you hurt so much.

SIGNS Often our anger registers in our body language; tightening of facial muscles, flushed face, sweaty palms, stiff body posture, grinding our teeth, piercing stare or scowl. It also may come out as sarcasm, a loud angry voice, insults, throwing things, non compliance or over compliance. It may be masked by an overly sweet attitude, nagging, nit-picking, whining or sulking.

TYPES People vary in their expression of anger. Some people have a short fuse. Their anger may even become rage. They may carry their anger to dangerous extremes, some even seeking revenge. Others have great patience and are very slow to anger. Some just let their anger smolder. Still others may be someplace in the middle or go from one extreme to another. It may be difficult for some people to even recognize, much less express their anger, while others find it easy to express. It is important to respect these differences.

SUGGESTIONS FOR COPING WITH ANGER

It is important to acknowledge the anger and to find ways to deal with it constructively. In the old days we performed hard physical labor which helped to bleed off stored-up anger. People had to dig ditches, chop wood, beat rugs, etc. Recently, one counselor suggested that using an old fashioned rug beater was worth ten bottles of Valium. Anger is a physical thing. The more physically demanding the better, because it forces a deeper release of pent-up anger.

- It helps to deal with anger physically-take a walk, the longer and faster the better...go for a bike ride...use an exercise bike...work out at an exercise/aerobic club...scrub floors by hand...wash walls...tear up old magazines.
- Imagine whoever or whatever you're angry at being on the other end of your blows - hang a tire in a tree and hit it with a baseball bat...beat boxes with a broom...hit a bed with a tennis racquet...pound nails...throw rocks into a lake or field.
- Write about your anger...in a journal or even in letters that you tear up.
- Crying releases anger and frustration. Do things which force the tears, such as listening to special music, looking at photos, visiting the cemetery, doing things that remind you of your loved one.
- Talking will help you to understand the specific cause of your anger. You often feel better after getting it out.
- Deep breathing, meditation, even counting to 100 helps muscles to relax and resolves the physical component of your anger.
- Fantasies are a safe way of handling anger. One idea is to stick pins in a voodoo doll.
- Become aware of the dangers and limitations of "inner directed" anger and "displaced" anger. Be careful of uninhibited expressions of rage. They may make you angrier and do harm, which is self defeating. It is critical to unleash your anger in safe ways. Set limits so that no one is hurt.
- Consider counseling if your anger and/or depression continues.

I FINALLY REALIZED I WAS ANGRY

In the beginning when I was having a difficult time, my friend/pastoral counselor would ask me if I was angry. I always said no. About six months after Mary died I finally realized that I was angry. I now say that I will always be angry - not a wild-eyed type of anger but an honest statement that I feel Mary had a life to live and things to do. I was angry in general, plus I was angry at the driver. My anger led to depression for a while. I feel it is much healthier to admit to my anger. It no longer colors my life. I learned to talk about it and to really enjoy exercising.

Two of my favorite stories from the bereaved have to do with anger. One lady spoke of purchasing baskets of odd crockery at garage sales. She placed plastic trash bags in front of her cinder block garage wall, put on safety glasses and threw the crockery. Afterwards she gathered up the broken crockery as well as some of her anger and threw it away. A neater version of this idea is to place an old glass in a ziplock bag and throw it at any wall. One man, who had three family members die, would beat on a mattress with a baseball bat. When he moved he brought the mattress and bat with him.

Work at recognizing your anger, expressing it safely and eventually letting it go. Then, hopefully, you will be able to turn your energy to the more enjoyable aspects of your life.

ANGER
by Kathleen Jacques

Anger can be one of the strongest and most disturbing of the many emotions we experience after the death of a loved one. So many people have been conditioned to suppress their anger, they think it is unhealthy or anti-social to feel angry, much less vent that anger. Yet when a loved one dies we can be consumed by anger. It is a normal response to a devastating blow. You want to shake your fist at the heavens for this injustice. You seethe.

Anger is protest. How can this be! Why! That first rush of anger is in direct proportion to the magnitude of our loss. Sobbing may dissipate some of that initial anger, by virtue of the great amount of energy expended as you cry violently. It is the more pervasive, brooding anger that builds up that you may later have more difficulty resolving.

We may have specifically-directed anger; at God, ourselves, a doctor, someone who caused an accident, or even the deceased. This anger gives us a target on which to focus our frustration, to try to ascertain our loved one's death. Somehow our directed anger lets us establish "who's at fault." This gives the event a measure of reality; we begin to accept that our loved one is really gone. The facts become irrefutable and we angrily accept the details. Somehow this gives an illusion of control. Our anger gives us something to DO, a means to feel less helpless.

It is less important that we feel angry than what we do with the anger that erupts. We do not choose to be angry; our emotions come despite our will. Once we recognize that these emotions are there, like it or not, we can go about the business of dealing with them. We can choose to ignore our anger - become walking time bombs; when will that suppressed anger detonate? Or we can seek acceptable outlets for our anger and frustration.

If you are angry at a person you can tell them so. Not the "let-em-have-it" kind of confrontation, but the "You upset me when you . . . " approach. Don't be a martyr, but don't be a bully either. Speak up for yourself, it feels great.

When many people think of expressing anger, they think of it in physical terms - because it works. Scream, run, walk, swim, throw something (be careful about what and at whom!), skate, smash a tennis ball, whack that golf ball, FLUFF those pillows, hit a punching bag. Do any of these types of things and your fury will subside. You may even end up laughing at the spectacle of yourself at war with your sporting gear or household "enemies."

The method of positive release that you seek is secondary. The most important thing that you've done is allow yourself the need to be angry. You have every right to be. Get it out and you can let go of it. Let go of it and you begin to heal.

I WANT TO BLOT IT ALL OUT... DRUGS AND ALCOHOL
by Margaret Gerner

One of the things bereaved people should be careful of is the use of drugs during the grief process. In the early weeks and months when our minds and bodies try to shut out the terrible reality of our loved one's death, we experience physical as well as mental changes. We may not eat properly. We may not be able to concentrate. We may be chronically tired but cannot sleep. Our nerves seem to be on the surface. We become upset at the slightest provocation. Our mood swings are extreme. Some of us experience different kinds of physical ailments, such as stomach pain or chest pain. It is at this time many of us are inclined to see a doctor. This is good, but be certain that the doctor knows you are in the early stage of grief.

Drugs for the physical symptoms are at times necessary, but drugs that mask the pain of normal grief are dangerous. Grieving is necessary to readjustment. If grief is not fully worked through it is buried and will show itself destructively at some future time.

You must have confidence in your doctor, but be aware that not all doctors are knowledgeable on the grief process and its effects on the griever.

You must use your own good judgment as to whether mind-altering drugs are necessary. Any drug which produces a state of euphoria, causes us to sleep for long periods or makes us feel "better" in a short time should be looked at carefully.

There is also a danger in dependence on another drug that can be bought easily and legally at your corner liquor store. Alcohol, because of its easy accessibility and acceptability in our society, may be the first thing we reach for.

For those of us who have never drunk much, who do not care for the taste or effect of alcohol, there is little danger that alcohol could become a problem. But for those who have an already established drinking pattern, moderate though it may be, there is a strong possibility that we may seek escape or solace from our grief in the bottle.

In many ways alcohol is worse than the prescribed medication. Alcohol requires no prescription and no one is controlling how much we consume. Another common problem is that no one thinks of alcohol as a drug. It is; it's name is ethanol. It is a central nervous system depressant.

Grief itself has a debilitative effect on our bodies as well as our minds. Grief sends us into a state of depression, then to add the depressant drug ethanol, further complicates the problem. Alcohol increases the intensity of the symptoms of grief.

To fall asleep is difficult for most grieving people. We reach for alcohol to help us sleep. There is no worse drug than alcohol for the relief of sleeplessness. Granted, enough alcohol may cause us to go to sleep, but as soon as the blood alcohol level is gone we wake up.

Actually, findings indicate alcohol causes insomnia. With alcohol, as with sleeping pills, we build up a tolerance and more alcohol is needed to produce the same effect. When the alcohol cannot get us to sleep we may turn to sleeping pills. There again the tolerance is soon reached. Many times this leads to a combination of the two. Mixing alcohol and sleeping pills is extremely dangerous. People die from the combination. Not sleeping is one of the worse aspects of grief, but it is only temporary and will ease after a period of time. Addiction to alcohol will not.

The grieving person is intensely sensitive to outside stimuli. The least little irritation sets us off in fits of anger or paroxysms of sobbing. Our nerves are shattered. Again we reach for alcohol to settle them. On the contrary, alcohol does not help our nerves. It may sedate us for a few hours, but when the alcohol is gone it leaves us more jittery than before. Eventually our nervous system is in shreds.

The biggest danger in drinking for our nerves is that those of us who drink to calm our nerves are likely to take pills for our nerves also. This can be a lethal combination.

Some bereaved people may experience physical symptoms. The most common is stomach problems. Alcohol aggravates this. Stress of any kind results in stomach disorders for many people, but add the additional strain put on the stomach by the drug ethanol and there is trouble.

Grief causes a loss of appetite in many people. This, in addition to heavy drinking by the bereaved, can cause malnutrition. The vitamin deficiency created can itself cause an increase in many of the symptoms of grief.

Almost every bereaved person experiences the inability to concentrate. Minor decisions become major ones. Alcohol renders us less able to think, both when we are sober or directly under the influence of alcohol. While drinking, our mind is slowed down by the depressant effect of ethanol. When we are sober we are hyperkinetic. We can't sit still. We tremble. Our heart beats fast. Everything is racing, including our minds. With this reaction alone, we cannot concentrate.

Grief work, along with emotional pain and its physical manifestations, is necessary to constructive resolving of our grief. Any chemical we use to alter the normal process of this grief work only serves to prolong it or create other destructive problems.

The practical question is, how much alcohol makes the difference between a couple of drinks that makes us comfortable for a short time - and harmful drinking? There is no exact amount in ounces or frequency. We are all affected by alcohol in different ways. Body structure plays a large role in our capacity. A two hundred pound person can consume much more alcohol before he experiences the same effect that a hundred and twenty-five pound person can. Our individual metabolism is a factor, as is our emotional condition. Also, whether the alcohol is taken in conjunction with pills is important.

The frequency of drinking, whether it is every day or once a month, is not important. Individually we have to decide what effect the amount of frequency has on us. What is important is the role alcohol plays in our life and in our grief. One of the simplest tests is to ask ourselves if we feel a need for alcohol, not how much or how often.

What should we do if we find ourselves having a drink or two before going to bed or to calm our nerves now and then? STOP the couple of drinks now. Stop it before it gets to be a habit. From habit it becomes addiction. That addiction is called alcoholism.

There is disagreement among professionals as to the cause of alcoholism. Is it a learned response? Is it caused by our environment? Is it a physical craving that one is born with? But there is no disagreement with the fact that in almost all cases, the person started drinking occasionally and slowly progressed to heavy drinking and then to alcoholism. In most cases, a stress situation precipitated the heavier drinking which resulted in alcoholism. The bereaved surely do not need this complication.

HELP IS AVAILABLE: There are those individuals who can stop their drinking without help because they realize the danger before it becomes an addiction. But for those of us who find we are already in this situation where we need to drink or feel we cannot cope without alcohol, we must get help to stop drinking. Help is available.

First we must be honest with ourselves. We must admit to ourselves that we have become dependent on alcohol. Then we must be honest with our doctor. He may recommend treatment in a hospital or a self-help group such as Alcoholics Anonymous.

If you are newly bereaved, be aware that the use of alcohol can be very dangerous for you. For those of you who are farther along in your grief and alcohol has already become a problem, see your doctor. As hopeless as you feel your dependence on alcohol is, there is help. It is never too late. People do not die from grief, painfully but properly worked through. They do die from alcoholism.

Margaret Gerner's six year old son, Arthur, was killed by an automobile in 1971. He was the seventh of eight children. Her grief was long and hard, complicated by drugs and alcohol. She lived in a pit of grief and depression for five years. It wasn't until June, 1977 Margaret and her husband began meeting with other bereaved parents to constructively work through their grief. In December, 1979 they started the St. Louis Chapter. They feel it has been the most rewarding experience of their lives.

Permission to reprint from Margaret Gerner, The Compassionate Friends, St. Louis Chapter. Article has been edited

****

In this sad world of ours, sorrow comes to all . . .
It comes with bitterest agony . . .
(Perfect) relief is not possible, except with time.
You cannot now realize that you will ever feel better . . .
And yet this is a mistake.
You are sure to be happy again.
To know this, which is certainly true,
Will make you feel less miserable now.

Abraham Lincoln

****

Three of Abraham Lincoln's sons died: Edward, age 4; William, age 11 and Thomas, age 18.

NO TIME FRAME

"People are forever changed by the experience of grief in their lives. We, as humans, do not `get over' our grief, but work to reconcile ourselves to living with it. Anyone who attempts to prescribe a specific time frame for the experience only creates another barrier to the healing process."

- Alan Wolfelt

I HURT SO MUCH I WANT TO DIE

Authors Note: The topic of suicide is difficult for someone to read about when they are already grieving. We panic at the thought of another loved one dying. However, this is an important article because one of the reasons that people die by suicide is UNRESOLVED GRIEF. I know of at least five people who died by suicide after the death of a family member. For a long time after our daughter was killed I would wake up at 5:00 a.m. I can remember hurting so much one day that I could understand that people die by suicide. That scared me. I never made any plans or really wanted to die by suicide, but I came to realize that others in grief experience similar thoughts.

The death of a loved one is devastating. At first we don't believe it. As the hours, days and months go by we are left with the cold reality that our loved one is dead. Some of us have more support than others, but either way grief is lonely and seems to stretch ahead of us forever. Often the pain is so great that the grieving person thinks "I want to die." Missing our loved one intensities our feelings of wishing to be with him or her. Thoughts about wanting to die may range from just the idea to actual plans to take one's life. Bereaved people have shared how they thought of ending their grief...swimming into the middle of a lake until they just sank... driving a car at 80 miles an hour on a road that has a sharp turn. When you are grieving, facing the idea that you or another member of your family is at risk to die by suicide is a difficult concept. Yet it is CRITICAL that we realize this may be a possibility. We need to be on guard for ourselves and for our remaining loved ones.

Many times the adults have their hands full of grief and do not realize that their children need help with their grief, too. Teenage suicide has become a national epidemic. We need to discuss the tragedy of suicide with our family and become aware of ways to prevent it and to intervene.

People die by suicide because the fear of living seems more painful than the fear of dying. They want to get away from the pain they are experiencing and to escape from their inner torment. Suicide is an act of total despair and hopelessness, an act which the person thinks will bring peace. Most people who consider suicide have "tunnel vision," which is the inability to see anything else in life except the loneliness and pain of that particular moment. They are not crazy, just unable to step back, think the situation through and know that almost always, things will get better.

The grief that follows the death of a relative or friend by suicide is devastating and lasts a long time. It is often filled with guilt, questions and real pain. Realizing this, no one would want to cause those they love such deep grief.

> Suicide is a PERMANENT solution to a TEMPORARY problem.
> There are many other CHOICES besides death by suicide.

PREVENTION: HOW CAN I HELP MYSELF AND MY FAMILY?

FIND SOMEONE WHO WILL LISTEN: A friend, family member, counselor, teacher or clergy - anyone with whom you are comfortable. Call a community hotline. In Syracuse call CONTACT, 425-1500, or Crisis Center, 474-1333. You will find a good listener, someone who can help with referrals.

DON'T EXPECT TOO MUCH OF YOURSELF: Don't be tougher on yourself than you are on your friends. Bereaved often expect that they should handle grief better or faster than is really possible.

HELP OTHERS: By helping others you will get to see the pain and difficulties others are suffering and it will allow you to see that there are ways to cope. Volunteer at HOPE FOR BEREAVED, help a neighbor, etc.

BE A FRIEND: We all need friends, and being a friend makes friends.

LOOK AT WHAT YOU ENJOY: Spend more time doing things you like to do: sports, hobbies, etc.

AVOID DEPRESSANTS: Drugs and alcohol just complicate problems. They do not make you feel better permanently.

LEARN COPING SKILLS: Life is not fair and it is frustrating and difficult at times, but it is worth living. Even those who are not bereaved are depressed and disappointed sometimes.

JOIN A SUPPORT GROUP: You find others with a similar experience who offer suggestions for coping, understanding, friendship and HOPE.

LEARN ABOUT GRIEF: Read, attend workshops.

REMEMBER: "Love your neighbor AS you love yourself."

> THERE IS HELP, FOR YOURSELF OR YOUR FRIEND. LOOK FOR HELP . . . CALL SOMEONE FOR HELP. IF THE LINE IS BUSY, CALL AGAIN . . . AGAIN . . . AGAIN, UNTIL YOU *ARE* HELPED!

WHAT ARE THE WARNING SIGNS?
  PREVIOUS SUICIDE ATTEMPTS
  THREATENING TO COMMIT SUICIDE
  BEHAVIORAL CHANGES - sleeping, eating, neglecting appearance and health.
  DRASTIC MOOD/PERSONALITY CHANGES - unusually hostile, reckless, anxious; excessive moodiness, helplessness, sadness, worthlessness; unusually calm, passive.
  LACK OR LOSS OF FRIENDS - withdrawal from people, less communicating.
  DRUG AND ALCOHOL ABUSE
  DEEP DEPRESSION OVER LOSS
  ON-GOING DIFFICULTIES
  PREOCCUPATION WITH DEATH
  RECENT SUICIDE - of a family member or friend
  ABRUPT CHANGE FROM DEPRESSION TO LIGHTHEARTEDNESS
  GIVING AWAY PRIZED POSSESSIONS - making final plans
  PLAN FOR SUICIDE - getting a weapon
  YOUR "GUT FEELING"

> MYTH: "THOSE WHO TALK ABOUT SUICIDE DO NOT TRY IT"

INTERVENTION: HOW CAN I HELP?
  NEVER IGNORE SUICIDE THREATS - you might say "you seem really down, let's talk about it" or "what's wrong, you seem depressed lately?"
  IDENTIFY - the source or cause of distress.
  PUT PERSON AT EASE-they need to know you are trying to understand, that you take them seriously, that you will listen and try to help.
  DO NOT - moralize, scold, act shocked or argue about the value of life.
  MAKE SUGGESTIONS - they need to know where to turn for help; offer to go with them. In Syracuse suggest they call Suicide Prevention Hot Line, 474-1333, or Contact, 425-1500.
  DON'T BE AFRAID - talk about suicide, ask if the person plans to kill him/herself. Communication is the key to suicide prevention.
  DON'T LEAVE PERSON ALONE - if you think the risk of suicide is imminent. REMOVE WEAPONS - including drugs and alcohol.
  DON'T PROMISE NOT TO TELL - if you think someone is thinking of suicide, get help for him/her IMMEDIATELY!

> People want to kill themselves for a relatively brief period of their lives. Help them to see that they have alternatives and CHOICES!

I CAN'T SLEEP ! !

Many people suffer periods of insomnia after a death. For some, sleeplessness lasts a long time. Sleeplessness often accompanies depression and since many bereaved tend to be depressed, it further complicates their ability to sleep. One adult in four has trouble falling asleep or staying asleep. It is no wonder that insomnia is a big problem for many bereaved people.

The inability to express your grief and the increasing anxiety that grief brings is often the cause of insomnia. A person who has chronic insomnia finds it hard to turn off anxiety and tension and often keeps the grief and problems to himself. Not expressing anger and disappointment is another cause of insomnia. The stress of bereavement often makes our thoughts race, making it more difficult to get to sleep. Some bereaved suppress their feelings of grief during the day. When they try to get to sleep they relax and their defenses are lowered. It then becomes impossible to avoid these thoughts and sleeplessness results.

One of the most lingering problems I had after our daughter died was not being able to sleep. The days and weeks after Mary's death I had trouble falling asleep and would awaken early. It seems I was always tired. Eventually I was able to fall asleep fairly soon, but I would awaken at 5:00 a.m. My first reaction was, "What day is this? What things are going on?" Then it was as if someone stood above me and dropped a cannon ball on my stomach and I would realize that Mary was dead. I could not get back to sleep. At camp the next summer I would fall asleep, but awaken at 2:00 a.m. At first I didn't understand. Then I realized that it was the time that Mary had died the summer before when we were living at camp. After that I couldn't even fall asleep until after 2:00 a.m., but I still awoke at 5:00 a.m. When we returned home I fell asleep more easily, but continued to awaken early.

At one point I grew desperate about my lack of sleep that accompanied my depression. My doctor gave me sleeping pills. After taking the first pill I didn't awaken until 11:30 a.m. the next morning and I still felt tired. Then he changed prescriptions, but I really didn't feel good about taking pills. So I cut them in half, and then gave them up entirely. In my research on sleep I found most experts agree that sleeping pills should be used only for occasional sleeplessness, IF AT ALL. They say that barbiturates and sleeping pills don't help in the long run. Pills can wreck normal sleep if used regularly. They suppress the central nervous system activity, but they do not permit the natural vital stages of sleep to occur. Sleeping pills can be dangerous because their long lasting effects can impair coordination for such tasks as driving.

I have found that I can not drink beverages that have caffeine in them. Caffeine definitely keeps me awake. I drink decaffeinated coffee or tea - even in the morning. Grief is difficult enough without being able to get adequate sleep. Difficulty sleeping lasted much longer than I thought possible. Other problems and worries that entered my life made me anxious and affected my sleep. Eventually, as I worked on my grief and with the passing of time, my sleeping improved. I found that a glass of milk before bed and reading an interesting book every night helped me to sleep. If something is worrying me I may have trouble sleeping, but basically I can sleep again. I try not to concentrate on problems or let worry become a way of life. What a relief to be able to sleep!!! Hold on to HOPE that you, too, will be able to sleep again.

SUGGESTIONS TO AID SLEEP

1. Try not to become overly upset about not sleeping, as this just perpetuates your inability to sleep. Have confidence that EVENTUALLY you will sleep again.
2. Go to bed and get up about the same time everyday, including weekends. A regular routine keeps your inner clock set. If you always awaken early it may help to go to bed earlier.
3. Don't try to force sleep. If you cannot fall asleep after 30 minutes, get up and do something unexciting or peaceful, like knitting. Then go back to bed. Repeat this if necessary.
4. Take a warm bath and/or drink warm milk before going to bed. Warmth is soothing and milk contains an amino acid that may help you to sleep. Even cold milk may help.
5. Take time to unwind. Do not go to bed after a flurry of activity, either physical or mental, like balancing your checkbook.
6. Read light books, so the last thing you're thinking about is the book instead of your grief and other worries. It helps to get your mind off your insomnia.
7. Learn some kind of relaxation technique, such as meditation or biofeedback. Try alternately tensing and relaxing your muscles as you lie in bed.
8. Exercise daily, but NOT close to bedtime.
9. ALWAYS AVOID ALL SOFT DRINKS, COFFEE, TEA (HOT OR COLD), COCOA, CHOCOLATE AND ANACIN WHICH CONTAIN CAFFEINE!! (DRINK WATER, HERBAL TEA, DECAFFEINATED COFFEE OR TEA OR JUICES.) CARRY YOUR OWN TEA BAGS!!
10. Don't watch television in bed. Even dull, boring shows may keep you awake.
11. Be aware that sleeping pills, alcohol and cigarettes may even cause insomnia. Alcohol or sleeping pills may help us to go to sleep, but as soon as they are out of our systems we wake up. We build up a tolerance and need more to get us asleep. Barbiturates can cause death when taken with alcohol.
12. Try not to spend daytime hours in your bedroom. Reserve that room for sleeping at night. Do not nap during the day. Avoid heavy meals before retiring.
13. Try sleeping in a comfortable bed (possibly a water bed) in a dark, quiet room.
14. The hum of an air conditioner or special bedside machines that produce soft noises may induce sleep.
15. Watch the temperature and humidity of the room. Warmth helps to relax muscles and induce drowsiness, but overheating and excessive dryness from high temperatures interferes with sleep. A cool room and an electric blanket may be a good combination.
16. Try curling up in bed with a pillow or large, soft stuffed animal. It may aid you as it did when you were young.
17. Lie on your side. Place a second soft pillow over exposed ear, leaving your face out between the two pillows - or use ear plugs.
18. If problems and anxiety are causing you much sleeplessness, consider talking them over with an understanding friend. If this doesn't help, consider counseling.
19. Widowed people suggest sleeping in a different room; sleeping on your spouse's side of the bed so your side is empty instead; putting a pillow behind your back as you lie on your side.
20. Try mind games - counting sheep, recalling a nice day, plotting a novel, planning a trip, etc.
21. You may find the repetition of prayers to be sleep inducing.
22. Remember that many bereaved people have difficulty sleeping. Concentrate on the sleep that you do get. We often sleep more than we realize. Try to keep an optimistic attitude about sleep.

GRIEF IS BAD FOR YOUR HEALTH

The experiences of grief are emotionally grueling. It can seem to take every bit of energy you have just to make it through the simplest daily tasks. It is understandable then why so many people neglect their health at this time. It's hard to get adequate rest and nutrition when you just can't fall asleep and food is the furthest thing from your mind. Yet if we ignore our health, it is likely that we risk illness or discomforts that will complicate our grief even more. It is much harder to deal with the realities of the death of a loved one when you are plagued by insomnia, feeling weak from lack of a proper diet, suffering the consequences of too much alcohol, medication or caffeine, or leaving chronic medical conditions unattended. Grief takes work, and you'll need all your strength and resources. All the available literature on grief and your health points to the importance of rest, exercise, good nutrition and proper medical attention.

Some physical symptoms may occur as a result of your inclination not to take care of yourself after the death of a loved one. However, some problems are brought on by the severe emotional reaction of shock. Tension headaches, stomach and body aches, nervousness, nausea and skin disorders have all been reported as immediate reactions to the news of the death. It is widely held that grief weakens our resistance to disease, which can have serious, and in some cases fatal, results. The emotional period following the death of a loved one triggers suppression of the immune system, allowing a host of ills to complicate the grieving process, doctors say. You may experience gastro-intestinal problems, asthma, sleep problems, flus, weight loss or gain, frequency of colds, arthritis, palpitations or increased blood pressure.

"The death of a spouse has been associated with increased illness and death particularly among widowers," said Dr. Steven J. Schleifer and colleagues at Mount Sinai School of Medicine in New York. Studying a group of widowers, Dr. Schleifer's research team found a significant decline in the activity of lymphocytes (white blood cells involved in the body's defenses against disease) during the first two months after the death. "The present findings are consistent with a hypothesis that changes in the immune system following bereavement are related to the increased mortality of widowers." A study conducted at the Yale Medical School by Dr. Adrian M. Ostfeld indicates that widows and widowers experience hormonal changes that increase their susceptibility to infections and cancer.

Suppression of the immune system may also be affected by the neuro-chemical mechanisms that have been associated with depression and anxiety, both commonly found in the grieving. In the Journal of the American Medical Association, Drs. J. Trig Brown and G. Alan Stoudemire of Duke University Medical Center cite studies showing bereaved individuals feel sicker, spend more time in hospitals and use alcohol, cigarettes and tranquilizers more than non-bereaved individuals in age-matched control groups. Normal grief may lead to long term depression that requires professional help.

A fairly common, but mostly misunderstood, physical reaction to the frustration and anxiety of bereavement is "bruxism" or grinding of the teeth. Often a bereaved person grinds his teeth at night and is therefore unaware of the process. They only become aware of the problem when it causes marked periodontal disease, severe muscle pain, or headache caused by nerve impairment of the jaw. Once diagnosed the problem is often corrected with a special wedge worn in the mouth to prevent the nightly -gnawing and gnashing. Chronic jaw-clenching also occurs in bereavement. This may include pain in the face, neck or shoulders, pressure or sounds in the ears, periodic loss of hearing, pressure in the eyes, sinusitis or chronic sore throat.

There have been a lot of general interest articles lately about the debilitating effects of excessive stress and ways to alleviate that stress. These articles offer advice that certainly pertains to the bereaved, who are facing the greatest stress of their lives. We are urged to exercise, vent our feelings, and foster a positive outlook. The single most important antidote to stress, depression, and illness may very well be a sympathetic listener. Studies have shown that those who isolate themselves have greater incidences of becoming emotionally or physically sick. Reaching out to others, individually or in a support group, may be crucial in maintaining your health, both mental and physical.

by Kathleen Jacques

****

DEATH OF A LOVED ONE CAN HAVE PROFOUND EFFECTS ON YOUR HEALTH

The following was taken from a two-year major study sponsored by the National Institute of Mental Health. The findings from the 300 page report were published in 1984.

Each year, eight million Americans experience the death of a close family member. During that period 400,000 children under the age of 25 die and 800,000 become widows and widowers. Bereavement puts some survivors at increased risk of dying prematurely themselves or suffering physical or mental illness, even years later. Research also indicates that grief can produce changes in the respiratory, nervous and hormonal systems and may alter heart and immune system functions, affecting survival.

According to the report, a child whose parent or sibling dies is likely to grieve differently and longer than older people. This requires special attention because they may suffer emotional disturbances that carry over into adulthood. Children younger than five years and those in their early teens appear most vulnerable to long term disturbances.

The study found recovery from grief is long and irregular, lasting as long as three years and not following a uniform progression. (It may last longer than the study indicates.)

****

The following suggestions have been found helpful to reduce stress and would therefore apply to grief . . . a major stress.

GOOD NUTRITION: Try to eat balanced meals. Resist the temptation to skip meals or eat junk food. It forces your body to work very hard on a skimpy handful of nutrients and denies the body the resources it needs. Become aware of what you eat. There is too much fat, salt, sugar, meat, chemical preservatives and alcohol in our American diet. Fish, chicken, fruits, vegetables and fiber are better for you. Analyze what you eat. Is it to satisfy your hunger or to relieve loneliness and anxiety?

EXERCISE: You need exercise to stay healthy. Exercise increases your heart and lung capacity, strengthens your body and your immune system, reduces nervous tension, depression and anxiety, aids weight control and increases your ability to cope. Practice whatever exercises you choose regularly - at least 20 minutes a day 3 or 4 times a week.

REST: Try to get adequate sleep...If you are not able to sleep, at least rest. Work on learning to relax. It helps if you turn off your "thinking" and "doing" for short periods each day. Choose your own relaxation technique, such as finding a quiet place and thinking positive, pleasant thoughts or concentrating on slowly relaxing each part of your body, starting at your toes.

FUN: Build in time to play each day, to do what you want to do, to feel free and spontaneous, to have fun, to laugh.

POSITIVE THINKING: Take responsibility for your health and for working on your grief. Replace negative thoughts with positive thoughts and attitudes. Realize that there is a connection between what you think and how you feel.

OTHER SUGGESTIONS

At first, grief consumes you. You don't think about taking care of your health; in fact, you may not even care if you live or die. The following suggestions have been researched by the longer bereaved in the hope that they will help you to take care of yourself and your family, who do not need another illness or death:

- Have a complete checkup. Be sure to tell your doctor that your loved one has died.
- Realize you are not a hypochondriac if you have a psychosomatic symptom, which is a physical problem brought on by an emotional reaction. It is real. You really do feel the pain and distress.
- Pay attention to your breathing. Inhale and exhale in equal amounts. It is important to get new air in and stale air out. The deeper you breathe, the better.
- Listening to pleasant, relaxing music is often soothing.
- It helps to stretch, loosen up your body. Move your shoulders, rotate your neck, wrists, even wiggle your nose and jaw.
- Find a friend (support group members) that you can talk with about your grief and who will support you in your struggle to recover.
- Faith in God, yourself and others helps.
- Make a commitment to life. Find purpose for living. Become determined to work on your grief and to take care of your health. Hold on to HOPE.

LAUGHTER IS GOOD FOR YOUR HEALTH

In 1964, doctors told Norman Cousins that his chance for full recovery from a painful collagen illness was only 1 in 500. However, with Vitamin C, laughter and a generous dose of "the will to live," he was able to conquer his crippling disease. Norman Cousins was the former editor of the Saturday Review and is author of the bestseller, "Anatomy of An Illness."

He believes that creativity, the will to live, hope, faith and love have biochemical significance and contribute strongly to healing and well-being. He felt strongly that each person has a doctor inside him. He studied and analyzed his disease and, together with his doctor, formulated a plan to get better. Since it was medically recognized that negative emotions produce negative chemical changes, he felt that the opposite would also be true...that positive emotions would produce positive chemical changes. He watched films of Candid Camera and old Marx Brothers movies. His nurse read from books on humor. Ten minutes of genuine belly-laughter gave him two hours of pain-free sleep.

According to Norman Cousins, laughter is a form of internal jogging. It moves your internal organs around and enhances your respiration. His story demonstrates what the mind and body, working together, can do to overcome illness and improve your health.

Laughter and a sense of humor are important tools in handling your grief and maintaining your health. They help to make life worthwhile. When you can, laugh at yourself, at the humorous people and events in life.

TEARS
by Eunice Brown

TEAR *n* 1a: a drop of clear saline fluid secreted by the lacrimal gland ...

b *pl*: a secretion of profuse tears that overflow the eyelids and dampen
the face 2 *pl*: an act of weeping or grieving

Websters New Collegiate Dictionary

At a grief workshop I attended in the spring of 1986 given by Dr. Terrance O'Brien, I heard him say, "Tears are not a luxury, they're a necessity." During the last few days of our son's life and his long struggle against cancer, I found myself sobbing uncontrollably outside his hospital room. I know now that it was important for me to do this.

Our 30-year old son Keith died around 6:00 a.m. on November 10th, 1981. After I had called our other children, packed our suitcases and left the hospital room across from his (our home for the preceding four days), it was only about 7:30. The day loomed ahead of me like a dark cloud. I wanted so desperately to push the clock ahead. It wasn't easy sitting in an apartment in a strange city with literally nothing to do but walk from one room to the other; time hung so very heavily. I needed to do something - anything. I noticed a basket of clothes and asked our daughter-in-law if I could take them to the laundromat, along with our son's robe and things he had at the hospital. She said it was okay. At the laundromat I sorted the clothes, and was doing just fine until I went to put Keith's robe into the washing machine. I began to cry, hugging the robe, embarrassing my husband, and had the people there all looking at me. I'm sure they were all wondering, *Why is that lady crying in her laundry*?! I felt a need to tell the young woman next to me why I was crying and hugging the terrycloth robe. So I did tell her that our son had died that morning. To my surprise, she told me she knew exactly how I was feeling, because three years before she had a four-year-old son die after an illness. We shared some thoughts a few minutes longer, and I could see she was doing okay after three years. That in itself made me feel better.

"TEARS ARE NOT A LUXURY, THEY'RE A NECESSITY."

I have shed many tears, especially in my adult life. When we returned home after our son's funeral, I was shocked by the expression on our oldest daughter's face when she met us at the airport. It was a look of sheer pain, and after we had talked I realized she had not cried. Once she broke down and cried, the expression was gone! She released some of the grief in her tears.

I am moved to tears easily at times. I can cry reading a book or an article, watching television, or at the movies. My eyes well up with tears when I'm touched by a homily in church; and when someone else cries it is not unusual that I end up crying along' with them. Sometimes words fail and it's the only way I can empathize. I remember seeing a television show about children suffering with cancer. One teenager said people had told her that her doctor would go back to his office and cry after seeing her suffer. She said, "If only he had been able to cry with me it would have meant so much more."

"TEARS ARE NOT A LUXURY, THEY'RE A NECESSITY."

I saw my father cry just once, the day my 3-1/2-year-old brother was buried. I was 6-1/2 at the time, just starting second grade. I didn't cry; I was told that we had a little angel in heaven and I thought, isn't that wonderful?! When my mother died after 51 years of marriage to my father, he didn't cry (at least not in front of us), and I thought, isn't that strange?! Four years later when my father died, one of my saddest experiences was watching an 81-year-old man, who had been a friend of my father for almost as many years, stand in front of the casket with tears streaming down his face. And I thought, what a tribute to my father; he really cared about his longtime friend and was moved to tears by his death and didn't care who saw him crying!

I had a similar experience the summer of 1986 when my aunt, my mother's youngest sister, died. She was the last of her generation. I found myself thinking: Now they are together again; my grandparents, all their children, cousins who died at birth or in infancy, my little brother, my cousin's son,- our first grandchild and our son, Keith. Death is no stranger to me. And -

"TEARS ARE NOT A LUXURY, THEY'RE A NECESSITY."

When we watched the Kennedy family over 20 years ago after the assassination of our 35th president, many people marvelled at how strong they all were. All those hours of televised coverage and nary a tear did we see through any of their tragedy. For me, that was not real. I cried when our president was shot and killed, along with millions of others. If that family had shown their true emotions, what a help that would have been to so many who would grieve and want to cry, but wouldn't because they wanted to be strong like the Kennedys. As one of my friends put it, the Kennedy family managed to set back the grieving process about 25 years!

"TEARS ARE NOT A LUXURY, THEY'RE A NECESSITY."

In Chuck Swindoll's beautiful book, "For Those Who Hurt," he devotes a chapter to "Some Thoughts On Tears." He says, "Tears have a language all their own, a tongue that needs no interpreter. In some mysterious way, our complex inner-communication system knows when to admit its verbal limitations, and the tears come. Tears are not self-conscious. They can spring upon us when we are speaking in public, or standing beside others who look to us for strength. Most often they appear when our soul is overwhelmed with feelings that words cannot describe." He speaks of Jeremiah, nicknamed the "weeping prophet" ... "so tender and sensitive he could not preach a sermon without the interruption of tears. Even though he didn't always have the words to describe his feelings, he was never at a loss to communicate his convictions. You could always count on Jeremiah to bury his head in his hands and sob aloud."

There are many places in scripture where tears or weeping are mentioned. They tell all of us it is all right to cry. In John 11:35 Jesus Himself wept when His friend Lazarus died. My favorite is Psalm 56:9 where it says, "My wanderings You have counted; my tears are stored in Your flask; are they not recorded in Your book?" I wonder how many bottles of tears have your name and my name on them?

"TEARS ARE NOT A LUXURY, THEY'RE A NECESSITY."

I have thought of that incident in the laundromat so often over the past few years and of how close God had been to us that day, to send one stranger in a city the size of Minneapolis, who understood. That was the beginning of my belief in support groups. That's what it's all about. People helping each other, leaning on each other, talking to each other, crying with each other, hugging each other and - above all - really understanding. There is a bond between grieving people that is like no other. Our grief is a very personal thing and there is nothing as sacred as that space we move into, that place that is the core of who we really are.

"TEARS ARE NOT A LUXURY, THEY'RE A NECESSITY."

Eunice Brown is a bereaved parent and an active volunteer for HOPE FOR BEREAVED.

HOW TO HELP OURSELVES THROUGH THE HOLIDAYS
by Donna Kalb

There are many holidays or "special days," such as birthdays, anniversaries, graduations, weddings and Easter, to name a few. These are all difficult days for the bereaved, but for many, the most difficult holiday of the year is Christmas. This day, more than any other, means "family together." They are synonymous and it is at this time we are so acutely aware of the void in our life. For many, the wish is to go from Dec. 24 to Dec. 26. We continually hear Christmas carols and people wishing everyone "Merry Christmas." We see the perfect gift for our loved one who has died, and suddenly realize they will not be here to enjoy it. Eventually, the Christmas season will not be so difficult. This statement may not seem possible to those newly bereaved, but grief will soften and you will begin to enjoy life again, including Christmas.

SHOP EARLY!!!

Shopping may be extremely upsetting. It may help to shop early through a catalog, by phone or to make plans to shop with an understanding friend. Plan to relax over lunch or a cup of coffee. Friends or relatives might be willing to shop for you if they realize that just the thought of shopping is bothering you. Some people pretend Nov. 25th is Christmas and try to get whatever shopping, card writing, etc. done by that date. By shopping now you are able to avoid hearing the Christmas carols, seeing all the decorations and being wished Merry Christmas.

1. Family get togethers may be extremely difficult. Be honest with each other about your feelings. Sit down with your family and decide what you want to do for the holiday season. Don't set expectations too high for yourself or the day. If you wish things to be the same, you are going to be disappointed. Undertake only what each family member is able to handle comfortably.

2. There is no right or wrong way to handle the day. Some may wish to follow family traditions, while others may choose to change them. It may help to do things just a little differently. What you choose the first year, you don't have to do the next.

3. Keep in mind the feelings of your children or family members. Try to make the holiday season as joyous as possible for them.

4. Be careful of "shoulds"-it is better to do what is most helpful for you and your family. If a situation looks especially difficult over the holidays, try not to get involved.

5. Set limitations. Realize that it isn't going to be easy. Do the things that are very special and/or important to you. Do the best that you can.

6. Once you have made the decision on how you and your family will handle the holidays, let relatives and friends know.

7. Baking and cleaning the house can get out of proportion. If these chores are enjoyable, go ahead, but not to the point that it is tiring. This year you could either buy baked goods, or go without.

8. Emotionally, physically and psychologically, it is draining. You need every bit of strength. Try to get enough rest.

9. If you used to cut down your own tree, consider buying it already cut this year. Let your children, other family members, neighboring teens, friends, or people from your church help decorate the tree and house. If you choose not to have a tree perhaps you could make a centerpiece from the lower branches of a tree, get a ceramic tree or a small table-top tree.

10. One possibility for the first year may be to visit relatives, friends, or even go away on a vacation. Planning, packing, etc., keeps your mind somewhat off the holiday and you share the time in a different and hopefully less painful setting.

11. How do you answer "Happy Holidays?" You may say, "I'll try" or "Best wishes to you." You think of many answers that you don't say.

12. If you are accustomed to having dinner at your home, change and go to relatives; or change the time (instead of 2:00 p.m., make it 4:00 p.m.)   Some find it helpful to be involved in the activity of preparing a large meal. Serving buffet style and/or eating in a different room may help.

13. Try attending Christmas services at a different time and/or church.

14. Some people fear crying in public, especially at the church service. It is usually better not to push the tears down any time.   You should be gentle with yourself and not expect so much of yourself. Worrying about crying is an additional burden. If you let go and cry, you probably will feel better. It should not ruin the day for the other family members, but will provide them with the same freedom.

15. Consider not sending or cutting back on your cards this year. It is not necessary to send cards, especially to those people you will see over the holidays.

16. Do something for someone else, such as volunteer work at a soup kitchen or visit the lonely and shut-ins. Ask someone who is alone to share the day with your family. Provide help for a needy family. Donate a gift or money in your loved one's name.

17. Share your concerns, feelings, apprehensions, etc., as the holiday approaches, with a relative or friend. Tell them that this is a difficult time for you. Accept their help. You will appreciate their love and support at this time.

18. Holidays often magnify feelings of loss of a loved one. It is important and natural to experience the sadness that comes. To block such feelings is unhealthy. Keep the positive memory of your loved one alive.

19. Often after the first year, the people in your life may expect you to be "over it." We are never "over it," but the experience of many bereaved is that eventually they enjoy the holidays again. Hold on to HOPE.

20. Don't Forget: "Anticipation of any holiday is so much worse than the actual holiday."

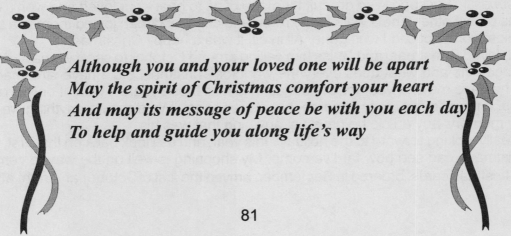

Although you and your loved one will be apart
May the spirit of Christmas comfort your heart
And may its message of peace be with you each day
To help and guide you along life's way

THE FIVE YEARS OF CHRISTMAS
by Eunice Brown

The Christmas holidays are approaching - for Christians, a very special time. I have always loved Christmas, and have always tried to make it very special; lots of baking, decorating, shopping, wrapping and trying to keep the true meaning of Christmas alive. I start shopping in January and continue all year long. This was very perceptive of me, because who would have dreamed that I would become a grieving parent and that the holidays, especially Christmas, would be so difficult? It is not the holiday itself - it's the family gathering and having one missing. Our children are all married, all live in New York State, the youngest in Syracuse. It has been customary that we spend Christmas day with our oldest daughter and family. Our "family Christmas" has always occurred whenever our children's working schedules permitted. This never mattered to me until our son died.

The first Christmas (a mere month and a half after Keith's death), our daughter-in-law planned on coming from Minneapolis but because of commitments couldn't make it until almost the end of January. Our tree stayed up and we waited to have our "family Christmas" until then. This proved to be disastrous for me. It was typical of me to try to please everyone else, and my own feelings got tossed - who knows where? I vowed I wouldn't accommodate anyone to that extent again. It is one thing to think of everyone else, but I went too far, and I suffered.

The second Christmas, I did very little baking, no decorating; just our artificial tree. I had the shopping done very early - sent Christmas cards, went to our daughter's for Christmas day and had our "family Christmas" the weekend of the 6th of January. It is vague in my memory.

The third year we did something different and spent Christmas day with our son and family in Schenectady, and our oldest daughter had "family Christmas" at her home. This change was good but the season was not especially a happy one. But as I look back it was just two years after our son's death. I know now this is normal.

The fourth Christmas we spent with our daughter and family and our "family Christmas" followed the next weekend, at our home. I wanted to do something a little different, which, by now, I had learned was a good thing to do. I bought an extra small gift for each of our ten grandchildren and had a good friend play Santa Claus. Needless to say, the grandchildren were delighted. We also hired a baby-sitter and took our children out on Saturday night for pizza and beer. Needless to say, the "children" were delighted. It also gave us the opportunity to spend some time with our children without constant interruptions from "little ones." Needless to say, Grandma and Grandpa were delighted!

Last year, my husband Dick injured his back and was confined to the couch. Our youngest daughter and family stopped over early in the day, and we had close friends in for a light supper in the evening. It was rather nice to spend the Holy Day, peaceful and quiet. It gave me time to reflect on what Christmas really is. There was a time when I would have been very disappointed in "changed plans," but it really doesn't matter anymore. I had time to rest and extra time to prepare for the following weekend and our "family Christmas." Only one little thing happened last year, when the boys, playing their guitars and everyone singing Christmas songs, picked "*I'll Be Home For Christmas.*" That song is so difficult for many of us to hear - our loved one won't be home for Christmas or any other time. I went to my room and cried, and then joined them in a short while. I don't think anyone noticed I was gone. All in all, it was a happy Christmas.

Keith loved Christmas, and I miss him calling around October to see if we have drawn names to exchange gifts and what does everyone want for Christmas, etc. I have stretched a bottle of perfume he gave me one year for Christmas to last all these years. I wear it only on very special occasions. It may sound crazy to some, but it's really not. We treasure anything we have left of him - any memory, any article he gave us, anything that was his.

I'm really looking forward to the holidays this year, and as I look back on that first, second and third Christmas I can see how far I've come. My shopping is well on the way to completion. My special Christmas cards, ordered in September, arrived the first ofOctober and right after Thanksgiving I'll start to wrap gifts. This works out well for me; I enjoy the week before Christmas more when everything is done early.

I wish I had realized earlier how important it is to change the way we do things, if only just a little bit. It's "a must" to be kind to ourselves. I don't do things just because someone expects it of me anymore. I now do things because I want to, and if what I want to do happens to be what someone else wants, that's a big plus!

"Life must be lived forwards; but can only be understood backwards."
Soren Kierkegaard

A HOLE IN THE SCREEN
by Eunice Brown

With the death of a child sometimes comes the death of a marriage. Love is work; it's sometimes a decision, not just a feeling. The grieving process is also work, sometimes a decision, and takes its toll on a marriage. Dick and I had our difficult times. When he was up I seemed down, and vice-versa.

We made a bargain with each other early in our grief that if either of us felt the need to talk about Keith we would, and the other would listen. We continued doing things we liked to do - he golfed and bowled, I've always been interested in arts and crafts. Together we went out to dinner or lunch frequently. We bicycled in summer, cross country skied a bit in the winter. We spent a lot of time at our camper in a peaceful campground where we enjoy canoeing. Getting away for a weekend with friends or alone has always been therapeutic.

One thing we differed on was a hole in the screen of our patio. Our son and his wife, on their last visit before his death, were playing ball and one of them missed - the ball broke the screen. The following summer I found myself unable to sit on the patio. I asked Dick to fix the screen - he said it was okay the way it was. What was painful for me was a happy memory for him, and the broken screen remained that way when we sold the house the end of that summer. It's strange how differently two people feel about the same situation. We both found satisfaction in this instance; he didn't fix the screen and, having sold the house that summer, I no longer had to look at it!

We would have come to a solution another way, had we stayed there, however, because we learned a lot about communicating through our grieving process. We learned to grieve alone and we learned to grieve together. Our marriage is important; it's a commitment we made thirty-eight years ago. We feel it is worth the hard work we put into it. We're grateful we have each other, and finally can count our blessings once again.

"Some wounds do not heal, even given an eternity. The scars they leave are permanent and can only be woven into the fabric of one's life."
Bernice Rubens from her book, BROTHERS

These articles were written by Eunice Brown, who is a bereaved parent and active volunteer for HOPE FOR BEREAVED.

ANNIVERSARY OF DEATH IS SO PAINFUL ... BUT IT DOES GET BETTER

The following stories show how two people lived through the first anniversary and how the grief did soften in the subsequent years.

I was genuinely surprised at how awful the first anniversary of my husband's death was. And it wasn't just that one date; I was a mess for over a month beforehand. I had terrible nightmares, insomnia at times, physical complaints, incredible irritability. It seemed I had undone all the grief work I had accomplished to date. My reactions came as a frightening, confusing development. It wasn't until about a week after the anniversary that I gained any perspective on what I had just gone through. In that week or so, I began to regain my equilibrium. I calmed down, I slept, I felt relieved. It seemed so obvious then; I had subconsciously relived all those events again and there was no way to avoid this. I had dreaded the anniversary date but had suppressed my feelings. As that first calendar year unfolded, each special day reminded me of the fact that just one year ago on that day my husband and I had been together. And I knew what was coming next -THAT day.

The inescapable fact is that the first anniversary date is going to be a fiasco. You are going to feel absolutely rotten. But one thing I learned is that if you accept this simple fact, then you won't feel so bad about feeling bad. In other words, if you expect to feel badly then you can face your fears and take action.

The next year, I was better prepared. I expected to feel lousy beforehand. I surely did, too, but for only about a month before the anniversary. The day itself I went to church and cried. It was a comfort to cry, it was appropriate.

After five years I still get anxious and unhappy before the anniversary, but each year the pain is less, the period of dread shortened. I've learned how to manage the pain, how to be nurtured by HOPE.

K.J.

As I write this on August 21, it has been eight years since our daughter died in a car accident. She was the passenger in a friend's truck. He failed to negotiate a curve, the truck hit a telephone pole and Mary was killed instantly. That began our long, devastating journey through grief.

On July 21, a month before the first anniversary, I started to get really anxious. I had trouble sleeping, eating, and it seemed that thoughts of the approaching anniversary were always with me. I dreaded the day, I was a shaky wreck...a basket case. The first eleven months had been horrible enough. I couldn't imagine what the anniversary would be like.

The last time that I had seen Mary alive had been on my birthday on August 15th. Mary, my mother, mother-in-law and I had all gone out to dinner. I was dreading that day as well as the anniversary, so my mother and our two younger children and I decided to take a trip to Cooperstown. We left on August 14th and returned on the 16th. It was a pretty ride. We stayed at a hotel with a pool, browsed in the shops and museums and went to the movies at night. It was fun for the kids, without memories for me. It helped to be away from reality and it was different from the year before. It also helped me to build pleasant memories with my mom, Margie and Steve.

In one way we wished that the anniversary of her death could be postponed. We dreaded it so, we found the day before to be absolutely awful. I couldn't imagine what the actual day would be like when the day before had been so bad. Surprisingly, the anniversary day wasn't as bad as we envisioned. I guess it couldn't be as terrible as we had pictured it would be. We had suffered every time we thought of THAT day, and the closer it got to THAT day, the worse it was.

The next year I started dreading the day once August arrived. It was a little better and at least it didn't start as soon as the previous year, nor was it quite as pain-filled. Each year the anxiety, pain and dread lessened. I couldn't believe how good we felt this year. I knew that the date was approaching, but it has become a fact in our lives that we have learned to live with. It was only the past few days that I thought about the up-coming anniversary. Even the day before was okay. I no longer dread the day and it is no longer painful. I don't like the day, but I am finally at peace-our family is at peace. I even slept well on the anniversary eve.

Over the past eight years I have learned ways of coping:

1. In the beginning years, the time before and the anniversary day will be difficult and even painful. It's a fact.

2. I take the day off from work and plan a simple day, reading, swimming, relaxing in the sun, being with family and friends.

3. As many of the family as possible try to be together, but there is no pressure to do so.

4. Some of us go to a special liturgy in the morning. We have the Mass said for our intentions. Mary doesn't need it said for her. She is in Heaven.

5. The few notes, calls or visits mean a lot to us.

6. It is important to be gentle and patient with ourselves and each other.

7. I don't expect so much of myself around the anniversary.

8. I concentrate on the fact that some day we will be together again, rather than on her death.

T.S.S.

HEARTBREAK IS LIFE EDUCATING US
George B. Shaw

THE GROOM'S FAMILY SAT ON THE LEFT

After a loved one dies you may dread family events, events where everybody is there but...There may be family birthday parties, anniversary celebrations, holidays, family picnics or gatherings to attend. You may become apprehensive if there is a wedding in the family. Attending a wedding is difficult enough; actually planning and holding a wedding sounds impossible. Many of us have had weddings in the family. We may have agonized over it but in retrospect it really was okay. In fact, most of us even enjoyed them.

I dreaded the first family wedding after Mary died. Everyone but Mary would be there. It also brought us face to face with the fact that this would never be a part of our lives with Mary. I really was anxious and full of dread but when the day arrived I found I was happy to be with the rest of my family. I still missed Mary but it dawned on me that "in her own way," Mary would be there, too.

Almost eight years after Mary's death our oldest son was planning to get married. Even though they purposely planned an informal wedding, we found that we were busy with all the cleaning, yard projects, invitations and wedding details. We talked about where we would sit in the church on the day of the wedding. Since the wedding was in the same church as Mary's funeral and the same priests on the altar, we did not want to sit where we had at the funeral. We made a family decision to sit on the left. I'm not suggesting this to others, but only pointing out that you may be creative about whatever is bothering you.

We were fortunate that the bride and her family were so understanding. (Although we were glad about the seating arrangement, I don't foresee that we will feel the need at the next wedding.)

Our son and his fiancee wanted the reception to be in our back yard as Mary had always planned. Rain was predicted for the wedding day but it turned out to be warm, sunny and with a pleasant breeze. We felt that was Mary's gift to her brother, her new sister-in-law and to us.

There were so many times that we missed Mary's presence and wished that she could be a part of the festivities...the showers, the rehearsal party, the church the picture taking and during the reception. We talked about her and felt her presence.

If you have family events to attend, realize that they will be difficult at first. Give yourself time to cry and talk before the event, and maybe at the event, with someone who understands and cares. Don't expect too much of yourself. Try to relax and concentrate on the positive aspects of the event. Your loved one would want you to enjoy yourself. You may be surprised at the fun you do have. With time and grief work, eventually you will find the events to be pleasant. You may even find that you are looking forward to them.

A WORD OF CAUTION: Any big event, and especially a wedding, entails a lot of planning and a lot of work. Often people mention that feelings are tender; there may be misunderstandings and even cross words. Realize this may happen at any event. When you are bereaved you are often even more sensitive. Be careful not to let wedding pressures get out of proportion. Keep the lines of communication open.

MEN DRIVING AROUND LOST
by Arthur Peterson

These are not pleasant times for men who are uncomfortable with criticism. You can hardly pick up a newspaper or magazine without finding an article about our inferior emotional make-up. Audiences on TV talk shows go on and on about our reluctance to communicate with our wives, to show any tenderness, or - for that matter-to discuss how we feel about much of anything. On top of this, the medical profession is telling us that our temperament is killing us.

The Fourth Principle of TCF is that "We never suggest there is a correct way to grieve." This is wise counsel for several reasons. First: all of us, male or female, are unique, and what works for one may or may not apply to someone else. Second: men are genetically and socially different from women, making it logical to have contrasting mourning styles. Third: if I am at all typical, the more you tell a man what he ought to do the more he is going to plant his feet and do it his way. Believing all this, my objectives in this workshop are not to tell bereaved fathers how to grieve, but to offer some options to men seeking to cope with the death of a beloved child, along with the problems that loss may have caused in their marriage or in some other important relationship with a woman.

In order not to clutter this presentation with repeated disclaimers, let me say just once that when I talk about men doing this and women doing that, I know very well that I'm referring to some men and some women, perhaps most of them, but not all of them. I should also make clear that my credentials are strictly experiential and not academic. I don't apologize for this, because I've had more than casual contact with loss. In my immediate family circle there have been deaths from drowning, suicide, long- and short-term illnesses and, of course, the accident that took the life of our beloved son. Moreover, when I read how men are reputed to react to serious loss, I can identify with nearly all of the characteristics described.

Men display a number of traits that have been analyzed fully in many articles and books. We tend to be competitors, placing great value on winning in whatever we do. We are overly conscious of projecting an image of strength and control. We believe we are responsible for protecting those in our charge, especially our families. We assume we can solve all problems arising in our jobs or our personal lives. We pride ourselves on being self-sufficient, dependent on no one. From our childhood, we have believed and have been taught that "big boys don't cry," that little leaguers as well as professional athletes ought to "play hurt." "Put me in, coach, I'm okay!" We all wanted to grow up to be Gary Cooper and say "Yup."

Many psychologists tell us that the main characteristics of temperament are shared equally by men and women. I am as apt to be an extrovert as is my wife. In only one area is gender a factor, that of how decisions are reached. This can and does result in contrasting mourning styles that have the potential for causing problems in our relationships with each other when we're both grieving.

There are some physical and emotional results because of our behavior. Alan Wolfelt, in an excellent article in the June, 1988, issue of Bereavement, summarizes these well: "Among some of the more common consequences of complicated mourning in the male are the following: chronic depression, withdrawal, and low self-esteem; deterioration in relationships with friends and family; complaints such as headaches, fatigue and backaches; chronic anxiety, agitation, restlessness, and difficulty concentrating; chemical abuse or dependence; indifference toward others, insensitivity, and workaholism."

There are social consequences as well when our male grieving style comes into conflict with that of the women in our lives. This is what Phil Donahue's female guests are telling us and what we hear at many Compassionate Friends meetings. "He won't talk to me" is the common complaint. Whether this criticism is fair or not makes no difference. It is very real, and we must deal with it. If we are, as psychologists tell us we are, all that rational and objective about solving problems, why not act logically about this one? To repeat the sports idiom, if we are inclined to "play hurt," why not do so in this case? What if it is painful to do what must be done to preserve that relationship with a wife or daughter or mother or friend? How much is that relationship worth to you? As much as winning a football game?

Where I part company with some workshop leaders is on what to do about this apparent conflict between male and female mourning. The face-to-face discussion group is one way - unquestionably an excellent way - to resolve grief, but it is not the only way. Perhaps you are more comfortable taking a walk in the woods, alone with your thoughts and distractions. Perhaps you are more comfortable sharing your fears and your sorrow privately with a very few, carefully selected confidantes. Perhaps you prefer to relieve stress as I did by throwing yourself into work or some other activity, at least for a time. You have the right to do whatever works for you.

Whatever choice you make, of course, remember that there are two parts to it. While resolving your own grief may be the primary objective, you must also think about what your decision does to the women you love. There's no sense to solving one problem by creating another. Suppose she wants to talk about the dead child and you don't. Maybe this means encouraging her to attend TCF meetings while you stay home. Maybe it means actually taking her to the meeting while you sit in the rear, a supportive but silent participant. Maybe it means setting aside a time when you will grit your teeth and talk about the dead child for her sake. Think about how you have resolved other problems in which what you'd like to do and what you're comfortable doing is at odds with what obviously ought to be done. Do that.

What if you are reasonably okay, but are interested in helping a buddy who is grieving? I think the key is to use what you know about the male temperament in general and about that specific man in particular, respecting his right to make his own decisions. The admonition to "please listen to what I'm not saying" is particularly applicable to strong, silent men. They won't come to you. Wolfelt puts it well in his article: "Having to ask for help or emotional support makes many males uncomfortable. How many of us know men who will drive around lost for hours without asking for simple directions? Actually, this analogy to grief works well - driving around lost he searches for a destination, assuming no one can help him. Many men, lost in the turmoil of grief, refuse to ask for the guidance and support that might well lead them in the direction of healing." My suggestion is that you make it a point to be there when and if your friend needs you, and to look for an opening. This could be on a walk in the woods, or between frames in the bowling alley, or during a coffee break. It probably will not be found in a formal, structured setting like a meeting.

A March, 1988, issue of U.S. News and World Report puts it to us succinctly and directly, telling us men we can "Be a real man and die young, or be a wimp and live as long as your wife." I know what they mean, but I'd like to think I have a choice somewhere between Sylvester Stallone and Woody Allen. Would you settle for Jimmy Stewart??

Art Peterson, a bereaved parent, was very active in The Compassionate Friends, before his death in 1989. Art and his wife Ronnie helped countless grieving parents.

THINGS HAVE CHANGED SINCE THEN
by Kathleen Jacques

Two years ago I rented out my house and took my nine-year-old daughter and my eleven-year-old son to Europe for the summer. By myself. Nine years ago, I never would have even fathomed such a scheme. Nine years ago when my husband died, I barely made it through the necessary routines of the day. Oh, how things have changed since then! I remember wishing I could go to sleep and accelerate the healing overnight. I wanted to wake up and have that horrible ache gone. But it didn't happen overnight, and it was the hardest work I ever did, to contain my grief and simply function. I didn't deny my grief- I let it run its course. I experienced all its variants: the anger, the sadness, the raw fear. Somehow, the intensity of these emotions diminished, little by little. I don't know when or how the pain lessened and my inner resources grew, and my pleasure in life returned. But somehow, the light returned.

I still miss my husband. I haven't remarried. Sometimes I'm lonely and anxious. But there is once again laughter and delight in my world, where nine years ago I thought it was banished forever. There was no magic turning point when suddenly I was at peace. There were only moments of peace here and there. Some days more, some days less. All the while, I guess there was a strength developing; a strength derived from the knowledge that I'd made it through yet another day.

I discovered that the second time I had to face certain events or people after his death was easier than the first. Surviving these first encounters made me realize that I would survive the next ones, and I became less apprehensive. You endure, and that gives you something to hold on to. Endurance itself is an accomplishment.

I would say it took me a full two years to merely stabilize. By stabilize, I mean to just be conscious of things other than his death for most of the day. After two years, my days were not dominated by thoughts of my husband's death. A shaky balance was restored. I could look back and see how far I'd come: After three years I'd begun to make new friends, and for the first time I felt I could really interact, not just observe. I was able to give something of myself in a relationship and not just worry about protecting myself from additional harm. I had spiritual and emotional energy to spare. This was a milestone.

In nine years I've learned much about myself, and people in general. I've acquired some humility; I know how easy it is to be smug and selfish. And I know what it is to really feel someone else's pain, because I've been there too. Life is a process; nothing ever stays the same. You won't feel exactly the same next year as you feel today. This terrible pain you are feeling now will redefine itself as time goes on. With hard work, you will find the burden easier to bear. Like exercised muscles grown strong, you will acquire the substance to withstand your loss. You will accumulate layers of understanding, acceptance, and forgiveness. And in time, you will find peace. But you must give yourself all the time it takes! This will be your hardest journey, and no two paths follow the same course.

STRONG AT THE BROKEN PLACES
by Rev. Joseph Phillips

I remember one of my grade school teachers saying once: "When one breaks a bone, the place where the broken pieces knit together and heal, is stronger than any other part of the bone. One doesn't have to worry about the bone breaking there again. It is stronger than ever at the broken place.

A human truth comes to mind. It is often in adversity that one becomes a stronger person. For example, bereavement may provide the crucible in which a deeper character and strength are formed.

After Burt's wife died, he was devastated and could not imagine ever feeling peace or happiness again. We saw him work on his grief, by attending support group meetings, talking with and helping others. We could see the grief soften, ever so slowly. This is an article of HOPE!

THE LAST JOB OF GRIEF WORK?
by Burt McKeon

An event happened in my life last week that has made me wholly reevaluate this business of grief. (Or perhaps I have grown.)

On a dresser in our bedroom is a phone and a pad for messages. You know the kind. Most teachers have them and they are very thick and they usually say *"From the Desk of . . ."* I suppose most people do the same thing in this age of multiple phones.

Upon arising one morning last week, I checked the notepad for a message I had written the night before. I further noticed that the pad was nearly out of paper, which allowed me to see that loose sheet that had been tucked in the back. My heart jumped as I recognized Phyl's handwriting. Upon closer examination, I found that she had written the following:

> Wow - 42 years
> What can I say
> They all add up
> To this happy day.
> You've been my laughter
> You've been my tears
> You've been my own true love
> For 42 years.
> Time passes quickly
> And I'm keeping score
> 'Cause if I'm real lucky
> We'll have 42 more.
>
> Happy Ann.

To say that I was bowled over would be the understatement of the year. Phyl had not made it to number 43, and I, for some reason, had never seen the little poem. Suddenly it hit me; waves of that love swept over me like a beautiful summer shower on the one hand - like a biting desert sand storm on the other. I gave myself up to the sensations completely, sank to my knees and accepted the moment

Later, when I found myself aware of my surroundings again, I tried to analyze what had happened. Of course the WHYs came: Why hadn't I seen the note on our 42nd anniversary? Why did I find it at this particular time? Why am I having feelings different than I have had in some time?

As I tried to analyze what had happened to me, I began to realize that a calmness, a serenity and a peace had come over me. It was a state which I thoroughly enjoyed. There was a contact. All was not "gone." Most of all the love which I missed so badly, was still in existence. Just below the surface. Scratch me and it's there.

Two years ago - no, even last year - I wouldn't have believed it possible. My contentment, since this happened, I would wish for everyone. Perhaps this is the final acceptance of death. Perhaps this is the last job of grief work. I don't know. I do know that the intense pain is now gone, "our love" still exists, and I am happy with my newfound peace.

WHAT HE LEFT BEHIND
by Kathleen Jacques

This is not a story about pain, or longing, or regrets. This is a story about the many things I absorbed from my husband over the years, how knowing him helped form my character. I would be a different person if I hadn't been influenced by Michael while he was here with me.

As you might imagine, I have thought endlessly about the death of my husband: The facts of his death have irrevocably changed me. I have gone the whole route with the "what ifs," the "if onlys," and the full aftermath of such a devastating loss. But I'd never really thought about how I'd changed over the years while Michael was still alive. I'd thought about our life together; I had my memories, I cherished my reminiscences, but that wasn't quite the same.

A woman whose name I didn't even catch started me thinking about all of this. Not too long ago my son Zachary broke his arm. There were complications and he had to be hospitalized. I waited with him for several hours before they finally took him into the operating room. I was a wreck. Any time there is a crisis with the children, I suffer the loss of my husband most keenly. Never am I more aware of being without his support. I may manage to look normal on the outside, but inside am a disaster, waiting for the cover of privacy in order to collapse.

Anyway, there I was pacing the halls of St. Joe's waiting for Zach to come back from the O.R., when a nurse approached me. This one had no forms, no questions, no instructions. She leaned back against the wall opposite from me with the wisest, caring smile, and said, "I see from the charts that you are a widow too." She was about ten years older than I which meant that she had also been young at the time of her husband's death. She'd walked in my shoes; she knew the language. We exchanged brief stories, only the facts of the deaths; we already knew each other's pain.

Then she looked up at me with the most beautiful smile and said, "What did he leave with you, what did he give you?" She explained: "My husband taught me how to laugh. I never really knew how to laugh until I met him. He had such a wonderful sense of humor that it rubbed off on me. He taught me not to take myself so seriously. He taught me not to fuss so much over the kids, to let them make their own mistakes. To enjoy life more." As she said these things, her face was radiant. I felt the presence of this man in her; he was there in her all the while. What a lucky man he had been to find her. There was nothing sad about her revelations; this was a tribute to life and the force of love.

I loved talking to this unknown woman in the hallway; she radiated peace and strength. I thought for a few minutes before I replied. "Mike gave me so many things. He taught me how to take a decent picture. We learned how to develop and print film together. He softened my harsh edges with his gentle humor. Mike never said a nasty thing about another person and his kindness shamed me into developing a more generous nature. He taught me to pursue all of my interests, not to just say 'I wonder why... wonder if...' I never would have done so well in college if it hadn't been for his good example and encouragement. He taught me to appreciate jazz and classical music. He was smart and he was funny and he was interesting, and somehow living with him made me a little more of these things too."

"Thanks, Mike." I stood there in that hallway and I said thanks in front of this stranger, because of this stranger. And I felt wonderful! I felt closer to Mike; I felt his strength; I felt him with me. He's always been there. And he always will be. The person that I display to the world is the result of many influences, and Michael influenced me as much, if not more, than anyone in my life. Everyday of my life I have been using something that Mike had given me. I was drawing on that influence, even in that hallway.

Zach still has a cast, but soon he'll be back to normal. He's learned not to be such a daredevil on the monkey bars, and I've learned to thank Mike more often for his gifts. And I will always be grateful to that extraordinary lady who helped me summon the strength and peace that was there, all along.

Kathleen Jacques is Editor of the HOPE FOR BEREAVED handbook and a free-lance writer. Her husband, Michael, died in 1980.

A MESSAGE TO SURVIVORS - ABOUT HAPPINESS

Every Christmas since 1977, I have placed a large 9 x 14 inch card with a picture of Santa on our mantle. The greeting on the front is "Merry Christmas." Inside it is addressed to "Davey, T. J., Margie and Stephen." The message is, "Do I hope you're MERRY? JOLLY and HAPPY too?? At Christmas time and always? "YOU BET YOUR BOOTS I DO!!" It is signed, "Love, Mary."

This card was sent by our daughter Mary to her brothers and sister the Christmas of 1976. She died in a car accident in August of 1977. At first I put the card up just because it was from Mary. Eventually, I read the message more carefully. Mary had picked this card and even underlined the last six words. I think all our loved ones who have died wish for our happiness at the holidays, and always.

In this world happiness is not possible all the time. Things happen in our lives that we cannot control, but we do have a choice - to forever remain in our grief or find that life is worth living. I don't mean to imply that it is easy, or happens in a short time. Grief is a normal reaction to the death of a loved one. It is painful, and requires a lot of grief work on our part. There is no specific time frame for grief; for most of us the pain of grief takes too long. Ask yourself this question: If I had died and my loved one had lived, would I want them to be as happy as possible? I'm sure your answer would be YES. Realize that your happiness is what your loved one would want for you. Therefore you need to work on your grief and work toward that attitude of happiness.

In a newspaper interview, Dr. Terrence O'Brien, a highly esteemed psycho-therapist in the Syracuse area (and friend of Hope For Bereaved), stated that "Happiness is more of an attitude than what happens to you. It's like a muscle. The more you use it, the better it develops. You have to look for the possibilities in life. If you get stuck in the mire, you stay there." As a psychotherapist, Terry likes to "unstick" people. He calls it "developing strategies for dealing with life" and believes you are not responsible for what happens to you, but you are responsible for what you do with it. You can learn new ways of coping. You can learn skills for getting unstuck."

As you journey through grief, hold on to HOPE and become determined to enjoy as much of life as possible. That is a real tribute to your loved one!

AFTER THE FIRST YEAR ... THEN WHAT?

The first year of bereavement brings raw pain, disbelief, the agony of reality and many other deep emotions - emotions many of us have never experienced or at least not to the same depth. The time period after the first year is usually not quite as pain-filled as all the firsts were. Although we may be a little better, often we are not nearly as healed as we would like. It helps to understand this next period and to learn some skills for coping. It is most helpful if we lower our expectations of ourselves, work on our grief and hold on to HOPE. Remember, grief is different for everyone. It is like fingerprints or snowflakes; no two are alike. Everyone grieves differently, so don't compare yourself to others or place yourself on a timetable. Some of the following suggestions/observations may help you:

1. Beware of becoming critical of ourselves, either consciously or unconsciously, due to unrealistic expectations.

2. A different level of reality may hit us. We usually no longer deny the death, but now face the reality and its long term implications.

3. If the death is unexpected, some say that the second year is even more difficult.

4. It may be the time to struggle with new life patterns. We may have handled grief by overactivity (workaholic, etc.). If our previous style of grieving has not been helpful, we must be willing to try new approaches such as: become more active in a support group; find telephone friends; read about grief; develop coping skills; become determined not to become stuck in our grief; do our grief work; HOLD ON TO HOPE.

5. It is vital to find a friend with whom you may talk. This is the one significant factor that prevents people from sliding into deep depression. You can find such help in a support group.

6. We should carefully consider the phases of grief. One or more phases may be giving us trouble, such as anger or guilt. If so, recognize the phase and work on it. Don't push it down or ignore it.

7. Other events in your life may also be adding to your grief (trouble with spouse, children, work, other family members or friends). Realize this happens to many grieving people and it does complicate your grief.

8. You may or may not cry as often, as you did at first, but when you do, realize it is therapeutic. Don't fight the tears. As the author Jean G. Jones says in TIME OUT FOR GRIEF, "cry when you have to - laugh when you can."

9. Physical symptoms may become more acute (stomach disorders, headaches, sleeplessness). Have a checkup.

10. Insufficient sleep plagues many bereaved. It may be helpful to give up all caffeine and alcohol. Physical exercise helps you to relax and makes you sleepy. See article, Suggestions To Aid Sleep.

11. Check frequently that you have balance in your life —work, recreation (including exercise, hobbies, reading), adequate rest and prayer.

12. Don't be alarmed if depression reenters your life or appears for the first time. Depression is normal and its recurrence is also normal. See article on Depression.

13. Our grief may seem "out of control." We may feel as if we are "going crazy." This is common to bereaved people. It is important to realize grief work takes time. Much more time than we think it should. Be patient with yourself.

14. Be aware of a lowered self-esteem. We might think to ourselves, "I don't like the person I've become". Often it is our unrealistic expectations of ourselves to be handling our grief better - no doubt we are doing better than we give ourselves credit.

15. We often hear "Time will heal". Yes, time does soften the hurt a bit, but mainly it is what we do with time: read, talk, struggle with the phases, get help when we become stuck in a phase, be gentle with ourselves, lower our expectations, build a pleasant time with family and friends, pray to our loved one.

16. It helps to consider that our loved ones are happy - free of pain and hassles - that we will be together again. Also, if you died, would you want your loved ones to mourn deeply the rest of their lives? You would want them to enjoy life as much as possible. They want this for you.

17. PRIDE may be one of your greatest stumbling blocks. You may think that you should be doing much better - you may not want to acknowledge that you need help.

18. Vibes from friends may openly or subconsciously be, "Shape up - you must be over it now. Get on with living," etc. You not only experience the death of a loved one, but you feel abandoned by friends and even family. Find others to talk with who understand. These friends may come from those who attend the support group meetings.

19. Loneliness may seem to engulf us as we look ahead to a life without our loved one. Find new friends, worthwhile work (support groups always need help with phoning, mailings, research, etc.) and connect with friends from the past. Pleasant memories can help, too.

20. If you feel guilty, it must be acknowledged - not suppressed. Really look at the "if onlys." Hopefully YOU and only you will be able to say to yourself, "I did the best that I could at the time - so did my loved one."

21. WHY??? If the "why" is bothering you, ask it again and again until you can come to terms with it. You may never know why. It may remain a mystery that you choose to let go. When you can, concentrate on your choice to get better.

22. Realize that anger may be at ourselves, God, the person who died, those in the helping professions who did not seem to understand or help. Acknowledging our anger is the first step in releasing its power over us.

23. Don't expect too much of your family. They too, have their hands full of grief.

24. Consider even though you are struggling with grief, you would rather have had the time with your loved one than not to have had them in your life at all.

25. Set realistic goals for the future - realistic is the key word. Pinpoint your most acute concerns. Think of all possible solutions. Choose one solution at a time and implement it.

26. So many of us have been brought up to be independent; "I'm going to handle this grief myself." We find it difficult to ask for help. Yet we need help. Asking for help from caring people can make a big difference in your working through your grief. Force yourself to reach out for help.

27. Often, when we slide back into the pits, we panic. We hate the feeling. Irrationally we feel that we will remain there. It is important to realize we have been in the pits before, and will be again, but we WILL GET BETTER.

28. Be a fighter against giving up and becoming stuck in grief, as 15% do. A determination to work through grief may be one of the common denominators of those who recover. It is up to you.

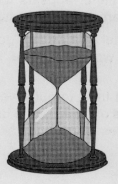

"Time heals," many people say.

It may.
It may help to dull your pain.

But the medicine of time,
taken by itself,
is not sure.

Time is neutral.
What helps is what you do with time.
                    EARL A. GROLLMAN

FINDING THAT LIFE IS WORTH LIVING

Especially in the beginning, it is difficult to think that you will ever be happy again. That is how I felt when our daughter died in 1977. What gave me encouragement were the people that I knew who had a loved one die and yet seemed to be happy again. I had been optimistic and genuinely in love with family, friends and life before Mary's death. My former enjoyment of life served as a pleasant memory, but I couldn't foresee that we would ever really enjoy life again. I was afraid that all we would have is endless days of grief. Eventually, the panic and physical pain did ease.

At first for many bereaved the only things that get done are the essentials, like breathing, going to work, shopping, cooking and paying the bills. It is such an effort and sometimes we even let the essentials slide. Eventually we do some small things, like bake a cake, clean off a counter, change the oil, etc. These things that we would have taken for granted are really big accomplishments. We begin to do some little thing above and beyond just existing. We begin to put a little more balance in our lives. Due to our own pain we may not have been aware of other family members' struggle. When we can turn some of our attention to them, it is a beginning toward returning to life.

About a month after Mary died we went to dinner with friends. There were young adults about Mary's age at the restaurant. Some of the background music were songs that Mary liked. It was difficult to chit-chat. I can remember thinking that we were not fun to be with. "I" couldn't even stand being with "me," so it must have been difficult for our friends. Over the years I found that special times with family and friends are very important. We need to build "oases" into our lifetimes to which we can look forward and enjoy: lunch with a friend, going for a walk with someone special, taking a trip, going to a conference or retreat, having friends over . . . whatever we enjoy. It also helps to find small ways to enjoy yourself every day.

About six months after Mary died I went to Florida with my mother. As I sat on the beach, I began to wish that Mary could sit with me just for the afternoon. I kept bargaining. If she couldn't be there for the whole afternoon, maybe just for an hour . . . a half-hour . . . 15 minutes. I asked myself, "What did I want to say to her?" I wanted to tell her that we loved her. As I thought about it, I realized that Mary knows we love her and we know that she loves us. I can't tell Mary in person that I love her, but I can and should tell the rest of the people in my life that I love them. I have since acquired a piece of marble with the inscription, "If you love somebody - tell them". I don't always do this, but I try and I have become aware of how important it is.

As I look back, another sign that I was gaining strength was the comparison of how we coped on the anniversary of her death, her birthday and various holidays. The first anniversary was devastating. From July 21 until the anniversary, August 21, I was anxious, depressed, full of dread, had difficulty sleeping, etc. The next year the dread and anxiety hit in the beginning of August. Each year the amount of dreaded anticipation lessened. In fact, by the seventh anniversary, August 20 and 21 were days of remembering, wishing, "if onlys," and feeling sad, but not like those pain-filled early anniversaries. Mary would have been 22 three weeks after her death. I remember shopping with a friend in Skaneateles that first year. I cried in every store - seeing cards or gifts that I wished I could buy for Mary. We still miss Mary, especially on her birthday, but as a family we concentrate on our happy memories and we are grateful that we had Mary for those almost 22 years. We still feel that she had a life to live and we wonder what she would be doing now, but we have learned to live with the fact.

Another idea that helped me was to think of how I would want my loved ones to live their lives if I had died instead of Mary. I would want my family to work on their grief and to be as happy as possible; to enjoy each other and life. I'm sure that our loved ones who have died want us to live this life to the fullest. One aspect of my life that has helped me to find that life is worth living is the Hope For Bereaved support group. I have gained understanding, suggestions for coping, HOPE, and a whole circle of friends who share my ups and downs of grief and life. They really understand - they've been there. They speak the same language of grief. Those who are longer bereaved give me HOPE. The newly bereaved help me to realize how far I have come from those early days of grief. I find in trying to help others, I am helped.

Our family does enjoy life again. We are not kept awake by grief. Our appetites have returned. We look forward to events. Life is good, but different. It will never be the same. We will always miss Mary. LIFE IS NOT FAIR and it sure has its downs as well as ups. I've learned to really enjoy the good things and to do my best with life's sorrows and trials ... of which there are plenty.

Many bereaved who have already had their hands full of grief, still experience more reasons for additional grief and worry - disappointments in relationships, physical or mental illness of a loved one, family member involved in drugs, separation, divorce, pressures at work, etc. It may seem that everywhere you turn there are problems and pain. It helps to face these additional problems and to talk them over with an understanding family member or friend. When our spirits are down anyway, additional problems may seem like the last straw. As difficult as it is, we should tackle the problems as best we can. Sometimes there are steps that we can take. Some problems involve other people. We may be able to talk with them about it, but they may be determined to stay on a possibly destructive course. If this is the case, we have a choice; to worry excessively, to grieve, to let it add to our pain - or we can work on our grief and try to build as good a life as possible. We only have control over ourselves. It is not easy, but we should realize that these problems are their problems and it is up to them to solve them. We can help some, pray and love them, but it doesn't help anyone when we take on their problems, too.

We have a choice to make-to exist or really live; to sit and grieve, to let our grief drag us down or to try to rebuild our lives. When you have experienced the death of a loved one you EVENTUALLY look at life from a more aware vantage point. Grief can be a teacher. We can become more understanding and more compassionate, with the desire to help others. As Dr. Elisabeth Kubler-Ross says, "Out of every tragedy can come a blessing or a curse, compassion or bitterness . . . the choice is yours".

I have always been interested in the concept of making each day count - living life to the fullest. This concept did not fit in with Mary's death. For a long time after her death it seemed all we did was exist. Eventually I learned to live one day at a time. I am now determined to make the best of each day and not to wish my life away. So often people say - I can't wait till "something" or "someday" is over. That can become a way of life and we end up enjoying very little. None of us know how long we have, so we should take the time each day to say and do the things that are important to us. Hold onto HOPE that as a grieving person you can and will get better. Be determined to find that LIFE IS WORTH LIVING!

THERE IS NO TIMETABLE FOR GRIEF. It is different for everyone. The depth, scope and duration of your grief depends on your relationship with the loved one who died, the support you receive, your personality and your ability to effectively work on your grief.

WHERE IS GOD??

That's a good question..."where is God?" When a loved one has died we have a variety of thoughts about God and not all of them are pleasant. However, many of us find great comfort in God...in our faith. Others may be very angry at God - blaming God for letting the death happen. Some reject God - reject their faith. Some just plain wonder where God is in this tragedy.

I don't consider the death of our daughter or of my father and grandparents as being God's fault. They died due to illness and accidents. My faith that my loved ones who had died were in heaven and happy kept me going. I pray to Mary and my Dad a lot - for help with our grief and now to help me reach out to help other grieving people.

Anger is a common and often very strong component of grief. Sometimes you might feel angry towards God. That is okay. "God can take it." He loves us and understands our hurt. Religious and secular taboos against anger and hatred have made many people feel only shame and guilt concerning their negative feelings toward God. If you are ashamed and repress your anger, it only complicates your grief. It is best to be honest if you do feel angry at God. Honest emotions can be dealt with and eventually worked through.

Pierre Wolff in his book MAY I HATE GOD? states: "Perhaps there is a hatred present as long as people are mute, but as soon as they decide to express what is in their heart to the other, something is already changing and may be even already changed. This expression is a desire for reconciliation. If I can tell you, my friend, that I hate you, and if you can accept my words and feelings, then love is present, working and conquering. You are still alive and present in my life, even though in sorrow; I am coming back to you, and you are welcoming me."

Intimacy with anyone is dependent on the proper expression of anger. When someone we love hurts us, no matter what the reason, it is natural to be angry. If intimacy is to be maintained, the anger must be expressed, not buried under a pile of platitudes. To deal differently with God is to push God ever higher, ever farther from our souls.

Some people are comforted by the statement, "It's God's Will," but many of us are not. If this concept gives you genuine comfort then continue with it. I felt that Mary had a life to live, people to love and things to do. Her death in an auto accident was not God's will, but the act of a careless young man who was driving while alcohol impaired.

I will never forget one bereaved parent, who described herself as an agnostic, telling me that after her son was killed in a bike accident her "Christian" sister-in-law asked her, "Don't you think that God was trying to get your attention?" She said if that was how He went about getting her attention, then she didn't want any part of Him. How grossly insensitive of her sister-in-law!

One bereaved parent was told when her daughter died that God needed a flower for His garden. Her answer was, "I wish He had picked someone else's petunia." How small we make God. God does not need nor randomly pick flowers for His garden.

God loves all of us very much. He gives us life, our loved ones and this beautiful world. Sometimes death occurs due to acts of nature, such as floods, avalanches, hurricanes, accidents, illness or man's inhumanity to man by wars or murder. Sometimes we even take our own lives. I do not believe that God causes our death. It helps me to remember that God gave us this life and the next life. A poster that was given to our younger daughter brought us much comfort; "His eye is on the sparrow so I know He watches me. To this we added "and our loved ones."

97

Where was God when your loved one died? He was in the same place He was when His Son died. God on the cross bears our pain, feels our hurt and conquers our death. I read in a Compassionate Friends newsletter that "God is a bereaved parent too." I had never thought about that before. In the Christian faith we often concentrate on the resurrection. We forget that Christ cried when His friend Lazarus died, that He grew weary, angry and discouraged at times, and that He was tortured and left to die on a cross. God knew pain and suffering. He embraced it out of love for us. He understands our grief and wants to help us with our suffering.

Don't be afraid to talk with God about your thoughts and feelings. God can handle your doubts and anger. Remember, if you're mad at God, tell Him. Only by expressing your anger and questions to God will you come to know the fullness of both His love and freedom. God, through His Son, has identified himself with us in the experience of human life. He has given us Someone to whom we can turn, Someone who will hold on to us and never lose us as we journey through the valleys of death and despair.

 His eye is on the sparrow so I know He watches me . . .

FOOTPRINTS

One night a man had a dream.
He dreamed that he was walking
along the beach with the Lord.
Across the sky flashed scenes
from his life.
For each scene, he noticed two sets
of footprints in the sand.
One belonged to him and the other one
belonged to the Lord.
When the last scene had flashed before him
he looked back at the footprints.
He noticed that many times along the path
there was only one set of footprints in the sand.
He also noticed that this happened during the
lowest and saddest times in his life.
This really bothered him and he questioned the Lord.
"Lord, You said once I decided to follow You, You
would walk all the way with me; but I noticed
that during the most troubled times of my life
there was only one set of footprints. I don't
understand why. When I needed You most,
You deserted me."
The Lord replied, "My precious child,
I love you and I would never leave you.
During your times of trial and suffering,
when you saw only one set of footprints,
it was when I carried you."

Author unknown

WHY ME?...WHY US?...
by Kathleen Jacques

You might not say it, but you probably think it: "We never hurt anybody...with all the really rotten people in this world...and this happens to us...why!?" This is such a common reaction. We seem so desperately to need answers, as if some answer could ever give solace! The fact is that your loved one has died and you feel the unfairness of it all. Where is the order, the sense in life if good people always fall victim to calamity? We expect fairness. But then again, nobody ever said life was fair.

It is futile trying to make "sense" out of the death of your loved one. These things happen, it is the way of the world. There is an arbitrary quality of life that makes for the essence of our experience here on earth. Anything can and does happen.

I do not believe that we are singled out for misfortune. I do not believe that we are chosen, or punished or used as an example. I believe death comes to everyone in a random, arbitrary way and that everyone faces the possibility of tragedy. It is only chance that some die peacefully while others do not. I cannot believe in a God who would deliberately inflict pain. Instead, I believe in a God who has given us the capacity to cope with the unfairness of life with love and sharing and hope.

In his book, "When Bad Things Happen to Good People," Rabbi Harold S. Kushner searches for answers to our question of 'why me?'. He rejects the most common responses that many people perpetuate:

1. Tragedy is not a punishment. God is just. He wouldn't inflict such a harsh punishment. An innocent victim could not have deserved such treatment. There can be no link between innocent victim survivors and senseless death.

2. Tragedy is not "God's Will." What kind of God would concoct some master plan of misery? How could the same God, who has endowed mankind with so much goodness and beauty, preordain our ruin?

3. Tragedy is not a "test." God does not sponsor competitions to see who can withstand the most heartache. He could not possibly want to test the limits of human endurance with such an evil plan. God has given us other capacities - potential for discovery, invention, for love and the celebration of life.

4. It is not true that God only gives you the amount of suffering that he knows you can bear. This again assumes that God plans our suffering. God grieved at the death of Christ, surely he would not wish to inflict this pain on us. What makes us think a God who recognized sorrow would find any comfort in the misery of others? Finally, some people do not bear their grief, some choose suicide. What of them? Did God err in how much suffering to allot to them?

All of these "answers" assume that God caused the tragedy. Rabbi Kushner writes:

". . . maybe our suffering happens for some reason other than the will of God. The Psalmist writes, 'I will lift up mine eyes unto the hills, from whence cometh my help. My help cometh from the Lord, which made heaven and earth.' He does not say 'My tragedy comes from the Lord.' Could it be that God does not cause the bad things that happen to us? Could it be that, rather, he stands ready to help us cope with our tragedies? No one ever promised us a life free from disappointment. The most anyone promised was that we would not be alone in our pain, that we would be able to draw upon a source outside ourselves for strength and courage.

Let me suggest that the bad things that happen to us in our lives do not have a meaning when they happen. But we can redeem these tragedies from senselessness by imposing meaning on them. In the final analysis, the question is not why bad things happen to good people, but how we respond when such things happen. Are we capable of accepting a world that has disappointed us by not being perfect? Are we capable of forgiving and loving God despite his limitations? If we can do these things, we will be able to recognize that forgiveness and love are the weapons God has given to enable us to live fully and bravely in this less-than-perfect world."

Finally, in dealing with your own tragedy, remember that we have been blessed with the most healing potential of all: HOPE.

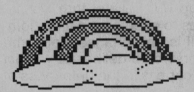 ## THERE CAN BE NO RAINBOW WITHOUT A CLOUD AND A STORM

WHICH IS EASIER? Sudden Death vs. the Expected . . . It is pointless to compare suffering. Who would want to weigh pain on a scale to see whose loss is "greater"? Indeed, there can be no scale, no form of measurement to compare each person's experience of grief at the death of a loved one. Yet the circumstances of the death can pose specific problems depending upon the manner in which death occurred. When death comes without warning, the shock is overwhelming. The first wave of shock is physical; we feel nauseous, shaky, cold. That first blow is crushing, like being hit with a massive weight to the chest. You fight the truth, you cling to unsupported bits of encouragement. When evidence verifies the awful reality you may give in to uncontrollable sobbing. There is so much unfinished business, unresolved issues, unsaid good-byes. You face the future and the past with equal anxiety. All those loose ends will never be tied, that vast future ahead with its frightening, uncharted waters to travel alone. Each succeeding day, the reality of the death gives you the time to ponder what happened, what will happen next. The initial shock lessens and grief commences. Some say that when death is instant the journey of grief may be prolonged.

If your loved one has died due to a lingering illness or injury, your grief may be complicated by emotional and physical exhaustion. Time spent at the sickbed may have drained you of your own health and energy. Seeing your loved one in pain is a terrible burden to bear. You may have already begun to grieve once the death was declared inevitable, although often a glimmer of hope remains. When your loved one finally does die you may feel a measure of relief. You did not wish their life to end, you wished for their pain to end. Guilt over this relief is common, but once again edged out by the other facets of grief. We cling to memories of better days, we focus there instead of on the final ordeal.

Regardless of which way your loved one dies, it may be helpful for you to sort out your feelings by having a "conversation" with your loved one. Ask forgiveness, pray to them for help and guidance. You'll feel their presence, and imagining what they would say to you can give you a sense of peace. Your loved one wants you to be happy, they would want you to make peace with yourself.

? QUESTIONS FOR A COUNSELOR ?
by Dr. Terry O'Brien

What can you do when people will not mention your loved one? Let's look at your options. You can choose to just let things be. I am not sure how satisfying this alternative is. You must decide this. Another option is to get upset with people for not mentioning your dead loved one. Make sure you consider the aftermath of this strategy before you choose it. Consider the outcome that could result. Finally, you could gently raise the issue that you sense them avoiding mention of your loved one. If you choose this option be specific; what have you heard or not heard, seen, or picked up with your senses that led you to believe they were avoiding talking about your loved one?

Remember, you cannot read minds. You do not know what another person is thinking or what may be motivating them. So don't guess! Share with them what you have sensed. Carefully say, "I wonder if you were not mentioning my loved one for any particular reason?" Notice you are not being incriminating or blaming, which could create additional barriers to communication. Let the other person share their own motivations and intentions. Only they truly know them.

You could raise the issue this way; "I've become aware that we don't talk about (your loved one) anymore. I'm sometimes uncomfortable about this and we don't seem to acknowledge it. What do you think and feel about this? I'd like to talk about how we might handle this situation more to our satisfaction." At this point the issue is out in the open and hopefully you can both clearly redefine how you would like to deal with the situation.

What can you do on the days you just can't stop thinking about the moment your loved one died? At first we need to listen to what this experience is telling us. It is so hard to let go of a loved one. Even acknowledging their death is so painful. The recurring thoughts are the proof of both these points. Acknowledging the death is painful. Letting go is even worse. Our recurring thoughts are unconscious attempts to cope with these tough realities.

Fighting against such recurring thoughts is often futile and adds greater frustration and anger to our pain. The often used phrases "lean into the pain" or "embrace your pain" have to do with picking up on another thread of its unpleasant fabric and listening to the pain at deeper levels. For instance, when the memory seers into you, reflect upon your beloved prayerfully - ask a blessing on them and somehow seek their help in continuing your journey. Then remember and be in solidarity with all those "new" or "old" bereaved who, like you, are faltering and all but overwhelmed by their burden. May your thoughts, prayers and inner energy connect with them in some way, making both of your burdens lighter. Finally, what is this recurring thought of my beloved telling me about my next step through this journey of grief? What do I need to do for me? . . . for other family members? In some way I can't rationally articulate, I believe and I sense that your beloved is beckoning you forward. This memory is urging you to look, to inquire, to reach out for support as our collective journeys continue. Our journeys are walked one step at a time. We must all pause at times, hopefully supported and sustained by those close to us; but be attentive to that next step.

How do you get the members of your family to talk? This is a question many family members would like to resolve. The essential premise to keep in mind is that I cannot change another person; I can only change myself. This may sound like we are back to square one - not quite! Consider a mobile. When the various pieces settle, the mobile is fairly stable and settled. Then move one piece or add some additional weight to a piece, and the mobile is energized. The mobile must accommodate to the change. Human families are constantly accommodating to changing events, attitudes and behavior patterns.

Our first task is to assess the established patterns for communicating in the family. When, to whom, and how does a particular family member talk? What attitudes or behaviors of other family members actually reinforce or support another's silence? Consider such factors as: gender; one's sibling position (birth order) and the ensuing roles each sibling establishes; the need to be different from other siblings; the lessons one learns in one's family regarding communicating feelings and differences; the day-in, day-out interaction patterns and ritual in the home that have become frozen over time with little or no communication yield.

Remember, if what you are presently doing to bring about communication is not working, discontinue it. Try something else. Often we must create a different context - go out to breakfast with your child...go to a movie of their choice and out for a pizza after...get the "Ungame" and use this board game to structure your interactions in new content areas ...read a book such as STRAIGHT TALK by Miller, et al, or PEOPLEMAKING by Satir...take an adult education course on communication. The rule of thumb is to interact differently with another family member to jog the stuck patterns of communication. You cannot change anyone else, but you can change yourself. As you do this, it will definitely influence others. Herein lies our hope for creating better communication patterns within the family.

"You must be over it by now..." is an often expressed or unexpressed thought of those who do not understand the dynamics of loss and grief. Let's look at the statement from a communication perspective. Making statements or judgments about others can be risky business. Making statements about oneself is more appropriate and results in less reactiveness. The above statement implies, "I really don't know what to say to you so I hope you are over it by now. I am uncomfortable dealing with your pain and/or tears. I hope you can get it together. It will make it easier for me to deal with you."

Consider the comment, "Aren't you over it by now?" as a very circular and indirect way of saying something about the speaker. It is so easy to get frustrated and angry at this person. Acknowledge your emotion, but consider where the other might be coming from. This may enable you to behave differently.

If you hear the comment, "You must be over it by now," respond simply but candidly, "No, I guess I'm still hurting - sometimes more, sometimes less." Then pause. If your friend does not respond but seems uncomfortable or uneasy, ask "Does it bother you to see me upset?" If the other says "Yes," then let him or her know the type of responses you would appreciate. If he or she says "No," respond "That's good. When I am feeling sad I sometimes need... (articulate desired responses)...from others." Either way you let your friend know a more appropriate response. Try not to be too harsh or upset with well-intended friends or relatives. Educate them. Use this as an opportunity to raise their consciousness so they in turn can be more helpful when such a situation arises again.

Dr. Terry O'Brien is a marriage and family therapist in private practice, special consultant/ trainer for HOPE FOR BEREAVED and a local/national presenter of workshops.

BE NOT DISCOURAGED, THE FARTHER YOU GO
THE LESS SEVERE THE WAY.

TASKS OF A FAMILY IN CRISIS
by Rev. Joseph H. Phillips, Ph. D.

Tragedy tests the very fabric of a family. The family experiencing a crisis commonly finds itself strained to the breaking point. Some steps can be identified that seem important for families to take in their struggle to cope with grief. A few of these tasks are described below.

Owning Up: One of the most difficult things in life is owning up to something. From early childhood, the urge to dodge or run from the hard or unpleasant is a part of our human make-up. It is almost instinct to shy away from taking responsibility for something.

When tragedy strikes, we naturally tend to deny what has happened and to deny that we are having a troublesome time living with our shocking loss. Despite all the pulls to the contrary, it is necessary for a family to work toward acceptance of the tragic event. Blaming is natural for a time, but at some point it becomes important to take responsibility for coping with tragedy. The healing process only proceeds when the family acknowledges that the death has happened and all are now faced with the challenge of living with unbearable grief.

Often a person will respond with a confused look when I remark: "You are taking a significant step in acknowledging that you are experiencing trouble in the family." The person wonders what can be important about saying we have troubles. Accepting that we have a difficulty is a necessary first step toward learning to cope with the trouble. In the words of the familiar prayer, "God, grant me the serenity to accept the things I cannot change."

Exploration: When a family suffers a severe loss, there is a normal tendency to withdraw in grief and to close out the surrounding world. If the loss is the result of self-inflicted harm, then a family may withdraw in shame and embarrassment. These instinctive reactions may afford a family time to recover a bit of its strength. In this way, the hiding is a temporary help. Yet, the disadvantages of withdrawal may prevent a family from gaining outside information and support. It is helpful for a family to search for information about the trouble they are experiencing and to seek out sources of support during time of tragedy.

Words of long ago offer a helpful reminder: "Ask and you will receive; seek and you will find; knock and it will be opened to you." In suffering, our attention and energies are usually fixed on the second half of these phrases; finding and receiving. Our first steps, however, need to be asking, seeking, knocking. Where might others be found who have suffered tragedy similar to our own? What might we learn from their experience? What suggestions have proved helpful to people faced with a situation like ours? What reading might be helpful?

An Individual Or Family Matter: When a family experiences grave hardship, it is common for family members to think in terms of themselves as individuals. "What is happening to me?" "What am I going to do?" The tragedy is experienced as an individual matter.

Tragedy tends to strike at the core of a family. There is a shattering effect that occurs. The extreme pain may prompt family members to withdraw from one another or to go off in separate directions. Anger and resentment about what has happened may cause family members to ignore or attack one another. Guilt can be like a poison, turning family members against one another. An attitude of "everyone for himself" may creep into the home. There is a frightening power in tragedy: one family may be drawn closer together, while another finds itself fragmented.

It is a help when the hurtful event is viewed as a family matter rather than as an individual matter. Here is something that is happening to us as a family, attacking us as a family, challenging in a grave way our very life as a family. How are we going to respond as a family? What might we do to help each other through this time of pain and sorrow?

Clear Versus Confused Roles: When a family member dies, confusion often reigns. It becomes important for the family to identify tasks to be accomplished, responsibilities to be carried out, and roles to be performed. How might we as a family organize our response to this crisis? What needs to be done and how will we take care of these needs? What are the parts that each might play? It sometimes helps to give even the smallest member of the family some part to play. Does each member understand their particular role? In crisis, the family needs to develop a plan of attack, to include each member of the family in the plan, and to spell out carefully the part each has.

Tragedy challenges the deepest resources of a family. Survival as a family may well be at stake. Certain steps described above are important for a family to take. In grief, each step is a strain; progress is so slow the end never seems to come into sight. The struggle to survive is, in fact, the very process of healing. The family struggling to come through crisis is opening itself to life's most precious gift: healing.

Rev. Joseph H. Phillips, Ph.D., was the co-founder of Hope For Bereaved.

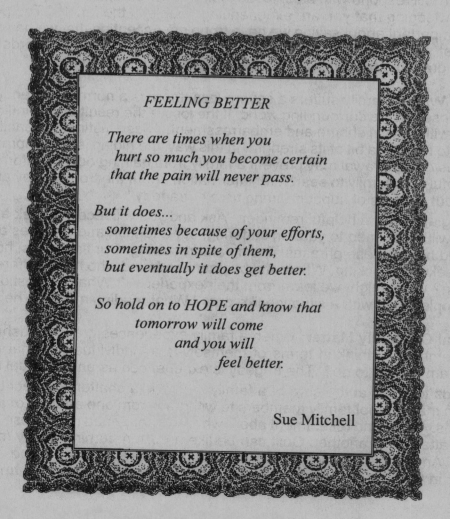

FEELING BETTER

There are times when you
    hurt so much you become certain
    that the pain will never pass.

But it does...
    sometimes because of your efforts,
    sometimes in spite of them,
    but eventually it does get better.

So hold on to HOPE and know that
    tomorrow will come
    and you will
        feel better.

Sue Mitchell

IS THERE LIFE AFTER LIFE?

Belief in life after death is found in the writings of the earliest civilizations. The oldest, clearly formulated beliefs in life after death appear in early Egyptian civilization (2000-1600 BC) as seen in their texts and tombs. In Christianity, life after death is central because of the resurrection of Jesus and His promise that His followers shall live on through faith in Him. Scientists are amazed by the number of predictions made about the dying experience in the Tibetan Book of the Dead (800 AD) that also appear in stories of 20th century Americans who have had death encounters and have never read the Tibetan book. There is something in our being that refuses to accept death as the end. It is an almost universal conviction that we are on a journey through this life to the next. Currently there is special interest in a life beyond this life due to the many publications about such experiences. The works of Dr. Elisabeth Kubler-Ross, Dr. Moody, Dr. Sabom and Dr. Ring, to name a few, are examples of studies that have been made and published within the past 10 years.

The first serious study of near-death experiences was by Albert Heim, a 19th century Swiss geologist, after his near-fatal fall while climbing the Alps. For the next 20 years, due to his own transcendent experience, he collected accounts from survivors of serious accidents (soldiers, roofers, workers on mountain projects, alpine climbers, etc.). His findings were presented in 1892. He concluded that the experiences in 95% of the cases he studied were similar, regardless of circumstances. He found that they felt detached from their bodies, heard heavenly music, saw magnificent lights, and were encompassed by feelings of peace and reconciliation. They said if given the choice, they would not have returned to this life.

Although most of the world's major religions hold that there is life after death, until recently people did not speak of their near-death experiences. In 1966 Dr. Elisabeth Kubler-Ross, an internationally known psychiatrist, began urging the dying to speak of their experiences. Dr. Kubler-Ross has pioneered work with the dying. To the well-known stages of dying (denial, anger, bargaining, depression, acceptance), she has added the transformation stage; from dying, to a happier, fuller life beyond death. According to Dr. Kubler-Ross, "I know beyond a shadow of a doubt that there is life after death." Before she started working with the dying, she did not believe in life after death. It is interesting that Dr. Kubler-Ross had not intended to publicly say this, but did it out of compassion in response to a question from a bereaved parent. Dr. Kubler-Ross keeps a file of the hundreds of stories of her patients and she personally checks the details. The following cases are examples:

One day a man came upon a hit-and-run accident. He tried to aid the young lady who was critically hurt. As he held her head on his lap, the lady said, "Please tell my Mom that I'm happy, I'm with Dad." With that she died. The man was so touched that he decided to drive the 700 miles out of his way to tell the girl's mother of her last words. He found the mother living on an Indian reservation. When he told her about his conversation with her daughter, she asked him what time her daughter died. Her husband had died one hour before, on the reservation, of a heart attack.

Dr. Kubler-Ross has chosen to work with dying children and often sits by their beds as they are dying. These children are always aware of those who preceded them in death. One holiday weekend there had been a tragic auto accident involving a family. Some members died at the accident, and others were brought to different hospitals. As one child was dying, he said, "I'm all right. I'm with Mommie and my brother, Peter." The child's mother had died at the accident, but no one had told the critically ill child. Peter was at a different hospital. After the child died, Dr. Kubler-Ross called the other hospital to tell them of the death. They said, "Oh, Peter died an hour ago we were just going to call you."

In another case a research chemist, who had been blinded the year before in an experiment, had a near-death experience. Despite his blindness, he was able to view everything that went on around him and report it after he was revived.

Another example is a young man in his mid-twenties who had a near-death experience after an auto accident. His leg was severed, and he showed no vital signs. He was pronounced dead on his way to the hospital. Yet, he did recover. He was able to report everything that had happened at the scene of the accident. He had floated out of his body and above the scene, where he watched the rescue team. He saw his own body in the street, minus one leg. He felt peaceful and had the sense that his whole body was intact, including his missing leg.

These cases give great comfort. They speak of an absence of pain and of our new bodies being whole, even if there is an amputation at the accident. The deaf hear, the blind see and the crippled can walk.

In a T.V. interview, Dr. Kubler-Ross spoke of the recollections of persons who had been brought back from a violent death (e.g., rape, beating, maiming). All of them related to her their experiences at the time of their death as strangely peaceful, with no physical pain. They spoke of being outside of their bodies, able to see what was happening, but completely detached from the violence. Even young children recalled only peace and beauty, no matter how badly they had been physically abused. Most of the persons she interviewed spoke of being with loved ones and friends already dead, of a beautiful light. Not one person she interviewed could remember any physical pain.

Albert Heim, in his 1892 study, found that sudden accidents are much more horrible for the observers than for the victims. Spectators may be deeply shattered, while the victim, even though badly injured, will be free of anxiety and pain. According to Dr. Bruce Grayson, psychiatrist and president of the International Association of Near Death Experiences, those who were revived did not mention anguish, fear or pain. During their clinical death, they were free of pain.

Dr. Raymond Moody's book, LIFE AFTER LIFE, published in 1975, was met with widespread interest. Originally Dr. Moody wasn't trying to prove life after life, but was collecting experiences to study. In a subsequent book, REFLECTIONS ON LIFE AFTER LIFE, Dr. Moody tells of people who, in their death experience, had brief glimpses of a separate realm of existence in which all knowledge, whether of past, present or future, seemed to coexist in a sort of timeless state. It was a feeling of complete knowledge of everything. Many people describe a city of light or being in a countryside with streams, grass, trees and mountains.

Dr. Michael Sabom, author of RECOLLECTIONS OF DEATH, was initially skeptical of Dr. Moody's findings, but as a cardiologist he worked with people in cardiac arrest. This led Dr. Sabom to examine these stories himself. He was especially interested in cases where patients reported seeing what was happening from above. He found that many patients could tell in detail and in correct sequence exactly what had happened to them on the operating table, even though they had no previous medical training or knowledge.

In his book, Dr. Sabom found that 40% of patients who had cardiac arrest had a near-death experience. In general, these patients felt less anxiety about death and an increased belief in life after death. Although many were in extreme pain right before or after the near-death experience, during the experience they felt calm and peaceful. One patient said, "That was the most beautiful instant in the whole world, when I came out of my body."

These researchers personally think that there is life after death. What convinced them were the common elements found in thousands of death encounters. People who have experienced a near-death experience or clinical death are convinced that they have had a look at what's to come and most don't want to be revived again.

Dr. Kenneth Ring decided to conduct an in-depth study of a new group of people who had come close to death and to collect and scientifically verify their stories. The men and women that he interviewed were of a wide range of age, education, background, temperament and religious beliefs. Yet they all told of a similar core experience which occurred when they were close to death or clinically dead. There was a sense of great comfort, peacefulness, beauty and they wished to remain. They felt tremendous happiness, without problems, worries or anxieties. It affected the rest of the person's earthly life. Most of the people were convinced they had been in the presence of some supreme and loving power and had been given a glimpse of the next life. He felt that these experiences caused a transformation in the lives of those who went through them; in their attitudes, values, their inclination to love and to help others. Dr. Ring is convinced "that these are absolutely authentic experiences."

In recent times, many apparently dead persons have come back to life through emergency medical procedures. These people who passed into a temporary state of clinical death marked by an absence of heart beat, respiration and other vital signs, had similar experiences regardless of culture, race, background or religion.

The common elements in these experiences include:

indescribable beauty - difficulty in describing the experience with our limited language; some said it seemed to be more than three dimensional.

absence of fear and pain.

noise - ringing; buzzing; beautiful music like wind, waves or bells.

movement - floating or moving rapidly through a dark tunnel, which is not frightening, usually with a light at the end.

outside the physical body - a convincing sensation of leaving the body, yet the distinct feeling of having an invincible body; the new body is different, with different powers; sense of wholeness, weightlessness, timelessness.

seeing their body - from a distance as a spectator, even watching the resuscitation attempt; not being able to communicate with those around them; able to hear what people say and think.

met and helped by predeceased - relatives, friends or spiritual guides (no one dies alone, we have guides/angels all our life and especially at the time of transition); sometimes they inform the person that he or she must return to life; communication may be nonverbal, instantaneous reading of thoughts.

immersion in a beautiful, pure light - brilliant, dazzling, blinding yet never hurting the eyes, "light" is one of the most common elements and the one with the most direct, religious symbolism. Jesus said, "I am the Light."

a Being of Light - encountering a comforting presence; many feel that the light and love people experience is God; a shining figure who radiates love, acceptance and warmth; who showed personal qualities of total compassion and a sense of humor.

life review - a panoramic review of life events, "seeing my life pass in front of me".

feelings of great peace, absolute love - comfort, joy, quiet, well-being, bliss, trust, relief, feeling trouble free, worry free.

approaching a barrier - which may represent the limit between this life and the next life; finding he or she must return to earth because the time for death has not come; resists returning because overwhelmed by intense feelings of love, joy and peace.

not afraid to die - because they know it will be a beautiful experience.

experience changes a person - becomes warmer, more outgoing, loving; has a positive attitude towards life, learns to appreciate this life; desires to do something for other people.

Recent findings discussed above are in harmony with theology; philosophy, psychology, mythology, archeology and thanatology of various civilizations and cultures. Significant research has reinforced our long-held ideas about the next life. These newly researched experiences of those who have been revived from a physical death give help and hope to many. Such experiences reassure us that death is not a fearful ending, but a wonderful new beginning - a passage from one life to another as Christ promised. With every dimension of my being, I do believe that there is eternal life after this life...it is a comforting belief for the bereaved.

REFLECTIONS

I have always believed in heaven, although I didn't always talk about it very much. I believe that my father, grandparents, aunts, uncles and infant sister are in heaven, and we will be reunited one day.

In 1970, I remember reading an article in LIFE MAGAZINE by one of the editors. He had an allergic reaction to medication and was rushed to the doctor. For a brief time he was clinically dead, until the doctor's emergency procedure revived him. He recorded his death experience as, "Something more beautiful, more gentle, more loving than the mind or imagination of any living creature could ever conceive." I was fascinated by the brief article. Although I had great faith in the next life, I found it intriguing to think that people could actually have a glimpse of heaven. It was very reassuring.

In the August, 1976 issue of McCall magazine, there was an article, "There Is Life After Death." After I read it I shared it with my family and friends. One son took a copy to his good friend whose grandfather had just died. One Sunday evening in January, 1977, as a family, we watched a television show on which people who had been declared clinically dead and resuscitated were interviewed. In June of that year, I attended our yearly staff planning meeting. At a break some of us went for a walk. Jean, one of my friends, had just read the book, LIFE AFTER LIFE, by Dr. Raymond Moody. She was so enthusiastic, it was all we talked about that afternoon. The next day I purchased the book and read it. Then I shared it with my mom, a friend, and talked about the concepts with other family members.

At 2:30 a.m. on August 21, 1977, at Community Hospital, I used the concepts that had so interested me. Mary, our 21-year-old daughter, had been killed in an auto accident. The accident had occurred in Tully, a village about 20 miles from the hospital. We live about 25 miles from the hospital, so some time had elapsed from the time Mary died until we saw her in that hospital room. I wasn't sure if she was still in that hospital room or if she was already in heaven. I even pictured her going through that tunnel to everlasting life. I kissed her and told her we loved her, and that I knew she would go to God. Since hearing is the last of our senses to go I felt she might still hear me, and if she was in heaven she would know what I said.

We believe that our daughter, Mary, has entered a new life - without loneliness, hurts, problems, fears or pain. She is indescribably happy. We will always miss her. I found the following quotes by Dr. E. Kubler-Ross to be helpful: "Death is not a permanent separation, but a temporary good-bye" . . . "Death is not the end of a loving relationship - our loved ones will always be there" . . . "Real love doesn't die - it is the physical body that dies."

As a family, we talked about death and we are not afraid to die. Although we will grieve again when the next family member dies, at the same time we will picture the reunion in heaven. Some day we will all be together again (what a reunion that will be!!). Meanwhile, we will try to love and live life to the fullest. As devastating as grief is, it has taught us to appreciate life and the people in our lives.

In my research I found the concept that God has a sense of humor to be very comforting and important. Man is made in the image and likeness of God, and since we have a sense of humor it makes sense that God does, also. It seems that if we could be more gentle and peaceful with ourselves and others and look at life with a sense of humor, we could glimpse in a small way the peace and love of our next life.

The following was taken from the book, ON CHILDREN AND DEATH, by Dr. Elisabeth Kubler-Ross: "Since the consciousness of the people on this planet earth is unfolding at an accelerated rate, it is only a matter of a couple of decades until all people of all creeds, of all cultures, of all places will know that this life on earth is just a small, yet the most difficult, part of our long journey from the source we call God, back to our final home of peace, back to God."

These two verses from the Bible mean so much more to me now: Jesus said, "I came that they may have life and have it abundantly." And from St. Paul, "Eye has not seen, nor ear heard, neither has it entered into the heart of man the things which God has prepared for them that love Him."   T.S.S.

WHEN A LOVED ONE WAS MURDERED   by Nan Newman

I've believed in life after death ever since my mother died. I was only eight years old. I could not understand WHY. The only thought that consoled me growing up was that God would one day bring us together.

When my son, Tom, was murdered four years ago, I asked my mother and other family members who had died to watch over him. Elisabeth Kubler-Ross, M.D. writes of interviewing people who had been brought back from a violent death and of most of them remembering being with loved ones and friends already dead, surrounded by a beautiful light. Not one person remembered any pain. I do believe there is life after death!

WHEN A LOVED ONE DIES BY SUICIDE   by Christine Beattie

I have always believed that there is "Life After Life." As a child going to Sunday School, much emphasis was put on heaven. At that time I formed my picture of the hereafter. I would walk through this long tunnel and would emerge into a bright, sunshiny place, all white and gold and soft and fluffy with clouds and there would be angels.

I thought about my grandfather being in heaven and that my grandmother would soon join him. I thought about how happy he would be to see her. They would not have any more suffering.

Dr. Michael Sabom tells of a 43-year-old man during his post-operative cardiac arrest (near-death experience): "I came to some place and there were all my relatives: my grandmother, my grandfather, my father and my uncle who had recently committed suicide. They came towards me and greeted me. They looked better than the last time I saw them and they were very happy." Dr. Kubler-Ross also states in her book that after interviewing many people brought back from a violent death (suicide), they remembered no suffering - no pain.

My son died by suicide in 1980. He hung himself. Had I not believed in life after life, I would never have been able to survive that terrible ordeal. I truly believe that our loved ones who had died would be at the end of the tunnel, waiting for him. He, too, believed in life after life. We talked about it a few months before his death. I knew he had to find some peace in his life. He knew that the after-life would give him this.

So many people who come to our Hope For Survivors Support Group wonder about loved ones who have taken their own lives: "Would they be able to enter heaven?" YES - God does not judge a person on the last act of his life, but on his whole life.

109

WHEN A CHILD HAS DIED

WHAT HAPPENS TO A MARRIAGE WHEN A CHILD DIES?

A married couple may suddenly find, at the time of the greatest tragedy in their lives and at the time of their greatest need, that each is an individual. They must mourn as individuals. This is an abrupt departure from the other things they have shared together; laughter, joy, vacations, achievements and minor problems. Separately, in the back of each of their minds, they believed they could lean on each other as they mourned. It is difficult to lean on someone already doubled over in pain according to author and bereaved parent, Harriet Schiff.

One doesn't expect to outlive their child; this seems a contradiction of nature. The death may be that of a baby, a school-age child, a young adult, or even a "child" in their middle or senior years. The grief of the surviving parents seems to go on and on.

Some marital friction is bound to occur in any marriage. Friction becomes compounded with the death of a child. It is not easy but it does help to understand the various problems that may arise. Eventually, with time and work, the grief will soften and the marriage can survive.

"Till Death Do Us Part" foretells the end of marriage when one spouse dies. It may also be true when a child dies. In our nation 50% of all marriages end in divorce. According to The Compassionate Friends, a self-help organization for bereaved parents, "over seventy percent of marriages where children have died end in separation or divorce. " Couples have shared tragedy, disaster and grief, but these emotions do not necessarily create a tighter bond. Often, instead of holding them together, the bond becomes so taut that it snaps. These statistics point out the devastating effect the death of a child can have on parents. They also point out the need to understand what you are experiencing and how important it is to value the marriage.

Severe marital friction in bereaved parents may develop out of the ordinary, everyday irritants of just plain living. Sometimes the trivia can pull a couple apart. You lose your patience, your sense of proportion. You hurt so much you have no tolerance. Allowing petty little things that you could handle before to become gigantic irritants is a major cause of marital breakdown.

Everyone grieves differently, and couples frequently grieve in opposite ways. This situation makes it harder for spouses to support or understand each other and requires a great deal of tolerance and respect for differences. However, this variety of grief in couples may allow the family to keep on functioning.

Some parents want to change everything, while others do not want to disturb anything. One parent may want to put all pictures, mementos and reminders away. The other parent may almost make a shrine of pictures and of the child's room and possessions.

When one parent is having an "up" day, they resent their partner being "down." The reverse is also true; when you are having a "down" day you can't imagine how your spouse is able to feel so "up."

Even something as basic as weather can affect the marriage. The sunny days bring hope and warmth into one partner's life, while the other spouse can't feel happy on such a nice day when their child isn't there to enjoy it. The spouse who doesn't like the sunny days isn't bothered by the gray rainy days, whereas the other spouse's mood matches the gray, rainy day.

Another problem is whether to discuss the dead child. Some parents can be at opposite ends about this. One may speak all the time about the child who has died and the other may never mention the child and may even refuse to let their partner speak of the child. Often the happy memories can be discussed by both, but not the death and grief.

On the other hand, mutual protectiveness may become a cause of marital friction. You may think that telling your partner how devastated you are feeling may make your spouse feel worse. There is the hurt from the death of the child, then the additional hurt to see your spouse in such pain. However, spouses usually do "read" each other even if nothing is said. It is better to speak than to suppress it, only to have it surface in other ways.

Socializing after the death can be looked at differently. Sometimes one partner will take the attitude that "we shouldn't enjoy ourselves now that our child is dead," whereas the other spouse may seek the opportunity to be with other people. Sometimes a spouse may even refuse to continue having sexual relations. These differences can have a serious impact on the marriage. Another consideration is that often some family members and friends will distance themselves from the grieving parents. This is not out of malice but more from not knowing what to say or do. Also, as bereaved people there are times that we are not the best company. This isolation by others adds to the marital strain.

Differing views of religion, even between parents of the same faith, can be a problem. One partner may turn away from religion or have a stock answer, while the other may search for answers within their faith and find immense comfort. It may look as if our mate is not hurting as much as we are. We may not realize it but we may feel jealous of how well our mate seems to be doing.

Unresolved grief turns inward and may become destructive, both mentally and physically. Sometimes one parent will internalize the grief, ending up in a severe state of depression. One parent may be so obsessed with grief that he or she cries continuously, causing much turmoil to the other parent and children.

It is crucial to recognize your vulnerability and not to take your spouse's reactions personally. With the death of a child the nervous system is raw. We experience deep and often mysterious feelings. It is scary and unnerving. This severe pain of grief brings out the humanness of both parents. We can see both the good and the bad sides of ourselves and our mates. The temptation is to dwell on the negative. It is important to recognize the feelings and to see the negative side, but then to work on the grief and to concentrate on the positive. Remember, marriage is challenging at its best. With the death of a child our ability to love is really tested.

We do not want to "overload" our spouse. By trial and error, in time a couple can learn to grieve together by developing ways of understanding each other's needs more fully and by committing themselves to the re-creation of their marriage. It is important to value one's marriage.

SUGGESTIONS TO AID MARRIAGE

1. Don't expect your spouse to be a tower of strength when he or she is also experiencing grief.
2. Be sensitive to your spouse's personality style. In general, he or she will approach grief with the same personality habits as they approach life. It may be very private, very open and sharing, or someplace in between.
3. Find a "sympathetic ear" (not necessarily your mate) - someone who cares and will listen.
4. Do talk about your child with your spouse. If necessary set up a time period daily when you both know that it is time to talk about your child.
5. Seek the help of a counselor if depression, grief or problems in your marriage are getting out of hand.
6. Do not overlook or ignore anger-causing situations. It is like adding fuel to a fire. Eventually there is an explosion. Deal with things as they occur.
7. Remember, you loved your spouse enough to marry. Try to keep your marriage alive: go out for dinner or an ice-cream cone; take a walk; go on a vacation.
8. Be gentle with yourself and your mate.
9. Join a support group for bereaved parents. Attend as a couple, come by yourself or with a friend. It is a good place to learn about grief and to feel understood. Do not pressure your spouse to attend with you if it is not his or her preference.
10. Join a mutually agreeable community betterment project.
11. Do not blame yourself or your mate for what you were powerless to prevent. If you blame your spouse or personally feel responsible for your child's death, seek immediate counseling for yourself and your marriage.
12. Realize that you are not alone. There are many bereaved parents, both locally and nationally.
13. Choose to believe again in the goodness of God and of life. Search for joy and laughter.
14. Recognize your extreme sensitivity and vulnerability and be alert to the tendency to take things personally.
15. Read about grief, especially the books written for bereaved parents.
16. Take your time with decisions about your child's things, change of residence, etc.
17. Be aware of unrealistic expectations for yourself or your mate.
18. Remember, there is no timetable. Everyone goes through grief differently, even parents of the same child.
19. Try to remember that your spouse is doing the best he or she can.
20. Marital friction is normal in any marriage. Don't blow it out of proportion.
21. Try not to let little everyday irritants become major issues. Talk about them and try to be patient.
22. Be sensitive to the needs and wishes of your spouse as well as yourself. Sometimes it is important to compromise.
23. It is very important to keep the lines of communication open.
24. Work on your grief instead of wishing that your spouse would handle his or her grief differently. You will find that you will have enough just handling your own grief. Remember, when you help yourself cope with grief it indirectly helps your spouse.
25. As Harriet Schiff states, "Value your marriage. You have lost enough."
26. Hold on to HOPE. With time, work and support you will survive. It will never be the same, but you can learn again to appreciate life and the people in your life.

A FATHER'S GRIEF
by Owen Peltier

"Fix it, Daddy" my son, Chuck, would say as a little boy, bringing me some broken toy. Over the years I fixed the broken toys, the malfunctioning appliances, the ailing automobiles, the carpentry projects, etc. But in July of 1979, I came up against something I didn't begin to know how to repair - a broken heart after the death of my son in an automobile accident. Dad, the fix-it man, had an insoluble problem. There was no way to make it better for myself or anyone else in the family.

After the numbness and shock wore off, I began to realize that he was really dead and all the bright hopes and expectations for the future were gone with him. The terrible pain of grief and a sense of helplessness set in. There were feelings of anger, frustration, guilt, trouble concentrating at work, and wanting to escape but not knowing where to escape to. I tried to bottle-up my emotions and be strong. I postponed my grief due to concern for other members of the family.

For men of my age group and often younger men, too, conditioning has given us an image of being male: Men should be strong - "big boys don't cry;" the male is the protector of the family, the provider, the problem solver and he should be self-sufficient and able to handle everything on his own; displays of emotion are taboo, even among close friends and family. When a man loses his child, these expectations are unrealistic and superhuman.

In October we began going to Bereaved Parent meetings. The outcry of another father hit home; "What is a father to do? You can't sit at your desk and cry." At the meetings we heard a different approach. Rev. Simon Stephens, who founded The Compassionate Friends, said, "Grief only becomes a tolerable and creative experience when love enables it to be shared with someone who really understands." From our support group leaders we heard things like; "Grief work is the hardest work you will ever have to do. Lean into the pain. You cannot go over, under or around grief, but only through it. We did not have any choice about what happened to our child, but we do have a choice about recovering from our grief."

We learned a lot about grief. Everything we learned indicated it is much healthier to admit to and talk about our feelings than it is to deny them. Suppressed or unresolved grief surfaces in one way or another. It can be physical ailments, such as high blood pressure, stomach disorders and heart complications, or it can result in divorce, dependence on drugs or alcohol, or mental illness.

Admitting that we need help and support, that we don't have all the answers, that our power is limited and that we are in emotional pain is hard - especially for fathers. The grieving process is exhausting and frightening. It must be faced at a time when all our physical and emotional resources are at an all-time low. Most of us believe that we are in control of our own lives and our children's destiny, and it is a terrible realization when we find out we are not.

There is no timetable for grief. Your grief may be longer or shorter than mine. As the sixth anniversary of my son's death approaches, I can say the raw wound has become a scar I can live with. How and when did I get here? What is a father to do? I am not really sure what the process was, and it happened gradually, almost imperceptibly. I know that being a part of the Bereaved Support Group was responsible for much of my recovery. How did sitting in a circle of people listening to all their pain help? I don't understand how, but in some way letting others' pain in enables you to let your own out. With the help of some very good friends, I have been able to get to the place where I can spend more time thinking about what I have left than focusing on what I have lost. I still feel cheated at times because I don't have my son, but life is worth living again.

Fathers hurt, too. We need to be allowed to be human. We need the chance to travel through our grief with the support of others. You are not alone. I have been there and so have many others. Sharing the burden lightens the load.

Owen and Carol Peltier are founding members of Hope For Bereaved Planning Committee and are active volunteers.

114

MY JOURNEY THROUGH GRIEF
by Sharon Rusaw

Our 18-year-old daughter, Darcy, was killed in a car accident in December, 1978. Since then we have traveled the long and turbulent road of grief.

Grief is something you cannot go around or ignore. There are no shortcuts on this long and sometimes terrifying journey. We each must go through grief in our own way and in our own time, but in order to heal we must face it.

With the news of the accident came shock. At first, I couldn't cry. I couldn't believe it was real. I felt like I was in the distance watching this happen to someone else. After the numbness and shock wore off then came reality. It's true - it really happened. For the first time in my life I had no control over what had happened.

The range of emotions you feel is hard to describe. Many times I felt like I was going insane. Along with this came panic like I had never felt before.

I always had pretty good control of my emotions, yet found I was crying all the time... in stores, in church, with my friends, without friends, and usually when I least expected it.

I read as many articles and books on grief and death as I could find. Some were helpful and some weren't. It was the same with family and friends. Some withdrew because they were hurting and couldn't bear to see us hurting so much, while others became closer even though they hurt as we did. They helped us to deal with our grief by sharing our experience... by being there when we wanted to cry or talk about Darcy. One friend in particular knew when I was hurting even when I didn't show it. She would make me talk about what I was feeling. This helped me to bring my feelings out in the open.

People don't always say the right things, but then neither did I before this happened and I'm sure there will be times when I will say the wrong things again. I had to learn to be as patient with people as they were with me.

One of the hardest things for me was my own expectations. I thought I should be doing better and tried to push a lot of my feelings down. This was the worst thing to do because I had to face those feelings eventually. Because I had set time limits for myself, it really hit hard when I hit bottom again.

Anger was another thing I had a hard time dealing with. I don't like anger and did not want to become a bitter and unhappy woman, so it was really hard to admit I was angry. I didn't know who or what I was angry at, but I finally had to face the fact that I WAS angry. Once I faced this, it was easier. I was angry with God, angry with everything. I think I was angry with friends because they still had their daughters and our only daughter was dead. Gone were all our dreams for her future - college, wedding, grandchildren, all the things we could have shared together.

When I read that a large percentage of marriages break up after the death of a child, I found this hard to believe. I had always assumed that most tragedies would bring you closer together. I have since discovered it is a very difficult time even in good marriages. You are both hurting so much that it is almost impossible to lean on one another, just as you can't stay afloat if you hold onto a boat that is sinking.

We couldn't talk about how we were feeling, because if my husband was finally having a good day I didn't want to bring him down into the pits with me, and he felt the same way. We could talk about Darcy, but not about our feelings.

My husband went to the cemetery almost every day and it was hard for him to understand why I couldn't. This was helpful to him but not to me. He never said anything but I sensed that this bothered him.

We also had to try very hard not to take our anger out on one another. I'm sure there were many times when we did this, but for the most part we tried not to. I felt better when we were away from home or on vacation. He felt better at home. No two people grieve alike, so we had to have a lot of patience with each other.

One thing that helped me more than anything else was becoming a part of a support group — Hope For Bereaved Parents. There, I was among people that could understand what I was going through, because they had been there themselves. I could say what I was really feeling without anyone being shocked that I was still grieving.

I also found that all the emotions I was feeling were normal—I was not going insane. If I felt like sharing my feelings I could, or if I just wanted to listen that was O.K., too. We talked about our emotions and what we could do to help ourselves through this difficult time.

One of the most important things I learned in the group is that THERE IS NO TIME-TABLE for grief. It was also the one place I could be completely honest about how I was feeling. Once in a while I cried at the meetings, but that was O.K. and something I certainly needed to do. These emotions have to come out or they can destroy us. We need to face our grief if we are to get better.

When I started going it was because I needed help; and even though I still need their support at times, I go now so I can help someone just as I was helped. It helped me so much when I first started attending just to see someone that had lost a child and was "making It".

I've also learned not to worry about tomorrow, to take one day at a time. If that is impossible, take a half day or one hour if that is all you can handle.

There is hope at the end of the long tunnel of grief. I still have bad days and probably always will. I think of Darcy every day and miss her, but at least now I know I will make it.

My faith has grown even stronger through this and I know someday I will see her again. I have had to learn to be a "LEANER" - lean on friends and, more important, lean on God. He cares and will help us if only we let Him.

I feel grief is one of the hardest things in life to deal with, but because of this we can grow and reach out and help others.

Sharon and Stan Rusaw are founding members of the Hope For Bereaved Planning Committee and are active volunteers. Sharon is one of our Support Group facilitators.

We highly recommend The Compassionate Friends, Inc., a national self-help organization offering friendship and understanding to bereaved parents. To receive a complimentary copy of The Compassionate Friends Newsletter or for further information about the location of the chapter nearest to you, write to The Compassionate Friends, P.O. Box 3696, Oak Brook, IL 60522.

Darcy Rusaw

    She bloomed on earth . . .
        She blossomed in heaven.

WHEN A BABY DIES....FETAL AND INFANT DEATH
by Lois Loucks Sugarman

The birth of a child is life's greatest celebration of itself. Yet when a child dies by miscarriage, stillbirth or as a newborn infant, the parents and family are often encouraged to respond as if the loss is less painful and has less meaning than the death of an older child or an adult loved one. It is upsetting to realize that those persons upon whom we depend may not be able to respond in a helpful manner because of the extreme anxiety felt when there is nothing "to do," which will change the reality of death so close to birth. Statements such as "You can always have another baby" or "It is God's will" are most frequently offered as comfort, but better serve to reduce the speaker's own discomfort.

The process of mourning with its predominant emotion, grief, takes considerable time. When parents do not have a chance to see, touch or to hold their dead child, family, friends and professionals alike too often expect their mourning to be short or absent. In contrast to such an expectation, the death of a child during pregnancy or the death of a newborn can be as difficult as the experience of losing an older child or an adult loved one.

The feelings experienced by the parents are not abnormal, nor do they indicate that they are losing touch with reality. Many parents may feel exactly that way! When an older child dies or when an adult loved one dies, the mourning process includes relating closely to the deceased by remembering times and relationships shared. When a child dies during pregnancy or as a newborn infant, there has been little, if any time to share a relationship with the child as a separate person. As a result the parents are obliged to mourn the loss of a part of themselves without the aid of memories and momentoes, or at best they may have very few. While the initial response to keeping footprints, pictures, a name bracelet, crib card or a lock of hair may be negative, these items take on special significance as proof that a child existed or was expected. Naming the child, which can be done at any time, can help to confirm what is reality. A funeral or memorial rite is appropriate according to the parents' wishes, as is remembering the child on anniversary dates of the birth and death.

The feeling of the mourner that he or she is "getting worse" may be an indication that the initial phase of mourning is breaking down. Shock and disbelief (lasting varying amounts of time) subside to be replaced by deep, real emotional pain and searching for answers to questions of "Why? What did I/we do wrong? What does this mean to me, my partner, our relationship, our children, living or not yet born?" There may be distinct changes in sleeping and eating patterns, changes in the desire for sexual activity and a reduction of energy and interest in usual activities. There can be strong feelings of anger, depression, sadness and a sense of confusion; all very frightening when you do not know that this is part of a normal and necessary process.

Expectations of ourselves and of others can be disruptive. We need to realize that while the loss of a child during pregnancy or the death of a newborn is "over" for some when the mother comes home from the hospital or when the funeral is over, for the parents the mourning process has barely begun. As mourners we need to trust our sense of what is best for us, such as declining to attend a major family gathering because it is expected of us. We need to ask for the support we need from others without feeling guilty for asking, and know that our needs are real. We may have to become educators of our friends and family members who probably have never had similar experiences.

Mothers and fathers can be expected to mourn and to grieve in different ways. One spouse may believe his or her role is to protect the other and, without meaning to, shut them out from important decisions in which they may need to have a part; such as funeral arrangements. One spouse may feel that if only he or she can contain expressions of grief, they will not add to the other's burden. That may then be interpreted as the absence of the need to grieve openly. With this misunderstanding each spouse may expect behavior which the other may be unable to carry out, such as entertaining or returning directly to work. At this point misunderstandings abound: "He or she doesn't understand; doesn't care." Communication is essential . . . honest communication. When you are able to share your feelings, there is permission given for your partner to share his/her feelings as well. Sometimes it is helpful for couples to set aside time for talking about their loss and their feelings about it. This may provide some sense of control in a situation where the feeling of having lost control is overwhelming.

An immediate desire for another child can be very strong. Like other parents who have had children die, parents who have lost children during pregnancy or as newborn infants know that one child cannot replace another. It is difficult to invest in a new pregnancy while working hard to resolve the feelings of loss from the death of an earlier child. Giving yourself enough time to mourn the dead child is caring not only for yourself, but also caring for the marriage relationship and for the future child or children.

Accepting the work of mourning and grieving is painful when we have lost not only a child, but a portion of our future. However, it is through mourning and grieving that we heal, that we can look to the day when we can remember that child and smile. The desire is not to forget, but to remember without pain. Have hope and believe that it can happen!

Lois founded SHARE: HOPE FOR PARENTS WHOSE INFANTS DIED BY MISCARRIAGE, STILLBIRTH OR NEWBORN DEATH. Lois is a psychiatric mental health nurse, clinical nurse specialist and has experienced the infant death of one of their children.

WHEN AN INFANT DIES SUDDENLY... SIDS

Sudden Infant Death Syndrome (SIDS) is the sudden, unexpected death of an apparently healthy infant. It remains the leading cause of death of infants between the ages of one week and one year and is responsible for the death of approximately 7,000 infants each year. SIDS, frequently called "crib death," is not a new syndrome and can be found as far back as Biblical times. Currently, NO ONE KNOWS WHY. Researchers now believe that SIDS probably has more than one cause. It is important to realize that the research to date has not found a way to determine which baby may die of SIDS. Current research does show that the risk of SIDS may be decreased by having a baby sleep on its back or side, by reducing cigarette smoking in the baby's presence, and by encouraging breast-feeding. There are currently no sure preventative measures to be taken for all infants. There are no specific symptoms and no cure. No amount of supervision can prevent the death. SIDS is not caused by suffocation, choking, neglect or changing modes of infant care. PARENTS ARE NOT TO BLAME FOR THE DEATH OF THEIR INFANT ... IT COULDN'T BE PREVENTED (*For further information write to the National Sudden Infant Death Syndrome Foundation [page 173]. In Syracuse call our telephone Helpline, listed on the back of the front cover.*)

WHEN A BABY DIES IT IS HELPFUL TO:
- Recognize that the grief you are experiencing is devastating and normal. You may feel guilty, angry, etc. Many parents mention "Phantom Crying" or "Aching Arms."
- Give yourself enough time to grieve and to recover your physical and emotional strength before considering another pregnancy.
- Choose new names for subsequent children.
- Realize that the anniversary of your baby's birth and death may be very difficult. Leave time for grieving but also plan for as pleasant a day as possible with understanding family and friends; be good to yourselves.
- Read about grief and infant death in order to understand what you are experiencing.

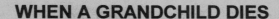

WHEN A GRANDCHILD DIES

No one expects to outlive their own children, much less their grandchildren. It is so difficult to raise a family, see your children do the same, and then see the cycle broken in this out-of-order way. No one is prepared for the grief that follows. As grandparents you have a double grief. You grieve for your grandchild who has died, as well as for your own child who is now a bereaved parent. You not only feel your own pain and sadness, but feel helpless and frustrated at not being able to help your bereaved child.

It helps to remember that there is no timetable for grief. Don't expect too much of your child, their spouse or of yourself. At first no one believes it. When the reality "hits" everyone feels even more devastated. It is important to consider your needs as well as those of your bereaved child. Acknowledging and working on your grief will help you and, indirectly, your grieving child.

As a bereaved grandparent you may feel great sadness, loss, guilt and anger. Some older grandparents have said, "I've lived my life. It should have been me." The fact that they are still alive while a young child or young adult is dead is difficult for many to bear. You may feel guilty if you live a distance from your child and, due to health or finances, you are not able to be with them at this painful time. Realize that you would be there if you could. It helps to write supportive letters and to make loving phone calls. You may experience anger at God, life, those in the medical profession, or any person you feel is responsible for your grandchild's death. You might even feel angry towards your own child for "letting it happen." Such guilt or anger is not always rational but may temporarily go with the territory of grief. (See articles on Guilt, page 61, and Anger, page 65.)

Some of you who now find yourselves grieving for a grandchild may have experienced the death of your own child years ago. Your grandchild's death may trigger memories and pain that you thought were long since forgotten. If your child died more than ten years ago, you may not have resolved your grief. In earlier years, and in some cases even today, grieving people were not allowed or encouraged to grieve. There were no support groups or books on grief. You were supposed to go on as if nothing had happened. If this is the case for you it is important to allow your grief to surface. If you can, talk about it with your grieving child. It may help both of you.

Be careful not to suppress your grief, and encourage your child not to suppress grief either. Suppressed grief can cause physical as well as emotional pain. In addition to being harmful to you, it may seem to your bereaved child that you don't really care and are not hurting, too. In reality, when our child suffers, we suffer. It is important for everyone to face the grief and work through it. Life will never be the same; but with time, effort and much love grief will ease.

> Don't be surprised if at first you can't reach out to help your grieving child. Remember, you are grieving! Be patient with yourself. Eventually you may be able to talk, listen and help. If you find that you can't help specifically with the grief, you can send cards, tell them that you love them, etc. Explain that you wish that you could be of more help but that you don't know what to do.

SUGGESTIONS FOR HELPING YOURSELF/YOUR GRIEVING CHILD

- Read about grief (HOPE FOR BEREAVED Handbook, The Bereaved Parent, Living When A Loved One Has Died). It is important to understand what you and your child are experiencing.
- It helps to be open and share your feelings. Your openness sets a good example for your child. Share the good memories and good days, as well as the pain of grief and the bad days.

- Talk about the dead grandchild. Mention his/her name.
- Find someone with whom you can talk freely- a friend, support group member, clergy or counselor.
- Be available to LISTEN frequently to your child. Respect your child's way of handling the pain and expressing the grief. Don't tell your child how he or she should react.
- At special times (anniversary of death, birthday, holidays) write and/or call your bereaved child (and their spouse). Mention that you realize what day it is. You are calling to say you love them and you wish that you could take some of their pain away.
- When adults are grieving, remaining siblings often feel neglected....plus they don't understand the grief that they are experiencing. Try to spend extra time with your other bereaved grandchild(ren), offering to listen and reminding them that they are very important and much loved.
- If possible, offer to take surviving grandchild(ren) for an afternoon or a day; help with practical matters, such as preparing food, doing laundry, shopping; spend time alone with your child.
- Most of us need hugs even if we don't recognize that we do. It helps to hug and hold your child if you both are comfortable doing so.
- Allow yourself and encourage your child to cry when needed. Crying offers relief.
- Let the family know that you care; that you love them.
- Hold onto HOPE that eventually you/they will enjoy life again. Offer HOPE to your grieving child and family.

TWO GRANDMOTHERS' REFLECTIONS

Our first grandchild died at birth. I never grieved over the loss of this baby. Ten years later, when our son died of cancer without having fathered another child, I found myself grieving for both of them. I realized that the part of him that might have been left to us was also gone. I had been under the mistaken notion that because we never knew or even saw this little life - there was no need to grieve. As a member of HOPE FOR BEREAVED PARENT(S) I have learned the importance of the grief process. The help that I received from the support group, plus helping others, has been the key to my recovery. It has been four years since Keith's death and I can now find great comfort in thinking of our son and grandson, together in heaven, getting to know each other.

by Eunice Brown

My beautiful granddaughter Mary died in August, 1977. When I was told, I did not believe it. Earlier that evening she had stopped to say goodnight. At first I was angry at everybody - particularly saints that I depended on. WHY? . . . was a question that I asked repeatedly. I had lived my life, why couldn't it have been me instead of Mary? I wanted to kill the driver of the car. Frustration was all I saw for a long time. Talking with others was helpful. As time went on, helping them helped me. Thanks to relatives and wonderful friends I began to slow down and to ask Mary to help us. I am sure she did. At last we all can enjoy life again.

by Mary Sharpe

OF SPECIAL INTEREST:

FOR BEREAVED GRANDPARENTS, by Margaret Gerner (*$4.25 includes postage and handling*). The author has experienced the death of her grandchild. Make check payable and mail to: Margaret Gerner, 7717 Natural Bridge Road, St. Louis, MO 63121.

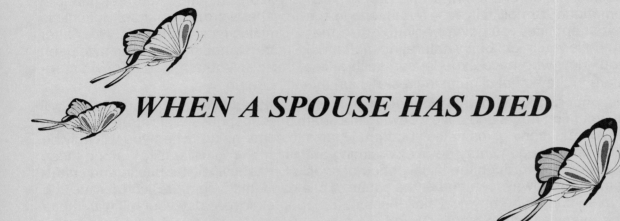

WHEN A SPOUSE HAS DIED

WHEN YOUR SPOUSE DIES
by Kathleen Jacques

As I write this, more than five years have passed since my husband was killed. I feel very grateful that I've made it this far, that I've come so far since those first dreadful days.

I won't presume that my experience is identical to anyone else's; I can't say what someone else will feel or how they will react. Yet I offer my reflections in hope that perhaps the reader will find something useful to help them cope.

Research shows that the death of one's spouse is one of the most devastating events in a person's lifetime. Studies point to the problems of survivors; health disorders, financial troubles, emotional turmoil. It is easy for anyone to see why these problems arise. But unless YOU lose your spouse, you never begin to grasp the full implications of the loss. No matter how sympathetic you might be by nature, no matter how understanding you might have been to those you know who have experienced such a loss, you'll still be amazed at how unprepared you are in the actual circumstances of your spouse's death.

Details, paperwork, the rituals of funeral services, the gathering of friends and family, will all structure your first hours and days following the death of your spouse. This structure buoys you, keeps you functioning; insulates you from what is to come next....when you will truly be alone. Your grief and agony may be overwhelming at this time. You will easily lean on those who come' to see you through the initial period of shock. Somehow, all the bustle and confusion is a comfort - I'll always remember the squeeze of a hand, the neighbors' kindnesses, the heartfelt "I'm so sorry," the physical closeness of the people I love. Busy yourself with these details, cling to any structure that is offered.

If there is just one thing I could tell people in this situation, it is this: FEEL WHAT YOU FEEL - it is appropriate for what you are going through. How can you expect to control and chart how you should feel, how you should react? Emotions will control YOU! Don't feel guilty because you can't stop crying or you can't feel grateful for the other blessings that may be in your life. This "grief' business is more than just a feeling of sadness; it is a physical hurt, like a punch in the stomach. It is a state of mind; you can't think of anything but this loss. It is a spiritual crisis; the universe loses its order. It's a loss of peace of mind - will I ever feel well, whole, normal again? Ease up on yourself. It's okay to be less than brave, calm, rational, collected, or gracious. Feel what you feel, then this aspect of the grieving process can work its way through and some other emotion will replace that one. If you suppress a feeling, say anger, it will surely crop up later, intensified.

Find someone to LISTEN to you. It's not as important for them to offer suggestions as it is to simply listen to you. You'll want to reminisce about your spouse, to gripe about all the things that will anger you now, to fret about the future, to challenge your religious beliefs. It is essential to find someone who will listen, not judge you. Most people have a very hard time dealing with a grieving person. You'll be stung by some very inappropriate remarks. Forgive those around you; remember how ineffective you felt in the past dealing with the tragedies of others. Don't expect people who have not lived with what you're going through to pull you through.

If you are not fortunate enough to have a friend or family member to use as your sounding board, seek outside help. You go to the dentist for a toothache, to the doctor for an infection, don't you? So why not a counselor for a life crisis, why not a clergyman for a spiritual calamity? It is easy to fall into the trap of thinking that simple industriousness (taking on extra work) will give you a means to a "cure." You may subconsciously think that your remaining family will "fill-in" in a way for your lost spouse, that they'll be able to give you the emotional support and sustenance that you received from your spouse. But "wellness" comes from within, not from without. You must recover from within yourself; strength comes from you working through those demons alone. And that requires work; the work of facing your fears and your disillusionment, and your anger, and your profound sadness. You need someone there for you to help you get it all out, to listen to you while you start to heal yourself. Many widowed people find such help in a support group.

There will surely be well-meaning friends who will irritate you by praising your strength. At the very time when you don't WANT to be strong, you wish someone would come along and take your hand and guide you through this misery (let alone someone to cook your meals, clean your house, pick out your clothes in the morning, make all your decisions, and make it all go away!). They'll assert, "You'll be fine, you're strong." You'll want to scream every time you hear it. I personally don't believe in this concept of "strength." I simply think we do what we must do to survive. Humans have the capacity for great adaptation. If this springs from an inner strength, then perhaps it is courage that asserts itself during these times and enables us to survive. But again, we do what we must. Feel what you feel; it is simply appropriate.

Expect the entire first year to be a trial. Each time the calendar shows a special holiday or other significant date you once shared, you'll feel a renewal of your worst fears and anguish. The days and weeks before the first anniversary of your spouse's death may be especially horrible. You may think you've undone all the progress you may have experienced up until then. Be aware that this process of recovery follows no straight path, but meanders backwards often before it loops back around and ahead. DON'T PUT A TIMETABLE ON YOUR RECOVERY. You'll never "get over it," but you do get through it, in time - your own time.

I realize that most women whose husbands die are older than I was at the time of my loss. There would be generational differences between us that shape our responses. I was used to sharing financial responsibilities, for instance. This made it easier for me to handle some practical matters that an older woman might find difficult. I had a great deal of personal independence and equality within my marriage. I am, after all, a product of the "liberating sixties." Given this, it was terribly frightening to me to discover just how "dependent" I had been on my husband after all. Until he died I never fully grasped how much our lives intersected, how much a part of my very soul he had become. Over nine years of marriage and two of courtship, we had indeed forged our identities; two separate parts of one whole being. His body that you come to know like your own; his thoughts that you anticipate before they're spoken; his dreams that you build toward together; his fears that you soothe; his joys that you delight in; his children that bind you through eternity. These and so much more, measure the vastness of the emptiness you now endure.

I'll never forget Michael. I'll always miss him. But now I can feel the joys and satisfaction of life with a new-found gratitude. Michael is a part of me, like my childhood, my school experiences, my children. My life with him has defined me, has become the substance of what I am. I cannot change or erase these things; I wouldn't want to. Whatever I do and think is an outgrowth of what I've been through and what I've learned.

Somehow, the ache dulls over in time. Years later, you might find yourself crying for no immediate reason. But you cry less and less. You do become capable of laughter again, of enjoying life. I remember closing all of the shades in my home, of isolating myself from people. I felt I had permanently lost my capacity for joy, my ability to appreciate the beauties of nature. The world held no comforts, no pleasures for me. Today, after the most difficult period of my life, I take supreme satisfaction in the view out my window, and the view within. Somehow, day by day I've been strengthened. I've found peace of mind. Life is more precious to me than ever before.

WHAT HAPPENS NOW?...AFTER YOUR SPOUSE DIES
by Kathleen Jacques

Facing the death of any loved one is devastating, but the death of one's spouse may force you to adjust to more changes than any other singular event you'll ever experience. All at once you may have lost your life's partner, lover, father or mother of your children, bread-winner, confidant, your best friend. So much of your time, of your own history has been centered around this one person. Where do you go from here? How do you ever adjust to the magnitude of this loss?

Much has been written elsewhere about the phases of grief and mechanisms for coping. Rather than duplicate that material, I offer some reflections and suggestions aimed at the special circumstances of the widowed.

FEAR Aside from sadness, the most overwhelming emotion I initially felt was fear. I didn't want to think, I didn't want to contemplate the consequences of what had happened. Time stood still for the first few days, moments felt like hours, I could not look ahead.

In those first few hours, few days, it is important to accept any assistance offered. Your family and friends need to express their love and concern, you need to conserve your emotional and physical resources. You need a 'safe harbor.' You become less afraid when you see the evidence of love and caring from those who gather around you in those early days; you are not alone.

PAINFUL REMARKS People will say some pretty amazing things; "Your husband/wife is in a better place." "It was God's will." "Well at least you had thirty years together." "You're young, you'll marry again." "God must have needed him/her in heaven." "At least you have the children." "Time will heal." Unless you've lost someone you loved, it's hard to grasp just how hollow these statements can seem. You did not want your spouse to die. You want him/her back. You hurt like hell. Period.

Believe it or not, the day may come when you'll laugh at some of those thoughtless remarks. Some of them can be pretty absurd. But please bear in mind that these remarks were indeed well-intended. People really struggle with what to say to the bereaved; they simply don't know what to say. Feel sorry for them because someday they may be quite unprepared for a loss of their own, and they will learn a painful lesson from their own mistakes.

DECISIONS There are so many details to attend to after the death of a spouse. Often the widowed plunge into these tasks, seeking refuge in time-consuming responsibilities. We ignore fatigue, nervousness, anger, moodiness, physical ailments. Perhaps we think the world expects us to be stoic, valiant, examples of courage. Rubbish! Give yourself a break. Take time to grieve. There will be time enough later for finishing household projects, learning to cook, spring cleaning, enrolling in school, for making all those monumental decisions (should I move, sell the house, hire a housekeeper, invest the life insurance proceeds, seek vocational counseling, get a job?). Let your family, close friends, clergyman or lawyer help with some of the more immediate tasks (the funeral and burial, child care, insurance matters, social security, the settling of accounts, bills), leaving you energy for the harder task of grief work that lies ahead.

Save major decisions for a later time when your vision is less clouded by anxiety and panic. Chances are you have far more options than you originally perceived. The world is full of stories of people who regret decisions they made in haste. Give yourself time.

REACTIONS For some reason I cannot fathom, society treats the widowed like victims. Something was done TO us. People pity you. This can be a very unwelcome response. The widowed are treated differently from other bereaved people, as if someone had abandoned you; you are now seen differently. (The survivors of those who have died by suicide might recognize this response as well.) Bereaved people who have lost a child, parent, another relative or friend are seen as they were before, only now carrying a heavy burden of sorrow. But the widowed are seen as having altered their identity. No one wants to be an object of pity, nor do they want to be put on a pedestal. It is not heroic to be in mourning.

If someone close to you begins to hinder recovery by treating you in any of the ways described above, you may find it necessary to clear the air. If, for instance, the room becomes hushed when you enter, you might want to initiate conversation yourself. You may have to "educate" the people close to you on what is appropriate behavior towards you.

FIND A LISTENER If it is difficult for you to tell others what your needs are during this period, you face disillusion and a feeling of rejection. The widowed often lament, "No one understands how I feel." When people start to treat you with kid gloves (or worse, avoid you altogether), you suffer a great loss of self-esteem. Instead of withdrawing, it is better for the widowed to seek out at least one other person to listen to what you may really be feeling behind the public facade of the "stiff upper lip." If you've been conditioned all your life to keep your troubles to yourself you may be headed for a backlash of pain when the suppressed emotions of grief emerge later, as they surely will.

WHERE ARE MY FRIENDS? How many times have you innocently said to a friend, "Let's get together for lunch/dinner/a movie/anything . . .," only to fail to follow through? Well then, why do we expect it to be any different now when these statements are made soon after the death of a spouse? Good intentions abound. Action on those intentions is another matter altogether. Sometimes you feel that you've lost your friends as well as your spouse. The hard reality is that you will indeed have lost some friends, too. Some people will not be able to deal with you; they cannot find the right things to say. They may see in your situation a foretelling of their own future; they avoid you so your "bad luck" will not rub off on them. Perhaps these were not strong friendships to begin with. Regardless, you must now concentrate on those relationships that remain supportive. Forgive people their weaknesses. Their expressions of concern, although not acted upon, were genuine.

LONELINESS Like Noah's Ark we see life's inhabitants as coming strictly in pairs. The checks still carry both names. "Couples Night" discounts, dinner parties for six / eight / twelve . . . always an even number. The years may seem to stretch out endlessly; all those events, all those occasions unattended, unescorted, alone. You feel like the proverbial square peg in a round hole. It takes a great deal of courage for a widow/widower to socialize again after the death of their spouse. That first family gathering or the company picnic can send you home in an agony of tears and loneliness.

The only effective way I've found to cope with and overcome this loneliness and alienation is to get out there and accept those invitations. Now of course, not all invitations, and not until you're ready. When you do socialize for the first time, expect it to be rough. Don't be afraid to leave early. If you start to cry, it's OK, it won't be unexpected, people will understand. The important thing to realize is that it will get easier. In time you will gravitate towards people who make you feel at ease, they will give you strength and help return laughter and pleasure to your life. Baby steps; start with social baby steps (tennis with a close friend, dinner with a co-worker . . .) and eventually you'll be able to handle larger groups, new situations.

ME, A THREAT? Have you ever heard the one about the "Gay Divorcee" or the "Merry Widow?" HA! Pure invention. Nevertheless there will be women who will treat you as a threat near their husbands. Of course you don't want their husbands, even though you may temporarily envy their intact families. If anything, you hope they appreciate the husbands they have because you have learned how fragile life is. So go ahead and feel annoyance at these insensitive sorts. Speak up if you are so inclined but better yet, turn to an understanding friend (or bring it up at your support group meeting, you're bound to generate laughter: "Why would I ever want THAT man?!") to vent your frustration. Consider that some of these women might be insecure in their marriages. This is their problem; don't make it yours by taking their actions to heart. Consider the source.

EXPECTATIONS The death of your spouse leaves you with a cornucopia of unfulfilled needs; emotional, physical, practical, intellectual and social. It is hard to imagine all the slots your spouse once filled until the gaps stand testimony to your loss. Yet our need for intimacy persists, and we may experience disappointment when we turn to others to fill some of these voids. For instance, we may assume that our families or children will automatically be there for us, telepathically sense our moods, our emotional requirements. Since they're already so close to us, shouldn't they be able to sense when we need to talk or need to withdraw? They should be able to "read" us somewhat like our spouse did. Well this just is not so. Probably no one will have that intuitive sense the way your spouse had. Family and close friends will not be able to fill all the roles left by the death of your spouse. Rather than becoming angry at those closest to you for failing to anticipate and meet your unspoken needs, remember that you're asking the impossible. We all have limitations; people give according to their capacities. Be thankful for what is offered, and then find ways to meet some of those more pressing needs. Counseling may be helpful; sometimes an impartial ear frees you to open up in ways that you can't with your family.

SUPPORT GROUPS One of the best things you might ever do for yourself is to summon your courage and attend a support group for the widowed. You'll discover a reservoir of sympathy, understanding, friendship and information from people who have "walked in your shoes." They "speak the language." You won't be pressured to say a thing if you choose not to. You'll find comfort in discovering that you're not going crazy, other people out there have survived this roller-coaster ride of grief. They have struggled with the phases of grief like you and have endured. When you see that you are not alone, you will feel less alone. You will discover HOPE. Many widowed who have participated in these support groups make treasured friendships sealed by a special bond of understanding.

I realize that most of this article has been directed at women. There is no reason to presume that men don't feel the same sensations or experience the same turmoil. I am limited, however, by my own perspective as a female, and I am sorry if I have neglected any special concerns of the widower.

Kathleen Jacques is a volunteer at Hope For Bereaved and is a free-lance writer.

Of Special Interest:

SURVIVAL HANDBOOK FOR WIDOWS (and for relatives and friends who want to understand) - Ruth Jean Loewinsohn, AARP 1984. Mrs. Loewinsohn writes with a rare sensitivity, in a clear, direct manner. This book is especially helpful. She offers detailed, practical advice on ways to start living in the present and to plan for the future, taking into account the strain and new lifestyle you are experiencing.

ABOUT WIDOWHOOD - A Scriptographic Booklet- Channing Bete Co., Inc. 1980. Highly recommended booklet. Only 14 pages but packed full of ideas. Helpful in understanding feelings.

FOR CRYING OUT LOUD - Jean Gannon Jones, Jones Books.

The following excerpts are taken from the book FOR CRYING OUT LOUD (How to Work Through Grief to Happiness) by Jean Gannon Jones. Although the book was written specifically to help the widowed, any grieving person could be helped by its practical, understanding approach to grief and depression and by the author's strong belief that happiness is possible. The book is strongly recommended.

Cry when you want to; laugh when you can.

When confronted with the death of a loved one we become deeply depressed and are likely to believe that we can never be happy again. Tragic circumstances, however, need not keep any of us from enjoying at least some of the good things in life after we have worked through our grief.

"I thank God I can enjoy people and life again, and that I came through my hell intact- I feel like me again but I'll never forget what It was like when I wasn't me at all - when I was a stranger to my self, standing on the sidelines watching other people live."

"I came through my grief a happier person than I had ever been before because I learned that happiness seldom just happens; we have some control over it. I discovered numerous techniques of behavior and thinking that work. It is ironic, and significant to me, that the biggest tragedy of my life forced me to learn how to be happy when I felt I had the least reason in my life for being that way."

HELPFUL QUOTES

"Instead of taking refuge in panic one learns to be willing to face, tolerate and endure discomfort."

"To live in the hearts we leave behind is not to die."

"Death is a new beginning to a life unending."

"Memories are yesterday's gifts to the heart."

ON DEALING WITH LONELINESS
by Kathleen Jacques

Loneliness, like all emotions, may mean one thing to someone, and quite a different thing to someone else. It is felt in a matter of degrees; some of us may feel it acutely and others may experience it only fleetingly. Keeping this in mind, it is important to note that there is no right or wrong way to handle loneliness. We must let these feelings run their natural course, a course which is as variable as our differing personalities and backgrounds.

It is not merely the physical absence of your spouse that makes you lonely. Many apparently happily married people speak of periods of loneliness within marriage. People who are isolated from their families or people who have few friends often feel lonely. But for the widowed it is the permanence of this absence that can make this brand of loneliness so difficult to endure.

Unlike any other relationship, your spouse is your companion, your partner in life. Your children may move away, your friends may also; but your spouse stays put. This is the one person you can count on, plan and share with. Two by two; it seems the world is ordered this way. When you've been "two" and you suddenly become "one," it's as if your very identity changes. "*KathyandMike*" becomes *Kathy . . . Kathy without Mike*. Your entire life changes. People will never treat you quite the same again once you've lost your spouse. Your identity has altered, the world sees you differently.

There is simple loneliness; no one to share a meal with; holiday festivities that seem bleak with no one to buy for, celebrate with. This is a quiet, dull ache, a time for appropriately felt self-pity. Fortunately, this sort of loneliness can be held at bay (not easily, mind you!). This type of loneliness often responds to simple diversion. Keep yourself busy, distract your attention away from the immediate problem. Invite someone to share a meal; read a book, go to a movie. I once knew a very wise, very brave lady who died of cancer after a long struggle. She said that one of the things that helped her cope with the pain was to get totally absorbed in a book. She said that she couldn't feel her pain when her mind was focused elsewhere. Dealing with any pain takes courage, and sometimes just plain good sense.

There is the panic-tinged loneliness when misfortune strikes and we must face a crisis alone. It is just plain scary to be alone when a mishap or tragedy occurs. Facing legal ordeals or financial upheavals (which often accompany the death of a spouse) alone serves as a poignant reminder that your source of strength has been lessened by one half. You can't lean on anyone the way you can on a spouse. In your time of specific, urgent need, you feel that much more alone without your spouse.

If you are a parent, there is the loneliness you'll feel when a milestone passes in your child's life and your spouse is not there to share the occasion. You brought this child into the world together - it feels so wrong that there should not be both parents to witness the joys and sorrows of their development. If your children are young when a spouse dies there is the awful loneliness felt when pivotal decisions must be made alone. 'Am I making the right choices for my child?' If only you had the feedback of your spouse to lend some judgment, some balance. Carrying the burden as a single parent can only intensify feelings of loneliness because of the constant reminder of the enormous responsibilities you must now face alone. If you are in this situation it is vital that you seek outside help. A relative or friend of the opposite sex can help give your children support and serve as a role model. Keep the children's lives as normal as possible; participation in sports, for example, can give children structure and security. This can also serve to lessen your fears of carrying the load completely alone.

Sometimes we feel lonely even in the midst of a crowd. It is common to feel that 'no one understands how I feel.' No matter how sympathetic a listener may be, we may feel isolated and deserted; they just don't understand. But think about that for a moment; everyone feels that way. Everyone feels adrift and alone from time to time. How can we expect anyone to exactly grasp the full depth and scope of our feelings in periods of extreme anguish? Grief and sadness and loneliness are a part of life. Everyone will have to experience some degree of these emotions sooner or later. Remember this and have patience with the rest of humanity, and know that sympathy is just as appropriate a response as `understanding.' You can't walk in anyone else's shoes, not really. And no one can walk in yours. Be grateful for heartfelt sympathy and understand that your experience of grief and loneliness makes you better able to understand the problem of others.

When your spouse dies you may feel you've lost your future. Hopes, plans and dreams may offer little pleasure. You were building a life together. Without your spouse there seems little point to all that hard work. Yet after the worst of the pain and shock eases, you may find that fulfilling plans made with your spouse is a way of keeping him closer. To see that addition built on the house, or that vegetable garden planted, or that trip taken, can be a continuation of your life together. Your spouse lives on in the achievements you make based upon those shared dreams. Know the delight he or she would have felt in those promises fulfilled. Life is a continuum. We carry on with what has come before. What you accomplish alone later will always be a reflection of the dreams you had together.

Perhaps the hardest form of loneliness comes in those quiet moments when you think of something to say to your spouse and you are gripped with the reality that you can never share another conversation with them. Never hear their opinion, their reaction, their observation, their advice. It is the permanence of the situation that hits so hard in these moments. This loneliness is so filled with sadness for that which we cannot change or understand. Since we cannot change what life has dealt, it helps to recall the Serenity Prayer: God grant me the serenity to accept the things I cannot change, courage to change the things I can and wisdom to know the difference.

GOD GAVE US MEMORIES
THAT WE MIGHT HAVE
ROSES IN DECEMBER

. . . Barrie

AH, BUT YOU'RE YOUNG . . . YOU'LL MARRY AGAIN!
by Kathleen Jacques

Easy for you to say! Every time I heard those words, I wanted to scream. Many more times this was the implied message, even though the actual words were never spoken. But I could always tell that that was what they were thinking. After all, I was just twenty-eight when my husband was struck and killed by a drunk driver. I was young, my children "needed a father." Surely I would marry again fairly soon ...

Even though I knew that people only expressed this idea out of heartfelt good will, I resented the whole thing: I resented the idea, I resented them for having it. How could anyone ever replace Mike?! What was I supposed to do - find a new man and live happily ever after, as if this tragedy had never touched my life? Replace and forget, like getting over a teenage crush? "You'll marry again." It trivialized everything our marriage meant, everything I'd gone through. My suffering was somehow deemed less serious because of my age. I would be fine, I would marry again, so it was okay to accord me only a half-measure of sympathy.

Its difficult enough to be mourning the loss of your spouse without having the burden of dealing with society's expectation that you begin anew with a second marriage. I had plenty to do each day and fitful night without carrying around this nonsense. It seems so silly now, to have even let this bother me. But it did. Somehow I felt unworthy, that I was letting people down by not remarrying. What was wrong with me that I couldn't find some-one new? So I not only felt the loss of my husband, but a general rejection as well because I had not conformed to the seemingly universal notion that "you're young, you'll remarry."

Despite my first-hand knowledge of being on the receiving end of this attitude, I must admit that I sometimes instinctively respond, "she's/he's young, maybe he'll/she'll marry again." I've thought about why I still have this knee-jerk reaction when I really ought to know better. The best explanation I can offer is that the death of a young spouse seems especially out of balance with the natural order of things. We expect widows and widow-ers to be elderly. We have no rational response to the young widow or widower. Perhaps in our desire to deal with the incomprehensible reality of the early death, we simply as-sume a remarriage will restore order to these lives gone awry. A remarriage puts things back the way they should be. You are once again safe as part of a couple. People who care about you see your youth as giving you access to a second chance. They want to see your happiness and security restored, and the prospect of your remarriage somehow seems to mitigate your pain, and consequently theirs.

After the worst of your grief work is over, the hardest task to face is learning to be "single" all over again. I still hesitate when someone asks me if I'm married or single. It just doesn't feel right to say "single," because it implies one was never married. I don't really feel unmarried, and I always worry that people will assume that I'm divorced. Now that both-ers me. So you can see there are all sorts of added considerations for the young widow/widower; societal expectations that put added burdens atop our grief. I liked being married, I'd prefer being married - to Mike. Instead, I must play the hand I've been dealt. The most important thing now is to stabilize after my husband's death, raise my children, and create the best life I can for myself. In the meantime, no one should assume that remarriage is inevitable, or even preferable. That is a bridge to be crossed if and when one comes to it.

HELPFUL INFORMATION FOR THE NEWLY WIDOWED

Consult your lawyer if you have one. He or she can attend to many of the following details if you so choose. If possible, take someone with you who is not entitled to a portion of the estate. It is not that you cannot trust your family, but a third party not as emotionally involved may be able to take notes and help you remember later all you have to do. A lot of information is thrown at you all at once and you may have trouble remembering it later.

YOU WILL NEED: Numerous copies of the death certificate, complete with official seal. You will also need copies of your marriage certificate and your spouse's birth certificate, military discharge papers, social security number, W-2 forms for the past year, birth certificates of any minor children. These records are needed to establish claims for Social Security, life insurance or veteran's benefits. Write letters to your spouse's former employer, to any unions or professional organizations with which he or she was connected. Ask them about group life and/or health insurance.

DEATH CLAUSES: Examine loan contracts, mortgages, credit card contracts and insurance policies to see if there is a death clause which pays the balance. Notify the responsible institution immediately.

SOCIAL SECURITY: Check with the Social Security office immediately to find out if you are eligible for payments and how much. Apply for the lump-sum benefit at the same time. If a Social Security check arrives after your spouse dies and it is payable to your spouse only, it *must* be returned. If it is made out to survivor and spouse jointly, take it to the Social Security office and they will stamp it "Payable to Survivor" so you can cash it.

MEDICARE: Widows are eligible for Medicare at age 65 if their spouse would have been entitled to monthly benefits. Application should be made for Medicare about three (3) months before your 65th birthday.

VETERAN'S BENEFITS: Apply for these if eligible. Consult your local Veteran's Administration.

CREDIT CARDS: Change all credit cards which were in your spouse's name to your name. If all cards were in your spouse's name, you may have to establish your own credit standing.

PROPERTY TITLES: If the real property is in joint names, there is nothing you need to do immediately. The property automatically passes to you as surviving tenant by operation of law. It will cost money to change the name on the title (search bringdown, new deed, recording fees, attorney's fees, etc.) and your money can be better spent in other areas. There is also a chance your bank will want to rewrite the mortgage in your name, or even call the mortgage due. You can still sell the property, and your attorney can obtain a release of the property for a relatively low fee when it is necessary.

INSURANCE: Policies on properties and on autos should be changed to the survivor's name. Notify all companies carrying policies on the deceased of the death of your spouse and inquire what forms need to be filed. Check records carefully so that claims are sent to all insurance companies. Change the beneficiary on policies covering you if your spouse is named beneficiary.

MEDICAL INSURANCE: If medical coverage was formerly obtained through your spouse's employment, inquire immediately to determine if you are still covered and for how long. If no longer covered, inquire about options open to you now from various companies.

BANKS: If the amount in a joint account is over a certain amount you will need a waiver to get the money. If less, then you may have access, but the name should be changed immediately to the survivor's only. As soon as possible, notify banks to change all joint accounts to the survivor's name only. A safe-deposit box will be sealed at the time of death if it is in your spouse's name or if both names were signed for accessibility. You can request access to the box to get insurance policies, etc., but this must be applied for and done in the presence of an Internal Revenue representative. If an account is in your spouse's name only, no one can have access to it until an administrator is appointed.

Adapted with permission from Widowed Persons Services Support Group, Auburn, N.Y.

ITEMS THAT NEED NOT BE CONSIDERED IMMEDIATELY, BUT ARE IMPORTANT:

MOTOR VEHICLE: (This does not have to be done until the current registration expires.) One vehicle automatically becomes the survivor's property, but when the registration expires you will have to bring a copy of the death certificate, vehicle title certificate, and new insurance form in your name (obtainable from your insurance agent) to the motor vehicle department. They will supply the necessary forms to fill out. Any additional vehicle(s) must go through the estate.

STOCKS, BONDS AND INVESTMENTS: Notify your broker or banker or whoever handles your business. Leave decisions about investments for a later, less harried time. Call companies for forms.

FINANCIAL RECORDS: You are personally responsible for your resources and must be prepared to account for them. Keep a record of every bill you pay and of all funds you receive. If you will need extra time paying current bills, inform your creditors.

CHILDREN: If you have minor children or dependents, you must have yourself or some bondable party appointed as custodian of their property. For instance, have yourself named as custodian on stocks or bank accounts.

SALE OF PROPERTY: Do not be hasty about this! Review all options carefully. Avoid persons who want to make you rich.

FINANCIAL REVIEW: When things settle down you should review your financial standing: Your net worth - the difference between what you own and what you owe; your budget - monthly income and expenditures; your future obligations.

YOUR WILL: If you own property or funds you should make a will. Keep a copy for your own records. Leave the original copy with your lawyer or in your safe-deposit box.

AUTO MAINTENANCE: If your spouse took this responsibility you should now consult a reliable service garage regarding things that need checking regularly; tires, gas, oil, battery, fluids, tune-ups, etc.

STATE AND FEDERAL INCOME TAXES: Review the income tax status of your spouse and the filing of next due returns. Visit the taxpayer service department of your state and federal governments for assistance if you do not use a private tax preparation service.

INHERITANCE TAXES: If there is any property involved it is advisable to file with the state within six (6) months, even though it is unlikely that an estate tax would have to be paid. At the present time only estates over $650,000 would have to pay New York State taxes. The limit allowed a spouse under the federal estate laws keep changing, so it might be wise to seek legal advice about the necessity to file. The limit for total assets at present is $300,000. For lesser amounts no federal estate tax need be paid.

WHEN SOMEONE A CHILD
LOVES HAS DIED

CHILDREN GRIEVE, TOO
by Kathleen Jacques

What happens to children when someone they love dies? They may inadvertently be shut out of sight of adult displays of mourning. They may be excluded from funeral services and sheltered from the details surrounding the death. Adults may feel it best to shield children from these things in an effort to ease their pain and confusion. However, it is just possible that we are denying our children the chance to work through their own grief. Depending upon their age and level of comprehension, children should be encouraged to discuss the death and participate with the rest of the family in funeral services.

My children were two and four years old when their father died. Just as I had no preparation for this journey of grief, neither had they. Through trial and error we sustained each other. I offer some things we have learned along the way:

1. When words fail, a hug is perfect.

2. Don't be afraid to cry in front of children. They must know that it is okay to cry. After all, we cry for those whom we loved very much; our tears are a tribute to the depth of that love. If we did not love we would not feel the need to cry. It may help to cry together; hold each other, but don't pressure the child to express his feelings.

3. Children think that they are immortal. "It can't happen to me." A child's first experience with the death of a loved one shatters this illusion. A child may become terrified that he or she will lose someone else they love or rely on. Let the child confide his fears. They are not far-fetched to the child. Reassure him that he is safe and that you are still here and will be for a long time.

4. Do not dismiss a child's feelings of guilt over the death. Of course the child is not to blame, but his feelings can be very strong. He may feel he was "bad" or "naughty" and this caused such a bad thing to happen. My son expressed this, to my horror. I held him in my arms and told him that Daddy's death had nothing to do with his behavior. Daddy loved him just the way he was and I loved him just the way he was. It is excruciatingly difficult to see your child struggling with such feelings, but you must allow them to express these thoughts or they will never be able to resolve theirguilt.

   Often children will think or say that they wish that someone was dead. If that person does die, the child may think that it is their fault because they wished for it.

5. A child may express anger over the death. They may throw things, ignore household rules, or becomedisrespectful. It is natural for children to respond this way. Children need to talk over any feelings of anger they may have, to be assured that these feelings will pass, that they are not bad because they feel anger towards other survivors or their loved one who has left them by dying.

6. Do not expect that your moods will mirror your child's. There will be moments when you are feeling relatively "normal," and out of the blue your child may begin to cry and lament. It becomes necessary at the expense of your own transitory sense of peace to delve into your child's expression of sorrow. Certainly this affects you, but it is far worse to suppress a child's spontaneous expression of grief.

Conversely, it may be difficult when you are having an especially hard day to see your child so (seemingly) indifferent to your mood. You may want to talk about the death of your loved one, but your child may be disinterested. The implied message, "Not now, Mom," can feel like the ultimate cold shoulder. Do not reproach the child. Allow him his moment of peace; you will have promoted his recovery.

7. Answer only those questions that the child actually asks. Volunteering unsolicited information about the death may only serve to overwhelm the child. Generally a child will let you know how much he can deal with at a given time.

8. Sometimes a child will become upset over an unrelated subject, but the source of the reaction is really unresolved feelings of grief. He or she may cry over a television program, or become unduly frustrated over a difficult task. Be observant; this may be a good time for you to ask your child if he would like to talk about his feelings. Give the child an opportunity to explore his feelings by acknowledging the real source of his stress; "Things really seem to be bothering you. I can understand. I sure do get mad at things myself."

9. Talk often about the person who has died, remembering happy times, recalling funny incidents. Laughter will come, and it is remarkably "medicinal."

Drawing by Zachary Jacques, age 10

Special mention must be given to two excellent books for children:
WHEN MY DAD DIED by Janice M. Hammond, Ph.D. 1981, and
WHEN MY MOMMY DIED by Janice M. Hammond, Ph. D. 1980 Cranbrook Publishing Co.
I HEARD YOUR MOMMY DIED by Mark Scrivani, 1994 Centering Corporation

In these books, subtitled "A Child's View of Death," children can see that what they are feeling is normal. Other kids have felt the same things. Read the book with your child. It can be the beginning of conversations that you may otherwise find too difficult to initiate.

HELPING YOUR CHILD THROUGH GRIEF
by Mark Scrivani

Grief is an extremely difficult process. We must focus on ourselves during this period and rightly so. Many times, however, we overlook the fact that grief comes to those of all ages. Therefore, children are often ignored during mourning, with the rationale that "they wouldn't understand." The grieving process in children is highly complex, since so much depends upon each child's stage of development. For instance, a 3-year-olds understanding of death and the mourning process will be quite different from that of a 10-year-old. Both of them would be very different from a 16-year-old. Yet, there are many fundamental similarities between a child's grief and the adult mourning process. It is important to understand that the grief work provides vast potentials of growth for all ages. If children do not work on their grief, behavioral and emotional problems may arise now or later. Following is a list of suggestions for helping your child through grief:

1. As soon as possible after the death, set time aside to talk with your child. Gently explain what is happening, why you are crying, etc.
2. Use the deceased person's name when referring to him or her.
3. Use basic words like "die" and "dead" to convey the message.
4. Avoid the phrases that soften the blow such as "sleeping," "went on a vacation," "God took them," "passed away," etc. These will confuse and scare a child.
5. Let your child ask questions. Answer truthfully! Be honest, simple and direct. If you don't understand something, let your child know that, too.
6. Be sensitive to the age and level of understanding of your child. Don't offer information beyond the child's comprehension, as it will only confuse matters.
7. Read or have your child read children's books relating to death.
8. Play with the child (e.g. dolls, drawing, imagining) in ways that will allow the child to express his/her feelings.
9. Watch for T.V. programs that might help your child's understanding.
10. Read books yourself on helping a child through grief. There are many excellent ones.
11. Talk about God with your child. Pray with your child.
12. Let your child participate if he/she wants to; e.g. going to the funeral, visiting the cemetery. However, it is very important that you don't pressure your child into doing any of these things or into expressing feelings.
13. Accept help from others to watch your children and talk with them — but remember, you are the most important person to your child!
14. You are a role model for your child—if you hide your grief, they will learn to hide it, too. Instead share your feelings with your child. Your example will set the tone for your child to do the same.
15. We should (as much as possible) have an understanding of our own grieving process, since these things are communicated to the child.
16. Help your child to vent and acknowledge his or her emotions.
17. Watch for tell-tale signs of maladjustments; e.g. eating and/or sleeping disturbances over a long period of time.
18. Seek pastoral or family counseling if the grief is unresolved.
19. Communicate to the child your appreciation of having had the deceased person in your life.
20. Discuss and have the child recognize changes in routine due to the death.
21. Plan something (e.g. a vacation) to which you and your child can look forward.
22. This is perhaps the most important of all—please do not be disappointed or angry if your child does not understand or appreciate death! They are going through a learning experience and discovery—give them time!

A BROTHER AND SISTER REMEMBER
by Tom and Margie Schoeneck

At the time of his sister's death Tom was 16. Four years later he wrote the following in response to an English assignment. The class was instructed to write about the best or worst experience in their life. I believe it shows vividly the depth of feeling that young people experience at the death of a loved one.

"The experience I am about to write was without a doubt the worst experience I had ever dealt with in my life. I would not wish this experience on my worst enemy or even the likes of a `Yotala Komanie. I am speaking of the death of my oldest sister, Mary. I am not looking for pity because it's over with and I have no problem talking about Mary or her death.

I was sound asleep, warm and comfortable, probably dreaming about a very pleasant experience. All of a sudden my pleasant dream was interrupted by a real-life nightmare. My mother asked me to come out to the living room. At that time I had no idea what was going on, although I did know there was something drastically wrong when I heard the earpiercing, heart-stopping cries of agony from my younger sister. My mother then looked me squarely in the eyes and said, 'At one o'clock this morning, your sister was killed in a car accident.' When hearing this and seeing the looks of disbelief on the other members of my family, I knew that this wasn't a sick joke. I felt a growing weakness in the back of my knees, accompanied by a sharp pain in my chest. For the first five to ten minutes I didn't say or do anything. My memory was carving a clear picture of the scene in my mind. Then I had a deluge of mixed emotions racing through my head.

At the time my family and I were living at the lake. I got a distinct surge of energy. I wanted to scream obscenities to the world. Then I wanted to swim the length of the lake.

I had a combination of thoughts and energies that frustrated the hell out of me. There was no way to funnel them into an act or words. I could go on forever, but I think I've made my point. The overpowering feelings of loss and frustration made this, without a doubt, the worst experience of my life."

His younger sister was thirteen at the time of their 21-year-old sister's death. Shortly after the death Margie wrote the following poem to the melody of a favorite song:

"Mary, our sweet Mary
You know the tears belong to you
Did you think your death could make us feel this way?
Mary, our sweet Mary
Did you know what you meant to us?
Did you know our love will never, never stop?
Mary, our sweet Mary
Those tears belong to you
And we'll never forget you all our lives."

WHEN A SIBLING DIES
Reflections On How My Parents Helped Or Didn't Help Me...

- Thanks for immediately telling me about what happened and the details of how, as soon as you knew.
- I needed to cry with you, and to cry alone. We all need to cry together, especially in the beginning of our grief.
- I needed your hugs to help me.
- Physical proof was what made me realize that he was dead. An open coffin sounds grotesque and morbid to others but was very important to me.
- When you see people who resemble him, tell me so I don't think I'm a little crazy. The first year this happened often.
- Let me share my nightmares with you until they go away.
- You helped me by asking me to help you.
- You helped me when you told me you were having trouble with the realization of his death.
- Talking about memories and what it was like when...is OK, but I'm here and I'm now and I need you to think about me. It's selfish, but necessary for me to feel needed, wanted, loved and near you.
- Understand that when I turn to my friends it's because I need to identify with them. I do talk to them about his death, more times than I talk to you. They're closer to my age and they help me to go on with my life.
- I loved my brother and always will. Telling me that he died young, that I'll never remember him growing old or going through some other hardships of adult life makes me feel better about his death. I'll never see him old or hurting.
- Thank God he didn't have to bear watching one of us die.
- When we talk, remember he was my brother and we had our sibling rivalries and fights. He wasn't perfect, but neither am I. You helped me to not feel guilty about the fights we did have and told me he'd forgive me and I should forgive him, especially if I get mad, because he died and left us.

22 years old

****

After my sister died I hated God. I threw things around my room and I cried an awful lot. My mother told me later that was my way of dealing with it and that was O.K. and I was O.K. too! Listed below are some helpful hints for parents:

- Let your children talk - express their feelings.
- Surround them with people - but familiar and comforting people.
- Don't put the deceased child up on a pedestal while putting down your other children. Talk of your child but talk of good and bad memories - be realistic and don't think you have to make your child out to be a saint - stay in perspective.
- Hug your kids - they're going to be feeling guilty about ugly words or arguments they've had with their deceased sibling.
- Give them choices about attending the calling hours. Your kids will let you know when it's too much.
- Never tell your kids to be strong for somebody else - I don't know anyone who can be strong at a time when their world is crashing down around them. Let your kids cry, scream, throw tantrums - this is the time for it.
- Be there for your kids - they'll need you at moments that you sometimes wouldn't expect. It might hurt you to talk about it but don't cut them off because that could lead to them holding it in.

13 years old

Talking helped me to realize my feelings more. It helped me to get my feelings out into the open. At first it was hard to talk but as I grew older it helped to talk. It brought us closer as a family. We realize each other's feelings and try to understand each other better now. I realize the importance of being nice. We don't know what might happen in the next hour or day.

9 years old

IN THEIR OWN WORDS

When someone we love has died we have our hands full of grief. Often we hurt so much that we can not think clearly. We may not realize that our children are grieving too. The following poems were written by children and show very clearly the depth of their sorrow. (*Permission granted to HOPE FOR BEREAVED to reprint the poems.*)

CHILDREN NEED US TO . . . hug them . . .

spend time with them . . . read to them . . .

listen to them . . . play with them . . .

build memories with them . . .

The first set of poems was written by Bethann Liberty, age 11, after the death of her mother.

THE ONE I LOVE

I wish things could be different,
Everything's going insane.
I wish things could be different,
I wish things could be the same
    as before.

But, that will not happen.
That was then and this is now.
I don't know how it all happened.
I can not see the one I love.
She's gone, but I hold her in
    my heart forever and always.

I remember her smile,
The way she smelled.
Nothing can bring her back now,
But I hold her in my heart,
I hold her in my heart.   Summer 1984

DUSK TO DAWN

When someone you love
Has left you and is gone,
You watch the sky from
Dusk until dawn.

You go and watch the doe
Care for her fawn,
Like your mother once cared for you.

She is now gone, and left you
Like a doe must leave her fawn.
You now watch the sky
From dusk until dawn.   Fall 1984

Imagination is the greatest thing for your sadness or loneliness.   Winter 1984

The second set of poems was written by Kirsten Van Meenan, age 12, after her friend Maribel died by suicide. Maribel grieved for her father who was killed two years before. Unresolved grief is one of the reasons that people die by suicide.

LOSS OF A FATHER

With a single shot, he was down;
A policeman's duty.
But now a husband and father is lost.
No one can bring him back;
Nor his eldest daughter who loved him so,
And grieved for two years after his death.

She grieved until she no longer could withstand the pain.
Then she changed her life with a 38.
Now a daughter and friend is lost.
No one can bring her back;
Nor the love and joy she brought into our lives.

DEATH OF A FRIEND

Death is so sudden.
How could this happen?
How could this happen to me?

Why is she the one?
Who chooses this fate?
Why my friend?

Is she happy now?
Is there peace there?
Does she miss me? I miss her!

But what about my life?
What will happen to me?
What will I do without her?

We were the best of friends,
But now she is gone.
My friend has died, she is gone.

SUICIDE VICTIM

She was gentle and kind; always smiling.
Her eyes always dancing to the beat of her own song.
She had much hope; held such promise.
But on a single night...all was changed.
Who gives someone the right
to take her own life,
And leave all the others behind?
If she was unhappy with her life,
Why not tell someone,
In voice, instead of blood?
Now we all grieve,
And beg for her forgiveness;
For not listening, not realizing.
Despite our pain,
We hope she is happy.
Good-bye. We loved you so.

The following are selections of poems and letters written by children in the "Hope for Youth" support group led by Mark Scrivani. The authors' ages range from 8-16 years, and the excerpts were written to the loved ones who died.

Dear Mom,

So how's it like up in heaven? Is it like they said it is? I hope so. I hope it wasn't as painful for you as it was for me for you to die. Well, I hope to see you up there someday.

Love,

Dear (Brother),

I really miss you. Everything has been different since you've been gone. Everyone thinks about you. Everyone thinks about us and they always are wondering how we are.

I'm really sorry if I was mean to you. I love you.

Love,

Dear Dad,

Thanks for a nice life. I miss you so much that it hurts. I love you.

Dear Mom,

I wish I could tell you that I really loved you, and that I miss (you) so very much. I wish I could tell how much fun I had talking to you and laughing with you. How much I enjoyed your company, your wonderful smile and laugh, how comfortable I felt when you were around. How good it felt to have a person such as yourself and how lucky I was.

Love,

DAD

My Dad was taken away from me,
and I was not prepared.
My Dad had meant the world to me
and now he wasn't there.

My Life was turned upside down,
and all I wanted to do was hide,
The pain seemed so severe,
and it never did subside.

The days went on without my Dad,
and life just did not seem fair,
Tears were always running,
and my heart was always bare.

But even though my Dad is gone
My memories of him still live on.
He'll always be a part of me
which some people may not see,
For he is deep within my heart
where he and I will never part.

Dad,

I wish you were here! I miss you so much and I know that I'm never gonna be the same again. You loved life so much and that's why I wish I died instead of you. It's so hard for me to accept because the doctors still haven't found the cause of your death. I just want you to know that I love you and I appreciate all the things you've done for me. I love you always.

Dear Dad,

Hi, How are you? I really miss you. But I know someday I will be able to see you again. It could be today or 90 years from now. But a few things I've always wanted to tell you are how much I loved you and how such a neat guy you were. We had a lot of fun at times. You gave a lot of people a new look towards life. You were really neat and I think you were the greatest father anyone could have. I love you.

Dear Dad,

I hope you're in a better place now but I wish you were back here. We all miss you. There is so much I wish I had said and done. I wish I had said "I love you" more often. I wish we hadn't fought over such little things and then never really said "I'm sorry." When I'm thinking about the future and I think about the children I might have I feel slightly sad for them because they'll never know what a wonderful man their grandfather was.

Love,

Dear Dad,

I've been thinking about you today. Today it has been two years since you were here, with us. I miss you a lot. And so do many other people. This Easter is going to be tough. But not as tough as it was last year. I miss you, but I learned that I can't just stay home and do nothing. I have to get on with my life. I've been wondering why you had to go but I know there isn't a reason. But maybe someday, you can tell me.

I love you a lot. And I miss you, too.

Love,

The following excerpt from a poem shows that crying helps and that eventually it is possible to accept the death. Remember, there is no specific timetable for grief. It is different for everyone. In time it is possible to enjoy memories and life again.

It's been almost a year since you've died
and somehow I found the strength to survive.

It hasn't been easy,
I cried a lot each day
But now I've learned to accept
why things must be this way.

142

A letter for bereaved youth, similar to the one below, is included in the HOPEline monthly newsletter. These letters have been compiled into two books which are available for purchase - "LOVE MARK: A Journey Through Grief" and "LOVE MARK II: Companions on The Journey Through Grief."

HOPE FOR YOUTH

by Mark Scrivani

Dear Friends,

People often ask me about what to do with grieving people your age. Sometimes people might want to protect us from hurt, or they might think that we don't understand what death means ♡. I always tell these people that just because you aren't older or don't understand all the big words 📖 doesn't mean that you don't grieve. I let them know that lots of times you are happy ☺, but it's O.K. for you to be mad ☹, sad ☹, or even not sure about your feelings sometimes ☹. Everybody has these feelings, and they become a lot stronger when somebody we love dies ♀.

Everybody has a lot of the same kinds of feelings, but it is important to know that we each have a different journey through grief. So, my dear friends, don't let anyone ever tell you how to grieve. Sometimes you will feel one way, then later you may feel differently ☺☺. The way you miss, and then remember, your loved one who died is yours alone. Let your grief help you to learn and grow. When you can do this, you can love and live better♡. I have always noticed that even very young people grow and learn about life after grieving the death of a loved one.

So it is important to talk about your feelings and let big people know that you grieve too. It's O.k. to write or draw pictures to help you to do this. It's good to cry and laugh when you want to. By doing this, you will never forget your loved one who died. When you remember them, they will become a part of you as you grow in your journey through grief. Love, Mark

WHEN A LOVED ONE HAS DIED BY SUICIDE

UNDERSTANDING SUICIDE

For the survivors, suicide is the cruelest of deaths. It is estimated that as many as 60,000 persons die in the United States annually as a result of suicide. If each of these persons has 8 close relatives or friends, that means at least 480,000 people are affected annually. You are not alone.

Thoughts of suicide are not foreign to us; they are a human reaction. Every study affirms that most people think about suicide some time in their lives. It is estimated that between 80% and 90% of us at one time or another think about our own suicide. It may be only a passing thought. Most do not plan the details. Still, suicide may be considered briefly as an alternative to some of the things we face in life. Grief and depression can bring thoughts of suicide. The act of suicide inflicts extraordinary pain on people left behind.

In the book AFTER SUICIDE, author John Hewitt states that suicide throws a triple whammy on everyone. In the first place, a close relative or friend has died. Secondly, there is the pain and shock of a sudden death. On top of all that, one has to deal with the fact of suicide with its additional pain and regret. The pain will last a long time. You cannot escape from it but you can help it run its course. The grief associated with suicide has many unresolved doubts; "What happened?" "What did I do wrong?" "Whose fault was it?" "What could I have done to prevent it?" "What do we do now?"

When suicide has touched your life, your emotions are intensified to unbelievable and unbearable proportions. Many survivors deny the death; and even more, the method. A flood of feelings engulfs the survivors - shame, anger, guilt, love, self-pity, bewilderment, rejection, self-blame. Suicide temporarily destroys your good feelings about yourself, about God, about life in general.

Most survivors say that their grief was complicated by severe feelings of guilt. Guilt presents us with a choice. We can either let it ruin our lives or allow it to diminish to the point where the guilt can be handled.

Survivors struggle daily with the question, "Why?" Suicide is usually caused by many factors that have accumulated over a period of years. There is no single explanation of why people take their lives. There can be physical, social or even economic factors, such as war or unemployment. Some researchers feel it is a biochemical imbalance, a serotonin deficiency, or a chemical imbalance due to the effects of drug or alcohol abuse. Serotonin deficiency and depression, in combination, increase the risk of suicide more than either factor alone does.

Your loved one may have been surrounded many times by what seemed like overwhelming internal struggles. Even though he/she wanted to quit, he/she persevered. Due to a combination of circumstances, it becomes impossible to cope. There doesn't seem to be any way out. Hopelessness and despair are common emotions of suicide. The majority of suicide victims suffer severe depression. Your loved one's sense of judgment was lost or distorted. Just before suicide the person's judgment becomes hazy, confused. He/she can't reason their way out of it. Even though others may see the many things that he does well, the person is likely to exercise extremely poor judgment about how he sees himself. If your loved one has lost sleep and not eaten, it makes things even worse. The last straw occurs. It may have very little to do with the death, but the person can't hold on any longer. Most likely the victims aren't fully aware of why they are choosing suicide; therefore, the question of "why?" is never resolved for the survivors. It is an escape from something, rather than choosing death. Since we don't know the victim's inner struggle, we can't answer "why."

There is much we do not know about suicide, but we do know there is a limit to the load any person can bear. Your loved one was not turning from you or God, but saw no alternative and felt that something had to be done.

Survivors should not feel responsible for the suicide. Suicide is an act completed in solitude and one person is responsible for it - the deceased. No person can make another person complete suicide. No person can single-handedly prevent a suicide, unless that person can live without sleep and spend 24 hours a day restraining the potential suicide victim.

Your life has been seriously wounded by suicide. Nothing can change that fact. You have your own timetable for coming out of your extended grief. When you are ready you can choose to live. It is comforting to know that many survivors recover to lead healthy, energetic lives. As one survivor states, "Ironically, we had no choice when our loved one died, it was out of our control; but we do have a choice in healing ourselves. It's the hardest task we will ever have to perform."

WHERE IS GOD WHEN A LOVED ONE DIES BY SUICIDE?

— Christ was very understanding toward people with personal problems. It is unthinkable that Christ would be unloving towards someone deeply troubled.
— Christ forgives us even when we don't ask, as seen in the accounts of the gospels.
— Christ offered acceptance to the heavily burdened. He summed up His attitude toward the overwhelmed by saying, "Come to me, all you who are weary and burdened, and I will give you rest."
— God understands the person who is confused and thinks that he/she can no longer carry his/her internal and external problems.
— Many people die suddenly without having repented of all of their sins. It is important to keep the last moments of a person's life in the perspective of their entire life. God judges our lives in their totality. To think otherwise is to misunderstand both the worth of our lives and the forgiveness of God.
— God loves us unconditionally. God's grace and mercy are not merited by us but given freely by Him. We don't earn His love, we receive it. Your family member receives the mercy and forgiveness of God.
— Survivors ask, "Why did God let this happen?" It is not unnatural for survivors to feel angry at God. It doesn't help to smother anger. It continues to smolder inside. We might as well admit our anger at God. He knows it anyway.
— God is compassionate and caring, but He allows us to make our own choices.
— God has created us as free persons, not puppets. We can freely choose the paths our lives will take. We can and do make wrong choices and destructive decisions. We can even choose to die.
— Remember that God didn't "take" or "need" your loved one. Suicide is a human act, done for human reasons, attempted and completed by human beings.
— When we look at suicide we confront a mystery. Only God knows just what goes on in the mind and heart of a person before suicide.
— Share your grief with God.

"We are children of God not because of what we do...
but because He loves us."

HELPING YOURSELF

— As soon as you can, start dealing with the facts of the suicide. The longer they are avoided or denied, the harder the recovery will be. Get the facts straight; it will relieve your doubts and let you face the truth. It is important to be honest with yourself and face the fact that the death was a suicide.

—Don't be afraid to say the word suicide. It may take time, but keep trying.

—It may be helpful to make reference to the suicide at the funeral.

—Don't assume that everyone is blaming you or thinking ill thoughts of you. They undoubtedly feel your pain and grief, but are uncomfortable about what to say and how to say it.

—Be prepared for seemingly cruel and thoughtless words from relatives and friends. They are experiencing their own anger, pain and frustration and may not vent their feelings in gentle ways.

—Read recommended literature on suicide and grief. The readings will offer understanding and suggestions for coping.

—Put a picture of the deceased on an empty chair. Verbalize all your feelings about the suicide, about the good memories you have, or about your guilt feelings. Articulating these confused thoughts and feelings will help to end unfinished business.

—You may want to forget about the suicide and not talk about it. Studies show this is the least effective and usually the most damaging approach to dealing with your feelings and questions. You need to express them so they can be faced and dealt with.

—It is best to be honest with your friends about the suicide. If you're not, you'll always wonder if, and how much, they know. It'll become harder to confide in them and isolation and loneliness may follow.

—Don't become discouraged that you are alone in your grief. Sometimes it is helpful to contact another survivor of a suicide. Support groups bring together people who have lived through what you are experiencing.

—Work on guilt. Something beyond your control has happened. Blaming yourself for the actions of another is illogical and dangerously self-damaging.

—If there is a suicide note, discuss, as a family, what should be done with it. If you all agree it will only cause more pain, have a private burning and commit its contents to God.

—Keep remembering that usually a suicide victim didn't want to die, but his/her problems became too overwhelming and in the confusion gave way to suicide.

HELPING SURVIVORS

Bereaved people, especially survivors, need the support, love and concern of their relatives and friends. Often a survivor feels completely isolated. It is up to us to reach out to help. Their basic needs are for kindness and caring. With time, understanding and the concern of their friends, the survivor's feelings of grief will soften. The following suggestions would apply to both the time immediately after the suicide, including the funeral, and for as long as necessary afterwards.

- Make an extra-special effort to go to the funeral home. The shock, denial and cause of death are overwhelming for the survivors. They need all the support they can get. In many cases the coffin is left closed due to the cause of death.

- When going to the funeral home do as you would normally do at any other type of wake. It will not be easy, since you sincerely want to comfort the bereaved person but really don't know what to say. Just a few words can be a help: "I am so very sorry." "Please accept my deepest and sincerest sympathies; my heart goes out to you." When the person is close, take their hand, by all means hug them and don't feel the need to say anything.

- Survivors may tend to be more sensitive, especially when people do not attend the funeral or send a card. A note or visit in the weeks and months to come is of great help to the survivors.

- Don't try to comfort the survivors by saying, "It was an accident, a terrible accident." The survivors need to start dealing with the fact of suicide.

- Do not say, "He or she was on drugs or drunk." You weren't there during the suicide, so how could you possibly know? It is not helpful or necessary to give reasons for the suicide.

- Be aware that the survivor's grief is so painful that sometimes it is easier to deny that it ever happened. Be patient and understanding. Sometimes this denial gives them a breather before the reality comes crashing in again.

- Don't say that the suicidal person was not in his or her right mind or was "crazy." The majority of people who complete suicide are ambivalent and tormented; they may have a character disorder or be neurotic.

- Survivors have every right to feel sensitive. Some people deliberately avoid the survivors. They will cross the street or pretend that they didn't see the survivors. This adds to their grief. Such actions are not done out of malice but rather out of confusion about what to say. It is important to make every effort to befriend the survivor and to reach out.

- Be the type of friend with whom the survivor can talk and feel comfortable and accepted. Don't be judgmental. Be available to spend time with the survivor. Most people find the best way to work through their emotions is to talk them out with someone they trust. When the survivor tells about their feelings, often they are helped in understanding what is going on. Talking also releases some of the pressures. Often while talking, the survivor comes up with his or her own solutions. Show genuine interest and concern.

- Vicious and cruel remarks are sometimes made. They hurt the survivor deeply. Don't repeat such remarks and try to help the originators of the remarks to realize the hurt that they are causing the survivor.

- Don't start telling the survivors that your child or friend "almost" tried to commit suicide and you "know" how they feel. Your loved one is still alive and theirs is dead: *you don't know*.

- Discussing the signs of suicide with a survivor is not helpful since the suicide is a fact. Telling them "there must have been signs indicating depression" only lays more guilt on the survivor.

- The anniversary of the suicide is a very painful time. Relatives and friends should make every effort to be available, to listen, to call, to visit, to send a note, to do little acts of thoughtfulness.

- Further suggestions are listed in the article, "*How to Help Grieving People*," page 40.

HELPING CHILDREN

"Children of suicides have a higher than average rate of suicide, not because the tendency toward suicide is biologically inherited, but because they grow up with a heritage of guilt, anger and a sense of worthlessness." (Klagsburn. TOO YOUNG TO DIE).

- Children have the same emotional needs as adults, but sometimes these needs are ignored or taken lightly. Many times adults are too full of grief to reach out to their children.

- Be honest with them. Give them clear, correct facts about the suicide in a compassionate, loving way. Be careful not to over-explain.

- Listen carefully to their questions, then answer truthfully. Remain consistent in your truthful answers about the suicide.

- Talk about the dead family member.

- Tell all your children about the suicide, even the youngest ones.

- Encourage your children to share their grief with you, and with trusted friends. Teach them to be selective about sharing the facts of the suicide with others.

- You can help them grieve by letting them see you cry and crying with them. Show them that crying is an acceptable and natural release for grief.

- Be aware of children's possible guilt feelings. Assure them that the suicide was not their fault.

- Discuss constructive ways of handling problems. Tell them suicide is a permanent solution to a temporary problem. Problems can be solved. Even if a family member chose suicide, the children have other options.

- Help your children to see they, too, have choices. They can choose to build happy, well-adjusted lives.

WHEN YOUR CHILD HAS DIED BY SUICIDE
by Iris Bolton

On February 19, 1977, our twenty-year-old son, Mitch, shot himself in his bedroom of our home with two revolvers. He was determined not to fail in the last act of his life. Apparently, he felt he had failed to reach the goals of perfection he set up for himself. I believe he saw death as a release from failure, loneliness and hopelessness.

The afternoon of Mitch's death a psychotherapist came to our home, and what he said had a profound effect on me personally. The first thing he advised was to use the upcoming days and weeks to bring our family closer in a way that is not possible under normal circumstances. He said, "Never close the door to your children or make decisions without including them." He suggested we be honest with each other, share our feelings-both positive and negative-about Mitch. He also said, "There is a gift in his death if you can find it. It won't jump out at you, but if you look for it, you will find it." My husband, Jack, heard his words and said they had no meaning for him. But I knew instantly that someday I would find the meaning of his words, and I have. I knew also that Jack and I would grieve differently and that difference must be honored and accepted.

Ultimately you must go through your grief alone, but it can bring you and other family members closer if you choose to do part of it together. It is easy and natural to blame yourself, your spouse, or anyone else at this time but to do so can be destructive and helps no one. Be careful not to blame in an effort to explain why this happened. It is hard to help your other children with their pain when your own is so enormous. But they need to know that it wasn't their fault and it wasn't anything that they said or didn't say to the sibling that caused his death.

In our own family, we included our children and Mitch's girl friend in immediate decisions that needed to be made. We talked about Mitch's good qualities and also about the times he overwhelmed us with his antics or his selfishness. Remembering him realistically helped us all and our family togetherness gave us much-needed nurturing and support at that time.

It is important to experience the pain and get it out. People release their emotions in different ways. Crying is helpful and necessary. Sometimes it is helpful to talk about how you feel to your spouse or a friend. The world we live in does not support your hurting. Well-meaning friends may offer you a drink or a tranquilizer and say, "Don't feel bad, take a pill, have a drink." I believe that in this tragedy, as in so many others, you have to hurt and allow yourself to hurt, without judgment, in order to someday get beyond the intensity of the pain. I believe I will not get beyond it until I go straight through it. There is no way to go around it, over or under it. To be with your feelings, to make no apologies for your emotions, is a very necessary part of the process. Then, one day, you will know that your healing has begun.

Many of our feelings may frighten us but know that all feelings are normal, natural and to be expected. You may think that you are losing your mind but even that thought is normal. So is feeling nothing, feeling hopeless, or having thoughts of wanting to die.

It is important to know that survivors of a suicide often do not want to go on living for a time and feel overwhelmed by these thoughts. This soon passes as the healing begins. Experiencing a sense of shame is common. For a few weeks, I felt "foul" - to myself, to my family and to the center where I worked. But, in time, I realized that I was still me; I had the same values, morals and principles I'd always had. I was the same person but I was different, too. I would never be the same but I had the choice of surviving or not.

I have been a counselor at THE LINK for nine years and have helped parents allow their kids to make choices and take responsibility for those choices. I have suggested that we, as parents, can only guide, advise, suggest, inform, persuade.

151

We can only offer ourselves, our humanness-our best selves and sometimes our worst selves. What our child does with that is his responsibility and his alone. We cannot insure that our child will have our values, morals or goals. Ultimately, it is the child's decision regarding what he does with what we offer him. He was responsible for his life and I am responsible for my life. I must stay aware of that fact.

I can grow with this event and survive or I can go down with it and destroy my own life. It is my choice and I have chosen to survive. So has my husband, Jack, and so have my three other boys. We have chosen to get **beyond** the pain by going **through** it and somehow making meaning out of its meaninglessness.

There is a need to ask, "Why?" The questions must be asked, even though you may never find the answers. It is an enigma **and** it is part of the process of healing that we all go through. But, ultimately, if there are no answers, you may need to stop asking the questions, for to continue only becomes an obsession which can be destructive to yourself and those around you.

I found I only had partial answers and nothing really satisfactory. I will never know all the answers as to why my son chose to end his life, but I came to the conclusion that **I didn't have to know** in order to go on with my own living. I finally chose to let go of the question but only after I had asked it over and over and struggled with the WHY. Had I not done that, I could have allowed mourning to become my life-style for the rest of my life.

I don't know why . . .
I'll never know why . . .
I don't have to know why . . .
I don't like it . .
I don't have to like it . . .

What I do have to do is make a choice
about my living.
What I do want to do is accept it and go
on living.
The choice is mine.

I can go on living, valuing every moment
in a way I never did before,
Or I can be destroyed by it and, in turn,
destroy others.
I thought I was immortal, that my
children and my family were also,
that tragedy happened only to
others . . .
But I know now that life is tenuous and
valuable.

And I choose to go on living, making
the most of the time I have,
And valuing my family and friends in a
way I never experienced before.

Iris Bolton

Iris Bolton is a Compassionate Friends Chapter Leader in Atlanta, GA, and the director of THE LINK Counseling Center.

Permission to reprint from The National Newsletter for the Compassionate Friends Winter 1981 and from Iris Bolton, author of MY SON, MY SON... A Guide To Healing After A Suicide In The Family, Bolton Press, 1325 Belmore Way, N.E., Atlanta, GA 30338.

WHEN A CHILD DIES BY SUICIDE...A PARENT'S GRIEF
by Christine Beattie

Suicide is ugly for onlookers, devastating for the family and harrowing for those professionally involved. Suicide is very often labeled "criminal" and religion has called it "sin." It is neither. On the surface, it would seem that a suicide has only one victim - the person who commits the act. But those who have lived through the emotional agony that follows know otherwise. The survivors, the parents, spouses, brothers, sisters and close friends are suicide's other victims.

1980 was a year I will always remember but wish that I could forget. Our beautiful, happy family of ten was dealt a blow that would change all of our lives. Our 18 year-old son, Donald, died by suicide. Donald had disappeared in June after attending a graduation party and having his girlfriend tell him that she wanted to date others. The endless waiting for some word had become a way of life. So in the fall when he was found hanging from a tree, twenty-five feet in the air, what none of us wanted to believe was confirmed.

We went through the rituals of burial. Young people joined us in our grief. How sad, quiet and confused they were. They needed to be with us, to share their tears and thoughts. We needed them, too - to bring us up to date on the many times they shared with Donald.

My children were much more accepting of the fact that their brother had taken his life. They knew he had not been happy those last few months and that there were many pressures on him. They knew him to be thoughtful, sensitive, caring and funny. He loved life! They missed the old Donald. My children realized long before me that Donald had choices - he chose to end his life. Apparently he felt he had failed to reach the goals he had set up for himself. How impossible everything must have seemed to him!!! How he must have been hurting! He chose to die rather than to suffer any more pain.

In the months that followed our friends tried to be there for us, but I found it difficult to talk to them. I felt that they didn't understand what I was feeling; after all, they hadn't lost anyone this way. I remember vividly our first social function that we attended after Donald's suicide. As we walked into the party, the room went completely silent. Time seemed to stand still before everyone relaxed and resumed talking. People turned away in grocery stores, or if they did talk to me they would say foolish things that hurt. But I realize now that it wasn't their fault. They wanted to be helpful, but they didn't know what to say. Many people are uncomfortable with death. There is such a stigma attached to suicide.

The children were careful not to mention Donald's name for fear it would upset me. My husband also was very careful not to mention him. We seemed to "unfold" as a family, each withdrawing into himself, tiptoeing around each other and rarely speaking to each other. If only we could have grieved as a family. I have learned since that this is almost impossible, because we all grieve in our own way and in our own time. Some of us take longer to get through the grieving process than others. Thanks to a good counselor we didn't become one of the statistics - 85% of all marriages in which a child commits suicide end in divorce. Through the counselor I found out that my husband blamed himself for putting too much pressure on Donald those last few months of his life - how foolish! I know now that it was a combination of things that contributed to his taking his life. No one person was to blame - no one incident, but many. I was often asked by well-meaning friends, "Didn't you see he needed help?" Of course I did and I tried to get it for him. But he didn't want it. A person has to want the help!!

Six months went by and I was still feeling numb and still experiencing that knife- piercing pain of grief. I thought I was going out of my mind. I needed to be with other people who had experienced the same loss. Through a friend I heard about a support group for bereaved parents. I went, but felt that I was the only one who had lost someone by suicide. A year later I went to the director, who listened and suggested that maybe I would like to form a support group for survivors of suicide. With much soul searching I decided how wonderful it would be for me to form this group in Donald's memory. I could turn this terrible tragedy into something positive. Thank God I did. I now conduct monthly support group meetings for survivors of suicide. Some come once, some attend many meetings. You can't put a time limit on the grieving process, but after a few years of grieving you can begin to see the difference. It takes two years at the very least to work through the process. With suicide, there is so much that dies with the person. Survivors come to the group with tremendous amounts of pent-up anger and guilt. They wonder if they could have prevented the suicide if they had said something different, forgiven some act, been at home when a call came that went unanswered. We let them talk. We can't take their pain away; that's an unrealistic expectation. But we can offer friendship, coping skills, understanding, support and a "home." That's what our support groups do.

In helping the many survivors I, too, was helping myself to heal. In the past five years I have learned a lot about suicide. I no longer feel alone. I learned that I wasn't going crazy - I was GRIEVING for my son. I learned that there is HOPE - that I would someday be a whole person. The experience of suicide in one's family changes the perspective of the survivors. You try to enjoy every minute with your remaining loved ones. You tell them often how much you love them. You hug them more. The pain of the experience is so great that you can only go one of two ways: stagnate and give up, or overcome it through grieving and growth. It is important for survivors to remember that those who died made a choice. Now the survivors have to make a choice, too - a choice to go on living, to start again. It's their choice to get better, to heal.

We never forget our loss. There will never be an occasion that they aren't missed. They live in our hearts and memories forever.

Christine Beattie is coordinator of Hope For Survivors: Those Whom Suicide Leaves Behind.

AFTERMATH! WHEN A SPOUSE DIES BY SUICIDE
by Mary Jane Meehan

It's been almost one and a half years - as I look back, the first year was a confusion of disbelief; "Why am I here - where I don't want to be?!!" The whole world had changed because of my husband's suicide. There were many weeks of not caring because of this awful, terrible thing that had happened, not only to me but to our children. Then little by little, the realization started to appear that this was the way it was and was going to be.

On top of my misery I discovered that in order to meet my financial expenses as a widow, it was necessary for me to work at least part-time! I had brought up two families, and at age 64 I just couldn't- and still can't understand why there wasn't sufficient insurance or protection.

I have been working for a local department store, enjoying what I do because I am needed. However, I cannot see any real change in my immediate future and don't expect any unless I do something about it; but what???

In this second year the reality of my situation has set in. I sometimes feel it is never going to be any different - the deep hurt is here and will be here. It seems that when I am feeling "good," inevitably the word "suicide" will be spoken on T.V. or radio and that word brings tears to my eyes. I can't help it, and I get mad all over again. I don't like getting angry so I try to think of something lovely - like my beautiful grandchildren, the color of the sky, the trees turning color because it is autumn, the tiny animals hopping about, and remembering God is letting me see these beautiful things. I am so grateful, but being human I am sad and lonely and will always hope that perhaps the dear Lord will see fit to let me live my remaining years in peace and with loved ones, so that I don't have to be alone.

I am finding that to accept what has happened is a big step in the right direction. It is hard to do. The next step is to accept life as it is and is going to be. I find that praying helps me tremendously. Family and friends are there when you need them, but it is the hourly, daily, terrible loneliness that is the hardest to bear. My working four days a week is good for me I know...but it's opening that door to my apartment and finding nothing has changed and I am alone, that bothers me the most.

Take heart! Our need to go to the "Bereaved Meetings" is good for the soul. We can talk about our needs and share our misery. It makes me feel good when I can help someone. We will all make it - because we are survivors. I'm stubborn and Irish and I absolutely refuse to let this suicide ruin the rest of my life. It could if I let it but I WON'T.

In the past, Mary Jane Meehan coordinated support for those whose spouse died by suicide.

WHEN A SIBLING DIES . . . ANONYMOUS

Looking back upon my teenage years, I find the experience which altered my life more markedly than any other was the death of my sister. She was a suicide victim at the age of sixteen. I was thirteen at that time. Something that only happens to other people, and in other families, happened to me. To this day the memories haunt me; in my search for answers I find none.

Unless one has lived through this type of personal tragedy, it is impossible to understand the tremendous difficulties in not only coping with what has happened, but in facing the future. If one asks how did I manage, I would have to say that I am not exactly sure. I remember the struggles I encountered then, and still have to overcome today.

Certainly, the tragic death of someone so close forced me to grow up very quickly. Self-preservation demanded this. But by doing so, my problems were increased, not decreased. I became much more serious-minded than my peers. This, in turn, deprived me of what I needed most- the association with my friends and classmates. However, they were afraid and unsure of how to handle a relationship with one who had suffered such a loss.

During my freshman and sophomore years I was consumed with the need to find that special friend, someone to confide in, and to be socially accepted. My accomplishments in those two years were few. Now I wish I had been able to concentrate more on my studies which would have earned me better grades. But it was not possible.

My parents, who have been continually supportive, had set an example of facing a future forever different, but one in which life must go on. At some point I realized that I should adopt a more positive attitude. With a new outlook, my junior year was a wonderful and fulfilling one. The accomplishments of my junior year encouraged me to look optimistically toward my senior year, entrance to college and the future. To date I have managed to continue the progress.

My experience has made me sensitive to human suffering. I have learned that in order to interact well with others, I must think well about myself. No one can change the past, but God gives us the opportunity to change the future, for ourselves and for those we respect and love. I hope to help others, for I know only too well how much help I needed along the way. I desire to have my life count for something worthwhile. Not only for myself and my parents, but most importantly, for my sister, who did not have that opportunity.

A FAREWELL TO JAMIE
by Mickey Vorobel

The evening star shines on the grave
Of one I loved, but could not save
My son lies alone and with no other
He was once alive and with me
I know, because I am his mother
His troubled heart and his troubled mind
Brought him no peace to find
And so he chose to end his life
And leave me alone in this world of strife
Consuming waves of tears, anguish, pain and hurt begin
And nothing seemed to calm my hell within
I grieved, I mourned, I drank, I agonized each day
My heart would not then to let me pray
The shock, denial and bitterness became my quest
Pain-filled days and nights gave me no rest
The poets say that death leaves us a gift behind
Sometimes the pain of missing you blocks my open mind
I wonder if the gift you left behind will ever be revealed
Or does it lie within your grave, forever concealed?
I had no choice when you died
But I do have the choice to survive
And so it has been that I have tried
I do not want you dead, my son
I want you back whole and alive
But fate has played a different tune for me
And I am not the same as I used to be
Is this the gift you left for me, my son
That I would not be changed by your death?
Is thought of by only a fool
I seek to find some inner peace
And banish the pain and make it cease
And then there came a day that I was shown
A Light at the end of my tunnel of nightmares
That I had never known
I joined this group and they alone helped me to be strong
They accepted me for what I was, whether I was right or wrong
The healing process had begun
And the seeds were being sowed
And after every meeting my burden of grief lessened up the load
Our agonies in this group entwined
And we shared a comfort that otherwise we could not find
The memories of you will never die
Even tho' you chose to close your eyes
My love for you lives on, my son
Just as I chose to go on living as one
Maybe you did give me a gift, unknowingly
And that is to learn to live again-fully and completely
The pain of losing you will always be there
But there comes a time to let go and say good-bye
In my heart you will stay
Forever and a day
Farewell, Jamie, I'll love you always.

WHEN A LOVED ONE
HAS DIED BY MURDER

GRIEF IS COMPLICATED WHEN A LOVED ONE IS MURDERED
by Norma Griswold

March 6, 1981 started out to be a special day. We were enjoying all the beauty and excitement that Lake Placid could hold for us. We viewed the skiers on the slopes, not realizing that when we returned to our room and to a blinking red light that we would learn of our tragedy. A call from the Pasadena Police revealed to us that our youngest daughter, Barbara, age 29, had been murdered in the Holiday Inn where she had been leading a women's seminar for Allstate Insurance. In a single instant, the whole world around me went crumbling and I became strangely numb. Had we heard right? We asked to have the message repeated. Yes, we had heard correctly. It was truly information directed to the Griswolds, involving their daughter. Before packing to come back to Syracuse, we had the difficult task of calling our two other daughters to inform them of the news about Barbara. We also had to make arrangements to fly to California as soon as possible.

As I reflect back, all the details fell into place and the next day we were in California to hear just what happened. An unidentified person had broken into Barbara's room, beat her, bound her, gagged her and killed her with a sprinkler pipe. The thoughts of the violence still linger and probably will forever. It wasn't until February, 1983 that an eighteen year old was arrested, breaking in again at the same Holiday Inn. He confessed to Barbara's murder and was tried in June, 1984, but because of poor selection of the jury it ended in a deadlocked 11-1 verdict. A second trial on June 3, 1985 brought a guilty verdict; but according to California state law, because he was sixteen at the time of the murder they allowed him ninety days in a diagnostic center to evaluate his background before sentencing him in September, 1985. I have trouble calling that a justice system when his taped confession was evidence. Barbara had a host of friends, a family that loved her dearly, a job with good potential. It was difficult for even the investigating officers to understand why this happened to her. In all their research they couldn't find anything to discredit her.

I reminisce often of Barb. I am traveling through the steps of grief. Violent death brings anger so intense most people can't stand it. Dealing with the mutilation of the body is so painful. I wonder what her last hours were like. Memories of Barbara are triggered by a song, a graduation or marriage notice in the newspaper, and always at a family gathering. I still struggle with her birthday. Time doesn't recognize these milestones. I have found that I have to work through grief patiently; work through grief persistently; do what I can, let God do what I can't; work through grief purposefully, work through grief confidently. Finally, a remarkable thing begins to happen. I notice that for short periods the hurt is not so great, and now I realize that this is the beginning of healing. No griever ever truly returns to become his old self. I have the option to become stronger or weaker, with either a healthier spirit or a sicker one. I know Barbara would want me to be happy again, and to laugh and smile again.

I found it helpful to read books about what heaven is really like. I know I will see her again. God allowed Barb's death to happen, but I have stopped asking the unanswerable question - WHY? Barb's memories have crowded out bitterness and now enrich every day of my life. As December approached I wondered how I could ever make it through the holidays. I heard about a support group-HOPE FOR BEREAVED PARENT(S). At the meeting I received suggestions for coping with the holidays. I sensed that this group would help me to ease my grief. It has in many ways! In May, 1982 a new support group was formed - HOPE FOR THOSE WHOSE LOVED ONE DIED BY MURDER - which I helped coordinate. Working at HOPE FOR BEREAVED helped me to turn something ugly into something positive. Although I joined the group for the help that I needed, I remained in order to help others.

Norma Griswold was one of the coordinators of Hope For Those Whose Loved One Died By Murder, and was an active volunteer for many years.

ADDITIONAL PROBLEMS OF SURVIVORS OF A HOMICIIDE*

This excerpt was taken from a report on the first 18 months of operation of the Victim Services Agency's "Families of Homicide Victims Project," New York City.

"THE PSYCHOLOGICAL REACTIONS TO THE TRAUMA OF HOMICIDE -

In working with families of homicide victims, we have learned that homicide inflicts a devastating emotional trauma on the surviving relatives. Among the reactions we typically encounter are: shock and apathy; helplessness and terror; overwhelming rage; guilt; intense yearning for the one who is dead. It is difficult to overstate the intensity of these reactions. Moreover, surviving relatives (particularly parents) often continue in a state of acute grief for well over a year. Frequently the friends and relatives of the close survivors become uncomfortable and finally exasperated by this intense mourning. As months go by, those close to the survivors begin admonishing them to resume normal living — "It's time to go on with your lives." When admonishment proves fruitless, the friends and relatives often begin to withdraw emotionally from the survivors. Thus for the survivors, murder of a loved one is often compounded by isolation and increased loneliness.

LEGAL AND JUDICIAL SYSTEM RELATED
No arrest
Rude treatment by police
No information from police or prosecutor
No notification of trial date
Not allowed to attend trial
Plea bargaining with no explanation
Hearing the defense attorney slander the victim
Killer free on bail, awaiting appeal; possibly in the same neighborhood as the victim's family
Confession thrown out of court without explanation
Poor handling of case by prosecutor
Sentence seems too lenient
Murderer out on parole in short period of time
No sense of closure because no arrest
Feeling that the police are no longer working on the case
Feeling of being ignored throughout the whole legal/judicial process

FINANCIAL
Funeral and medical costs
Medical expenses for psychiatric care for family members
Medical care for health problems for family members
Cost of private investigators, private attorneys
Possible loss of breadwinner
Various costs and financial losses that others may not realize are related to the murder, such as: the sister who gives up a 4-year college scholarship because she needs to come home and spend time with her family; the family sells their house and moves away because their child was killed in their own home and they're trying to get away from those memories; the teen-age brother who has one car accident after another because his rage is coming out in his driving; etc.

JOB RELATED
Inability to function and perform on the job
Lack of interest and motivation
Demotion or loss of job
Added pressures and stresses
Need to spend more time on job to accomplish same amount of work
Loss of job because of a show of grief, such as crying at work

Using job as an excuse to avoid working through the grief and to avoid a grieving spouse

Running away from pain by becoming a workaholic

MARITAL / SEXUAL

Husband and wife grieve in different ways

Husband and wife blame each other

Depression resulting in no interest in sexual contact

Trying to bury the pain by divorcing the parent of the murdered child and starting over with someone else without painful memories.

Extremely high divorce rate after the violent death of a child

Trying to run away from the pain by selling house and moving away and eventually dissolving marriage

The emotional pain of sexual contact because it is a constant reminder of the dead child and all the hopes they had for this child at the time of conception and throughout the pregnancy

FAMILY / CHILDREN

Lack of communication/alienation

School drop-outs

Use of alcohol and drugs to ease the pain

Bitterness and wanting to get revenge

Withdrawal of family members

Fear of adding to the others' pain

Pressure from some family members to put it behind them and irritation if they don't

Myth that sorrow draws a family closer together

Suicide on anniversary date

Danger of becoming overprotective of other children

RELIGIOUS / SPIRITUAL

Guilt because of anger

Absence of expected response and support from others in their church or synagogue

Comments of clergy, other members, which indicate lack of understanding

Disillusionment with self that faith was not strong enough to carry one through the grieving process bravely

Being put on a pedestal by others and told what a good example they are

The shaking - and sometimes the crumbling - of one's religious or philosophical foundations

MEDIA COVERAGE

Sensational/pulp detective magazines

Inaccurate

Inflammatory and slanderous

Intrusive and/or prolonged

For offender only — almost glorifying the offender and carrying him through each stage of the proceeding while the victim and survivors are forgotten (at least this may be the perception of the victim's family)

TREATMENT BY PROFESSIONALS

All of the following frequently demonstrate that they do not understand the effects of a violent death upon family members: police, hospital personnel, funeral directors, clergy, school counselors and teachers, psychologists and psychiatrists

This article was adapted from original article by P.O.M.C. permission to reprint granted by © Parents of Murdered Children. For further information contact POMC, 100 East Eighth Street, Room 841, Cincinnati, OH 45202.

WHEN A PARENT HAS DIED
WHEN A FRIEND HAS DIED
GRIEF NO ONE TALKS ABOUT

WHEN A PARENT DIES

For an adult the death of a parent may have a much greater impact than anticipated. We expect our parents to die before we do; however, when it happens we are sometimes not prepared and may experience very deep grief. Parents may have been the glue that held the family together for holidays and special family events. For some adults their parent may have been the most significant person in their life, and they now feel orphaned. But it must also be noted that not everyone has a good relationship with their parents, and strong feelings of relief, anger, unfinished business, and guilt (to name a few) may emerge. When a parent dies it is important to give ourselves permission to grieve, to find others who understand, and to realize that our feelings- whatever they are - are normal.

WHEN MY MOTHER DIED in 1933, I was eight years old; she was only twenty-eight. I remember it all so vividly, like it was yesterday. It was devastating! When my grand-mother told me, I ran out of the house and ran and ran till I couldn't run any more, crying all the time, not wanting to believe that my mother was not coming home to us.

Her wake was in my grandparents' home; my mom looked so beautiful. My brother Chuck was six and my brother Don, three months old. Our dad was in such a state of shock that our grandparents became our caretakers. We grew up in our grandparents' homes. I remember people not talking about Mom's dying. I guessed that no one wanted to make us feel any sadder. I'm sure we cried and were as depressed as children could be. My brother Chuck and I just clung to one another for so long. We've always been very close to one another-guess it began all those years ago, the need for someone to lean on.

I was seventeen years old before I could say the word "Mother" out loud, and when I finally did one day, the tears just flowed. All those years, not being able to really express my loss, my grief. People didn't believe in allowing you to talk about your loved one who had died! They didn't know how to handle grief, how to even begin to work through it! Thank God we have come so far.

It's been almost three years since my dad's death. For years, and especially since my husband's death, I wondered what I would ever do if my dad died! He had always been there for me; my rock, my refuge, my friend! I was always his "little girl," his "sweetheart," even until the end. He had not been well for months before his death. We cared for him at his home and in the hospital. We knew that he wasn't going to be with us forever, but it didn't make his death any easier. It's funny - you think you are prepared, but you never are. When you've loved deeply, it hurts deeply! There were such differences between my parents' deaths. I could grieve openly, talk about my dad, cry as much as I wanted and knew that these feelings were all okay. I wasn't expected to be brave, to "smile," "get over it" in a few weeks. I miss him terribly, but I know he'll always be with me. My mom, too!

- by Nanine Newman

"A Journey Of
    One Thousand Miles . . .
        Begin With A
            Single Step"

MY PARENTS LIVED for 89 years. They met in third grade and were married for 67 years. They died less than two months apart. I did not really grieve for my mother after her death. She had suffered with Alzheimer's disease for about 1 2 years. During those years we lost the person who was my mother, bit by bit. For me there was a sense of relief that it was finally over and the physical body had gone to join the spirit, long ago departed.

My dad was the opposite. The spirit was still strong, independent and mentally sharp and clear. He was much loved by all. The body, however, was ravaged by cancer and old age. My mother had died, and he was anxious to join her. From the time of his diagnosis in June, until his death in November, there was time for many conversations, from which I realized he was ready spiritually and physically to say good-bye. The end of his physical pain had come-there was a sense of peace.

by Carol Peltier

MY PARENTS DIED four years apart. When my mother died, I felt I had lost not only my mother, but my best friend. I knew my mother loved me unconditionally-even though she never actually told me. I knew it by her actions. She never interfered and was always support-ive. I didn't feel as close to my dad, but his death brought about the loss of a "home" to go back to as well as the loss of a father.

For the last 10 years of my parents' lives, we lived 150 miles away. I think the distance prepared me somewhat for their deaths. When we lived in the same town I talked to my mother every day. That obviously ceased when we moved. I grieved; I missed them, and still do. But my grief was not as intense as when our son died; it is "normal" for your parents to die before you. I was always grateful that God allowed them to live and be a part of my life for as long as they were. I know they were "there" to greet our son, and that is comforting.

by Eunice Brown

RELIEF AFTER THE DEATH of a parent may come from two different sources: Relief because they are out of pain; relief because you are out of pain. Perhaps your childhood was very painful, and your relationship with your parent was still conflicted and stressful as an adult. When my mom died I felt just that — RELIEF! Relief that now we could enjoy holidays and not always dread them because of family fights. Relief that now I didn't have to be peace-maker in the family.

RELIEF-an honest emotion, but one that is hard to admit.

— Anonymous

THE QUIET OF AN EARLY MORNING in March was broken by the shrill ringing of a phone. Answering, I heard my mother's plea to come quickly. I raced the short mile to my parents' home, praying that my dad would be all right. As I drove up the ambulance was already there. Inside I found the paramedics working on my father. Part of me realized that he was dead, while another part was saying he would be all right. I wasn't ready to let go just yet. "Just a little more time" was my prayer. We followed the ambulance to the hospital in silence, only to be told that Dad had died. All too soon the feelings of grief that I had all but forgotten returned. That old, unwelcome companion called grief began to invade my body and life. My son died in 1973, so I knew the long journey through grief that lay ahead.

During the wake and in the following days the messages I frequently heard were, "He lived a good life"; "It's all for the best"; "If I lived to be 86, I would be happy!" The death of an older parent is apparently not perceived to be as significant a loss as others. The single, most common form of bereavement is the death of a parent. Why, then, did I hurt so much? Why did I feel such sadness, guilt, helplessness, and so vulnerable? Why was I so exhausted, with

163

sleep eluding me, only to fall asleep and be wakened by nightmares? Why did I not want to get up in the morning? I could have stayed in bed, closed my door and let the days go by, not wanting to communicate with anyone. When I forced myself to get up, go to work and perform my everyday tasks, I found myself moving in slow motion, almost frozen in time. Food seemed to lose all flavor. Why was there such a tremendous emptiness? Why did my whole body ache? Had I mistakenly thought that my grief over the death of a parent would not be as painful as it was?

When we experience the death of a parent we lose a part of our past. No one knows us better than our parents. No longer are they there to remind us of incidents that happened when we were too young to remember. Haven't we all heard our parents say, "Do you remember when and then go on to tell of some incident many years ago? When a parent dies you not only have that enormous loss and void in your life, but you also experience many secondary losses. I not only grieve my father's death but all of the many things we did together. No longer would I be able to share a cup of coffee with him in the morning, take him for a ride on a hot summer night and stop for ice cream. I will never buy another Father's Day card or again sit with him in the warmth of a late summer afternoon and enjoy that special relationship we shared.

Our parents are our first teachers. How I remember all the patient hours Dad spent teaching me to ride my first bike, to swim, to drive a car. But greatest of all, he taught me to value the right things in life, to believe in myself, and how to treat other people. So much that we are is the result of the efforts of our parents. Their wisdom and love will guide us through life. Our parents are our protectors. Are they not the ones we turn to in times of difficulty? I remember the many hours we sat on our front porch during the summer nights. Once in a while a thunder storm would strike. I would run and jump on my dad's lap for his reassuring words that it was only the angels bowling. And I knew I was safe in his strong arms. In some ways that child within never leaves us, but seeks a buffer or barrier against life's hurts and problems. They are the ones to whom we rush to share our accomplishments and important happenings. Their unconditional love allows us to share our successes and failures, our joys and sorrows. With our parents, our life is richer, more stimulating and a time of joy and love. When they die there is a tremendous loneliness.

As I think of Dad, another thought comes to mind. Our son died several years ago. I had never thought too much of it before, but now I realize how hard it must have been for a grandfather to bury his grandson. Not only was he grieving for his grandson, but over the effects the death had on me and my family. Never once did he give up; he supported, encouraged and gave us the peaceful strength to continue. Our parents are truly our source of inspiration. With Dad's death I have thought of my son Jim much more frequently. Dad shared that struggle from grief to a life again filled with hope and laughter. I realize that I have lost the one person I could talk to about Jim.

I know that eventually the pain and sorrow caused by my father's death will soften. Life will again be filled with happiness. I will be left with the beautiful memories of times shared together. In the recesses of my mind I will store those treasured memories; and when I find that little girl within me returning, I will open up my treasure box and return to know that he is with our son sharing in the joys of the promises of our God, and in time we will all be together again. For now, I thank God for giving me this very special man to be my dad. He was my source of encouragement, joy and love. His love bound us together during life, and while his death has caused much pain, his presence in my life will live within me.

by Donna Kalb

Freud . . . who coined the term "grief work"
. . . said: "People spend as much energy in
one day of grief as if they dug ditches for an
eight-hour shift."

A CHILD'S PERSPECTIVE
by Mark T. Scrivani

The most difficult loss a child faces is the death of a parent. Children have varying degrees of understanding death, since much depends upon the age of a child. Very young children will have difficulty understanding the finality of death, while older children may explore the reasons why their parent died. The important fact to remember is that grief knows no age; even infants are able to grieve! Children are not afraid to effectively grieve in ways that adults may consider "inappropriate."

For children and teens the death of a parent is devastating; yet by the time a child is 12, one in 20 have experienced the death of a parent. The very young child may worry excessively that the other parent will die and then "what will become of me?" Even though the death was the result of an accident or illness, the child may feel abandoned. Some of the secondary losses may be moving (from home, neighborhood, school, friends, etc.), change in lifestyle, adjusting to a step-family. The death of a parent is exceedingly difficult for teens. It throws their world askew. At a time of growing independence they need their parents' love and direction. Their peers don't know what to say or do, and the remaining parent is often overcome with grief. This leaves the teen to struggle alone with the unknown feelings of grief. Children and teens need help to understand and cope with their grief. If they don't receive support, their unresolved grief may last a long time and even cause problems in their adult lives. Young people need to find someone who cares and will listen to them.

Although there are many ways to express a child's grief, common elements do exist. Children often view their parents as infallible and/or immortal. The first crisis a child faces is realizing that his parent is merely human. This knowledge can bring about great insecurity, since the child must make fundamental changes in his life. No longer will "Daddy" or "Mommy" always be able to take care of things, no longer will they have all the answers, no longer can the child find respite in that parent's embrace. The child learns that the only constant in life is that it will change continuously. This is a difficult lesson to learn; one cannot be truly happy without knowing this. The child may become fearful of what the future holds without that parent. By working through the journey of grief, the child can learn to appreciate the past, look forward to the future, and live for the present.

In short, the death of a parent forces the child to "grow up" quickly. The child must deal with and resolve some very complex issues. Children who continue their journey through grief are often more mature than others their age. They tend to take small irritants less seriously, since they begin to realize the important issues of life. Over time, children of a dead parent have an enormous potential to grow and become "well-adjusted" or "level-headed" people. For this to happen, adults must allow the child to grieve in his/her unique way. Suggestions for helping children are found elsewhere in this handbook.

It is important to be aware of any special difficulties that may arise when a parent dies. For example, the child may be very resistant to anyone "replacing" their parent, and would be very opposed to the surviving parent remarrying. On the other hand, another child in the same family might want a "replacement" and may push for remarriage. In this example, both children are working through their grief, and these expressions must be taken in this context.

To summarize: No other grief for a child is as difficult as the death of a parent. However, the journey through grief will challenge the child to gain a positive life perspective.

I WAS "JUST A FRIEND"

Death touches every person, not just once in a lifetime, but many times. Our grandparents, parents, spouses, aunts, uncles, sisters, brothers, children ... and our friends ... die. We cannot escape the pain of loss. It is a major mistake to even attempt to deny the feelings of emptiness and hurt we feel when someone we have loved is gone.

It can be more difficult when the loss is "only" a friend. The pain is every bit as real, and can be even more than we might feel for a relative. Friends know each other in different ways than they are known by their families. They share special times together, cherished times. A friendship is not like a family relationship. Families tend to have several members; a friendship involves only two people. When a friend dies, the bond is forever altered and the support that families give each other is not there. When you go to your friend's wake your role is to comfort, more than to claim the comfort you need just as desperately. You can even fool yourself into believing that you have no right to grieve. Don't believe it!

My friend was killed in a van accident a year ago. It's been said in one popular song that we never see people, really see them, until they go away. The truth of those words became clear to me when Joe died. I did not know how much a part of me Joe was. I had no idea how much I would miss him and how much I loved my friend until it was too late. Death really changes things. All the words you wanted to say, the hugs you planned to give, the hours you hoped you would spend in each other's company, have suddenly vanished. Memories are all that is left; the regrets can be overwhelming. Joe's last words to me were to tell me that he'd be back in the area. Well, he was right, but neither of us expected he'd come back the way he did! We couldn't have known that a phase of our friendship was over, or that the way we parted the last time we met would be the memory that would have to last us forever. Time ran out!

Is there a lesson to be learned from this? YES!! The lesson is really quite simple, yet surprisingly hard to learn. Its meaning came alive to me as I struggled through the pain of knowing and accepting Joe's death.

What I say to anyone who feels love for someone today is this - tell the person NOW!! Don't wait! You can't hug a person who is in a coffin. You can't hold hands with a tombstone. You can't celebrate your friendship and love for others in a cemetery. Give the gifts of friendship and love while they can be appreciated. Flowers only make you feel better at the wake. Give them now, generously. Show signs of your love again and again. The one thing you can be sure of is that the time you are given to be with those who touch your life and those you love will be too short. You never know when the last word, the last hug, the last day will come. If you share your love now, there can be no regrets later about what you should have done. As it has been said many times, if there is any good you can do or kindness you can show, DO IT NOW!! You (or the ones you care for) may never pass this way again!

Pat Ward, of East Syracuse, New York, wrote this article to thank HOPE FOR BEREAVED: "The stories I read (in your newsletter and your handbook) were such a help to me. I could identify with the pain and hurt, and was able to realize that I was not crazy: I was grieving."

GRIEF NO ONE TALKS ABOUT

Editors Note: Originally this article was being written for those bereaved by an AIDS death. However, there are many other reasons that people experience an unacknowledged grief. Many of the concepts and suggestions within this article apply to the various unrecognized griefs.

GRIEF AFTER A DEATH BY AIDS. Death of a family member or friend by AIDS is, for many reasons, one of the most difficult griefs to bear. AIDS spares no one. It strikes the young, the old, women, men, straight or gay, blacks, latinos and whites. The majority of deaths are between the ages of 20 and 35, which means there are many survivors. In some cases survivors cover up what the illness/death really was.

AIDS abounds with fear. Fear of the stigma that is often attached to an AIDS death keeps survivors from readily identifying themselves or seeking help. Survivors fear having been exposed to a life-threatening virus. Many are concerned that the physical symptoms of "normal" grief, which they are experiencing, may in reality be ARC (AIDS Related Complex). Due to past experiences with the medical system, survivors may be reluctant to seek medical care.

In the gay community death is often serial and multiple, which complicates grief resolution. The survivor is still reeling from one death when another occurs. Guilt may come from not realizing how ill their lover was; from not being able to persuade the lover to get care sooner or from seeing the pain, the many tests and isolation their lover went through because he did go for treatment. The survivor may feel anger toward the health care system for often not treating their loved one dying of AIDS as well as they treated someone dying of an "accepted" death. Sometimes the survivor may experience feelings of anger toward the deceased, followed by guilt for being angry.

Although touch is very therapeutic, survivors often do not get hugs because people are fearful of contagion. The isolation experienced by many survivors may combine with bottled up anger and lead to depression. With death comes secondary losses . . . the loss of the activities that had been the focus of daily living . . . caring for their loved one who was dying of AIDS. Some survivors must assume new roles, even move to a new location, at a time when change just adds more pressure to their lives.

UNRECOGNIZED GRIEF DUE TO DEATH. When a relative or friend dies in an accident and is responsible (drinking and driving) for the death of someone else . . . when a loved one murders someone and dies by suicide (in both cases there is grief due to the death of a loved one and further grief because others died as a result of a loved one's drinking or actions) . . . when a loved one dies by suicide... when a baby is aborted . . . involvement in a non-traditional and sometimes secret relationship such as extramarital affairs, heterosexual cohabitation or homosexual relationships . . . within strained or non-communicative relationships (e.g., when an ex-spouse dies, when an absent, uninvolved parent dies, when a relative or friend dies to whom the survivor has not spoken and/or has had ill feelings for years) . . . when a pet dies . . . This is not an all-inclusive list. There are many other reasons and relationships where grief is most appropriate.

OTHER REASONS PEOPLE GRIEVE. Separation and/or divorce . . . losing a job . . . moving . . . break-up of a friendship . . . living in an abusive and/or alcoholic home . . . illness . . . loss of family closeness due to drugs/alcohol . . . bad grades... not making the team . . . retirement . . . young adult leaving home.

When grief is unacknowledged the bereaved survivors often do not receive support, understanding or acceptance. The bereaved may not be able to use formal or informal support systems. In some cases religion and rituals may constrain rather than facilitate grief work. If the close or primary relationship to the deceased is not accepted by others or kept very secret it frequently means social support from family and friends may be non-existent. This lack of support and isolation may result in complicated grief.

For those in non-traditional relationships it is more difficult to accept the reality of the death because the survivor is often excluded from the dying process, planning for and the actual funeral. Usually there is no time off from work (bereavement leave) for other than immediate family members.

There may be medical, financial and legal problems with wills, credit cards and joint purchases. Unfinished business abounds. There tends to be great isolation on the part of the survivors who are reluctant to tell their story or may be ignored and left to struggle alone. Survivors often experience strong feelings of guilt, shame, fear, anger and despair. Unfortunately, the survivor frequently does not know where to turn for help and understanding. Lack of support may lead to unresolved grief which could become chronic, delayed or masked.

HOW TO HELP YOURSELF WITH UNACKNOWLEDGED GRIEF

"Give sorrow words. The grief that does not speak, knits up the
o'erwrought heart and bids it break." - SHAKESPEARE

• The first step to healing is acknowledgment. You must claim the emotions and the relationship. Find someone you can trust who will LISTEN and accept your feelings. Honesty is important. However, it is not necessary to tell everyone everything. You must go public, at least to yourself.

• It is important to NAME THE PAIN. You must acknowledge that the loss took place and what aspects of grief are troubling you.

• Join a support group that addresses your specific loss-AIDS, abortion-or one in which you feel comfortable. The group provides safety, empathy, hugs and a place to tell your story again and again.

• Make time for yourself-for your grief.

• Take it one step (even small steps) at a time. Admit you are powerless.

• Create an opportunity to say good-bye. Hold a memorial ceremony with family, friends, co-workers or within a support group. Share pictures, thoughts and warm memories. Without a funeral or some type of memorialization healing will be greatly hampered. Look at the relationship as it really was. Reflect on both the good and bad aspects.

• Consider talking with an empathic counselor.

• If there is an estrangement with your God, find an understanding pastoral counselor or caring lay person to help you.

• Reconciliation is important. With the help of a counselor or support group, work through unfinished business.

• Allow yourself to grieve the death of the person who died, not necessarily the reason or circumstances for the death.

• Write an open letter to the one who died or use the empty-chair technique (see page 63).

• Activate your grief by becoming involved with a support organization. Raise money to help an AIDS organization, a local SADD group, etc.

• For more detailed articles, see the following pages. Depression, page 58; Guilt, page 61; Anger, page 65.

HOW TO HELP THOSE WITH UNACKNOWLEDGED GRIEF

• Examine your own religious, cultural and/or family biases and prejudices, in order to acknowledge and understand your own reactions and responses. Once you have acknowledged your reactions, put them aside so you can be receptive to those you are trying to support.

• Be there. Show your genuine concern by acknowledging their pain and your helplessness to eliminate it. Realize your calm presence is a truly wonderful gift.

• Encourage the survivor to tell and re-tell his/her story.

• Listen ... listen ... AGAIN and AGAIN.

• Help the survivors to acknowledge their grief, emotions, reactions.

• Encourage some kind of memorialization. We all need an opportunity to say good-bye and to share memories.

• Provide a non-judgmental, safe atmosphere for sharing.

• Help form specific support groups: a group for those bereaved by AIDS; groups dealing with abortion; survivors of suicide; etc.

• Accompany the bereaved on their journey from Grief to Hope.

• Remember that a single loss often creates multiple changes/losses on a variety of levels. A death may necessitate a survivor's job change, relocation, financial changes, as well as re-open any previous unresolved griefs. Help to foster reconciliation on the many levels on which grief occurs.

• If an employee dies, acknowledge that people are hurting; relax standards at work in order to let people talk about their pain. See if your employer has an EAP program that offers information and support for grieving employees. Acknowledge the loss.

• Remind the survivors that they still have dignity and value. Help them realize that, even though they have suffered a painful change, they are still valuable human beings.

• Help the survivors (and yourself!) hold onto HOPE.

Many of the concepts in this article came from printed material and a day-long conference, "A Time To Heal ... Providing Outreach and Support To Those Bereaved By AIDS," presented by Patrick Del Zoppo.

Helpful Resources

Videos: *Too Little, Too Late*; *Mother/Mother (Mothers Who Give Care to Children Dying of AIDS)* - both from Fanlight Productions, 47 Halifax Street, Boston, Mass. 02130; (617) 524-0980.

Disenfranchised Grief - Kenneth Doka, Lexington Books, D. C. Heath & Co., 1989. Grief Counseling and Grief Therapy - J. William Worden, Springer Publishing Co., 1982.

A Time To Heal . . . Providing Outreach and Support To Those Bereaved By AIDS - (5) audiotapes of above conference. Available from HOPE FOR BEREAVED, Inc. *(see order form)*.

OTHER HELPFUL INFORMATION

SUGGESTED READING

What follows is a list of books and other resources that provide information on a variety of subjects. It isn't a complete listing, and it doesn't mean that a particular item is the best thing for you. It is important to know that resources are available, and that you find the resources that you need. There are many other materials and subject areas not listed here. A note to HOPE FOR BEREAVED can provide you with information on other resources.

GENERAL READING

Living When A Loved One Has Died - Earl Grollman, Beacon Press, 1977
HOPE FOR BEREAVED: Understanding, Coping And Growing Through Grief - HOPE FOR BEREAVED (see brochure, back of book)
Don't Take My Grief Away From Me - Doug Manning, In-Sight Books, 1979
The Courage to Grieve - Judy Tatelbaum, Harper & Row, 1980. (also available on video)
Why Are The Casseroles Always Tuna? - Darcie Sims, Big A & Co. Productions, 1990. (also available on audio cassette)
Living With Dying; A Guide For Relatives and Friends - Augsburg, 1990
Understanding Mourning - Glen Davidson, Augsburg, 1984
Does Anybody Else Hurt This Bad . . . And Live? - Carlene Eneroth, Otis, 1991
Footsteps Through the Valley - Darcie Sims, Big A & Co. Productions, 1993
Living Through Mourning - Harriet Schiff, Viking, 1986

PARENTAL BEREAVEMENT

The Bereaved Parent - Harriett Schiff, Penguin, 1987
The Grief of Parents ... When A Child Dies - Marg. Miles, The Compassionate Friends, 1978
Healing A Father's Grief - Bill Schatz, Medic Publishing, 1984
Comfort Us, Lord. Our Baby Died - Centering, 1985
Children Die, Too; A Book For Parents - Joy & Marv Johnson, Centering, 1978
Bittersweet . . . Hellogoodbye; A Resource In Planning Farewell Rituals When A Baby Dies - Jane Marie Lamb, 1988

FETAL / INFANT DEATH

Empty Arms; Coping After a Miscarriage, Stillbirth and Infant Death - Sherokee Ilse, 1982
Planning A Precious Goodbye After A Miscarriage, Stillbirth or Infant Death - Pregnancy & Infancy Loss, 1985

SUICIDE

Mourning After Suicide - Lois Bloom, 1986
My Son . . . My Son - Iris Bolton, 1983 (also available on audio cassette)
Andrew, You Died Too Soon - Corinne Chilstrom, 1993
Suicide - Earl Grollman, 1988
Suicide, Your Child Has Died - Adina Wrobleski, 1984
Suicide: Survivors - Adina Wrobleski, 1994

WIDOWED

Widower, When Men Are Left Alone - Scott Campbell, 1987
Learning to Live Again - Sue Carpenter, 1979
When Your Spouse Dies - Kathleen Curry, 1990
Cowbells and Courage - Patrick Page, 1992
Interlude of Widowhood - Patricia Stefano, 1983

BOOKS FOR AND ABOUT CHILDREN

GENERAL READING

Love, Mark: A Journey Through Grief - Mark Scrivani, 1986
Love, Mark: Companions On the Journey - Mark Scrivani, 1990
Thumpy's Story - Nancy Dodge, 1984 (Story book, workbook, coloring book, video, English & Spanish)
Tell Me, Papa - Joy and Marv Johnson, 1978
Lucy Lettuce - Patrick Loring and Joy Johnson, 1994
Emily's Sadhappy Season - Stephen Lowdan, 1993
Sarah's Journey - Alan Wolfelt, 1983
I Heard Your Mommy Died - Mark Scrivani, 1994

ADOLESCENTS

When Death Walks In - Mark Scrivani, 1991
Straight Talk About Death to Teens - Earl Grollman, 1993

SIBLINGS

Where's Jess? - Joy and Marv Johnson, 1982
Children Are Not Paper Dolls - Erin Levy, 1982
Am I Still A Sister? - Alicia Sims, Big A & Co. Productions, 1986
Sibling Grief - Marcia Scherage, 1987

MURDER / VIOLENT DEATH

What Murder Leaves Behind - Doug Magee, 1983
No Time For Goodbyes - Janice Lord, 1987
I Wasn't Ready - John Mundy, 1991

MAGAZINES

Bereavement: A Magazine of Hope and Healing - Bereavement Publishing, Inc., 8133 Telegraph Drive, Colorado Springs, Colorado 80920

TO LOCATE RESOURCES

Centering Corporation, 1531 Saddle Creek, Omaha, NE 68104
Rainbow Connection/Compassion Books, 477 Hannah Branch Road, Burnsville, NC 28714

NATIONAL ORGANIZATIONS THAT OFFER HELP TO THE BEREAVED
providing literature, information and assistance

DEATH OF A CHILD/INFANT

THE COMPASSIONATE FRIENDS
P.O. Box 3696
Oak Brook, IL 60522-3696
(312)990-0010

The Compassionate Friends is a self-help organization for bereaved parents and siblings, which offers support groups a quarterly national newsletter and a quarterly sibling newsletter, books to order and national/regional conferences.

NATIONAL CATHOLIC MINISTRY TO THE BEREAVED (NCMB)
9412 Heath Avenue
Cleveland, OH 44104
(216)441-2125

NCMB offers ongoing education, resources and assistance to dioceses, parishes and caregivers throughout the United States by providing JOURNEY (newsletter), lists of recommended resources, a Starter Kit and an annual national conference.

THE NATIONAL SUDDEN INFANT DEATH SYNDROME ALLIANCE
1314 Bedford Avenue, Suite 210
Baltimore, MD 21208
(410) 653-8226   (800)221-SIDS

The national office supports community chapters for parents whose infant died because of SIDS (crib death). Information available upon request.

PARENTS OF MURDERED CHILDREN (POMC)
100 East Eighth Street, Room B41
Cincinnati, OH 45202
(513)721-5683

POMC supports community chapters for all family members when a loved one has died by murder. They provide emotional support by phone, mail and literature.

SHARE
St. Joseph Health Center
300 First Capitol
St. Charles, MO 63301-2893
(314) 947-6164

SHARE aids in the establishment of community support groups. These groups focus on the needs of parents whose baby has died due to miscarriage, ectopic pregnancy, stillbirth or newborn death. Educational materials and referrals to local Support Groups are available.

DEATH OF A SPOUSE

THEOS FOUNDATION (They Help Each Other Spiritually)
1301 Clark Building
717 Liberty Avenue
Pittsburgh, PA 15222
(412)471-7779

THEOS offers self-help assistance to widowed persons through support groups and educational materials.

WIDOWED PERSONS SERVICE (AARP)

601 East Street NW
Washington, DC 20049

(202) 434-2277

Call for list of publications and for information about services in your community. They offer one-to-one outreach to newly widowed by trained volunteers who themselves have been widowed. Group meetings may also be offered.

SUICIDE

AMERICAN ASSOCIATION OF SUICIDOLOGY

2459 South Ash Street
Denver, CO 80222

(303) 692-0985   (9:00 a.m.-5:00 p.m. Mountain Time)

AAS provides a Directory of Survivor Support Groups, a Directory of Crisis Centers in the United States as well as a listing of resources for survivors. It is not a crisis line.

OTHER

THE ELISABETH KUBLER-ROSS CENTER

South Route 616
Head Waters, VA 24442

(703)396-3441

The center provides workshops, seminars, newsletter, books and audio/video tapes on bereavement.

NATIONAL SELF-HELP CLEARING HOUSE

33 West 42nd Street, Room 620N
New York, NY 10036

(212)840-1259

To obtain information about self-help groups throughout the United States, send a self-addressed stamped envelope to the above address.

RESOURCES

HOPE FOR BEREAVED, INC.

4500 Onondaga Boulevard,
Syracuse, NY 13219

**Rosamond Gifford
CENTER OF HOPE**

(315) 475-HOPE (4673) Helpline
(315) 475-9675 Business Line

HOPE provides four resources for sale (*see order form in the back of the book*):"HOPE FOR BEREAVED: *Understanding, Coping and Growing Through Grief*," "LOVE, MARK: *A Journey Through Grief*," "LOVE, MARK: *Companions On The Journey Through Grief*," "How To Form Support Groups For Grieving People"; The HOPEline, a monthly newsletter; telephone help; workshops and consultations.

ACKNOWLEDGMENTS

I want to express my deepest gratitude to everyone who provided encouragement and ideas in the preparation of this book. Without their help and support this handbook would not have become a reality. It would be impossible to mention everyone by name; however, I do wish to give thanks to the following people:

I am most grateful to my family: to my husband David, who is so special, for his love, support, patience, humor and helpful ideas; to our children - Davy, his wife Jodi, grandson Brando, Tom, Margie and Stephen who were very understanding during the years and especially the past few months when the preparation of this handbook absorbed so much of my time. They offered encouragement as well as very practical help. I also owe special thanks to my Mom, Mary Sharpe, for her example of determination and love which have been needed ingredients to accomplish this book and for her countless hours of proof reading.

My friend, Peggy Dupee, stood by me in my grief from the beginning. She LISTENED patiently and encouraged me to recognize and express my inner feelings. She also helped me to laugh. It was Peggy who first suggested that I put the articles together in a handbook. She gave valuable suggestions throughout its preparation. Peggy, her daughter Brenda and Christine Beattie mimeographed the first handbook.

I appreciate the unfailing encouragement and support in my attempts to write, given by my colleague and friend, Christine Beattie. She filled in for me on countless occasions, handling more than her share of office responsibilities.

There are many writers whose insights have been invaluable to me. The year before Mary died I read a published interview with Dr. Elisabeth Kubler-Ross which helped me greatly, as did Life After Life by Raymond Moody. Rev. Simon Stephens, founder of the Society of The Compassionate Friends in England and author of Death Comes Home gave me the idea to meet with other bereaved parents for support. The Bereaved Parent, by Harriet Schiff helped me to understand my/our grief. Earl Grollman took the time to review our original manuscript and offered his professional advice and encouragement. I have gained many insights from his excellent books.

I will always be grateful to the ROSAMOND GIFFORD CHARITABLE CORPORATION for a grant in 1985 which enabled us to make major revisions in the original handbook and to have it professionally typeset and printed as well as to Dean Lesinski, Director, for his interest and guidance in helping us to reach out to the bereaved.

I extend heartfelt thanks to a talented lady and friend, Kathleen Jacques. Kathy added many new articles; she read and dissected every page with me. Her skillful editorial help, sensitive observations and suggestions greatly enrich this book. I am grateful for all the time that she devoted and for her enthusiastic encouragement.

I appreciate the support of Rev. Joseph Phillips. He has been with us as pastoral counselor since that first meeting in 1978. He helped me to understand the grief I was experiencing. The staff of Family Life Education helped so much in those beginning years.

A special thank you should be made to those who contributed articles, in order of appearance in the book: Rev. Kenneth Czillinger; Mickey Vorobel; Mark Scrivani; Pat Fatti; Eunice Brown; Mary Ballard; Dr. Terry O'Brien; Peggy Dupee; Donna Kalb; Margaret Gerner; Kathleen Jacques; Rev. Joseph H. Phillips; Nan Newman; Christine Beattie; Owen Peltier; Sharon Rusaw; Lois Loucks Sugarman; Mary Sharpe; Widowed Persons Services Support Group of Auburn; Tom Schoeneck; Margie Schoeneck; Bethann Liberty; Kersten Van Meenan; Members of Hope For Youth Support Group; Iris Bolton; Mary Jane Meehan and Norma Griswold. Many of the above are volunteers with HOPE FOR BEREAVED.

I purposely saved our beautiful bereaved volunteers for the last. I value their support, understanding and especially their friendship. They were, and continue to be, so generous with their time and gracious about all the work. They have contributed to the contents and growth of this handbook as well as to the support groups and services. I am grateful to Judy Sugar and Nancy Devine for their fastidious proof reading. I offer my THANKS and APPRECIATION to ALL the volunteers - in particular: Helen Paul; Carol Peltier; Dick and Eunice Brown; Patricia Fatti; Stan Rusaw; Helen Walker; Leo Needham; Margaret Rathburn and Bessie Paloumpis.

Finally, to Mary I offer my everlasting gratitude that you enriched my life; that you continue to enrich it. After your death I eventually learned to more fully appreciate life and the people in my life; to share my grief as well as my joy. As devastated as I felt, I was determined that something good must come out of your tragic death. Mary, you gave me courage to carry on because life, as you lived it, was always full of HOPE.

> *In memory of*
> *Mary T. Schoeneck*
> *whose cheerful spirit*
> *touched the hearts*
> *of all*
> *who knew her*

The above plaque was dedicated to Mary by her coworkers. Mary was adventuresome, thoughtful, compassionate, hardworking and fun loving. She left a lasting impact on her family, friends and patients.

HOPE FOR BEREAVED

SUPPORT GROUPS AND PROGRAMS

For those whose loved one died by

- *ACCIDENT*
- *ILLNESS*
- *MURDER*
- *SUICIDE*

For those who want to help them

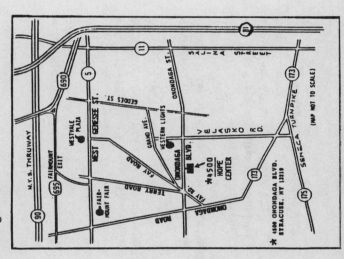

Rosamond Gifford
CENTER OF HOPE

HOPE FOR BEREAVED, INC.
4500 Onondaga Blvd.
Syracuse, NY 13219

The death of a loved one is devastating. Most of us are not prepared for the long journey of grief. Often by the time the reality hits us, friends and relatives think that we are okay and go back to their busy lives. We may have physical symptoms that we do not understand - sleeplessness/oversleeping, loss/gain of weight, tightness in throat, inability to concentrate, headaches, stomach aches, etc. Often we push down feelings of anger because of the mistaken idea that "nice people don't get angry." This is very harmful. Degrees of depression may enter our life and we may think that we are "going crazy." This is normal. It is important to understand grief, to learn coping skills and to have a determination to survive the loss. Hold on to HOPE and join us at a HOPE FOR BEREAVED support group meeting.

DIRECTIONS TO THE HOPE CENTER

FROM THE NORTH: Route 81 south to exit 22, Bear St. (Rt. 298). Right on Bear, follow signs to Rt. 690 west. 690 west to Rt. 695 (towards Camillus). **FROM ALL DIRECTIONS:** Take Fairmount exit, turn left on West Genesee St., go 2 blocks to Terry Road, right on Terry 1.3 miles to Onondaga Blvd.

HOPE FOR BEREAVED
Understanding, Coping And Growing Through Grief

January 1995

A Handbook of Helpful Articles Written by Bereaved People for Bereaved People and Those Who Want to Help Them ...

A helpful gift for families, friends, clergy or funeral directors to give to bereaved people.

The handbook includes suggestions for coping with grief, anger, holidays, guilt, depression, etc. It contains specific articles regarding bereaved, parents, grandparents, widows/widowers, friends, youth, AIDS, murder, suicide and infant death. ($13.50 plus postage; 10 or more copies, $12.50 plus postage)

HOPEline Monthly Newsletter contains helpful articles plus a special letter for children; 11 issues. ($12.00 per year, outside USA, $15.00)

"LOVE, MARK: A Journey Through Grief"; "LOVE, MARK: Companions On the Journey Through Grief." Each book contains hand-printed letters for grieving children/teens. Adults also gain helpful insights. (each book, $7.00 plus postage)

HOW TO FORM SUPPORT GROUPS FOR GRIEVING PEOPLE contains practical ideas, suggestions for publicity, sample notes, etc. ($15.00 plus postage)

ITEM	HOW MANY?	PRICE EACH	TOTAL
HOPE FOR BEREAVED Handbook ★ (see shipping charges)			
The HOPEline NEWSLETTER - 1 year subscription			
"Love, Mark: A Journey Through Grief" ★			
"Love, Mark: Companions On the Journey" ★			
How To Form Support Groups ★			
Donation to help the bereaved			
*Postage & Handling TOTAL ORDER			
$2.50 first book;		POSTAGE	
$.50 each additional book. TOTAL CHECK OR M.O.			

Enclose check or money order
Make check payable to: *HOPE FOR BEREAVED, INC.*

Mail to: **HOPE FOR BEREAVED, INC.**
4500 Onondaga Blvd.
Syracuse, New York 13219

Name _____
Address _____
City _____ State _____ Zip _____
Phone: (___) _____

THE ORGANIZATION

HOPE FOR BEREAVED was founded in 1978. HOPE is an independent, incorporated, not-for-profit community organization dedicated to providing support and services for the bereaved. The staff and volunteers at HOPE are here to help. We have known the pain of grief, struggled with and worked on our grief and finally have made peace with that grief.

Our purpose is to offer understanding, suggestions for coping, support, friendship, and HOPE. We are willing listeners. Families, friends and professionals who wish to help the bereaved turn to HOPE FOR BEREAVED for guidance and resources.

HOPE's services and resources are used locally, nationally and internationally. The help given by HOPE can add greatly to the physical and mental well-being of the grieving and, therefore, to their family and friends. Facts show that unresolved grief may lead to major physical and/or emotional problems, absenteeism, alcoholism, suicide and marital breakup.

Although there is no charge for some of our services, we do have expenses. HOPE's financial support is derived entirely from individual contributions, sale of resources, newsletter subscriptions, grants from foundations, businesses, corporations and service clubs and special events. HOPE does not receive church, state or federal funding. People may designate HOPE FOR BEREAVED on their United Way pledge. Currently, HOPE is raising funds to purchase its permanent bereavement center.

Therese S. Schoeneck
Executive Director
Donna Kalb
Associate Director

TELEPHONE HELPLINE
LISTENING, COUNSELING, REFERRALS
(315) 475-HOPE (4673)
Business (315) 475-WORK (9675)
Monday-Friday, 9:00 AM - 4:00 PM

SUPPORT GROUPS & TELEPHONE HELP
(area code 315)

- **HOPE FOR BEREAVED PARENT(S)**
  David & Bonnie Alsever: 475-4673 (office)
  695-2712 (eve./wknds)
  Ron & Kathy Spencer: 487-2939

  -Meets 3rd Wednesday

- **HOPE FOR YOUTH**
  Who Have Had A Loved One Die
  Mark Scrivani: 656-7846 (office)
  Terrie Conrad: 469-3302

  -Meets 1st & 3rd Wednesday

- **HOPE FOR SURVIVORS**
  Those Whom Suicide Leaves Behind
  Christine Beattie: 488-9902 (eve./wknds)
  Sarah Taisey: 638-7988

  -Meets 2nd Wednesday

- **HOPE FOR BEREAVED:**
  A General Support Group For Anyone Experiencing Death Of A Parent, Relative or Friend
  Sharon Rusaw: 475-4673 (office)
  457-7793 (eve./wknds)
  Terry Pelose: 472-7513

- **HOPE FOR THOSE WHOSE LOVED ONE DIED BY MURDER:**
  Nan Newman: 475-4673 (office)
  455-2800 (eve./wknds)

  -Meets 2nd Tuesday

- **RAINBOW: For Younger Widows/Widowers**
  Eileen Essi: 445-0734
  Judy Sugar: 622-3695 (eve./wknds)

  -Meets 2nd Wednesday

  -Meets 1st Wednesday

- **S.I.D.S.: Hope For Parents Whose Infant Died**
  by SUDDEN INFANT DEATH SYNDROME:
  Maureen O'Hara 478-7937

  -Meets 1st Thursday

- **SHARE: Hope For Parents Whose Infant Died**
  by Miscarriage, Stillbirth or Newborn Death
  Kathie Huffer: 458-8081

  -Meets 1st Thursday

- **PALS: Pregnancy After Loss Support**
  Denise Cote Arsenault: 682-9325
  Nancy Feinstein: 682-7974

  -Call regarding meeting date

- **HOPE FOR THOSE BEREAVED BY AIDS:**
  Donna Kalb: 475-4673 (office)
  474-3745 (eve./wknds)

  -Meets 2nd Monday

- **HOPE FOR WIDOWS & WIDOWERS**
  Helen Paul: 673-3231
  Jeanne Bosch: 673-3195

  -Meets 2nd Thursday

  Daytime Group 10:00 am - 12:00 Noon 3rd Wednesday

  NOTE: HOPE's Telephone Helpline (315) 475-HOPE (4673) is available MONDAY - FRIDAY 9:00 am - 4:00 pm. We are not a 24-hour hotline. If you need to speak with someone from 9:00 pm to 9:00 am, please call CONTACT (315) 425-1500.

SUPPORT GROUPS

Evening Meetings are from 7:00 - 9:00 pm. Facilitators are available at 6:30 pm to those attending their first meeting. The bereaved, their relatives and friends are welcome to attend meetings, ask questions, make suggestions or just listen.

OTHER SERVICES

- *HOPEline monthly newsletter contains helpful articles*

- *Community Education: presentations for hospital personnel, church groups, students, teachers, clergy, agencies, funeral directors, etc.*

- *Letter of condolence with articles sent to newly bereaved*

- *Counseling visits (up to three) at our Center (we are not therapists; we are trained bereavement counselors and have the lived experience.)*

- *Direct mailings to professionals*

- *Mailings of requested materials to individuals*

- *Presentations/materials/consultations to individuals to aid in the establishment of new Support Groups/Services locally, nationally and internationally*

- *Published resources:*
  - HOPE FOR BEREAVED: Understanding, Coping and Growing Through Grief
  - LOVE, MARK I and II (books for children)
  - HOW TO FORM SUPPORT GROUPS AND SERVICES FOR GRIEVING PEOPLE

- *Garden Therapy - Memorial and volunteer opportunities*

- 6TH EDITION -

"HOPE FOR BEREAVED"
Understanding, Coping and Growing Through Grief

A Handbook of helpful articles written by bereaved people for bereaved people and those who want to help them. A superb gift to give to bereaved. Also recommended for counselors, funeral directors, support group leaders, teachers, and church or hospital personnel. *($13.50 plus postage; 10 or more copies, $12.50 plus postage—see shipping charges)*

LOVE, MARK: A Journey Through Grief and *LOVE, MARK: Companions On The Journey Through Grief.* Each book contains handprinted letters for grieving children, teens and young adults. The letters cover different aspects or problems of grief. People of all ages will gain helpful insights. *(each book, $7.00 plus postage—see shipping charges)*

HOW TO FORM SUPPORT GROUPS AND SERVICES FOR GRIEVING PEOPLE. Newly revised book contains practical ideas, suggestions for publicity, sample notes, newsletters, funding, volunteers and various brochures. *($15.00 plus postage—see shipping charges)*

HOPEline NEWSLETTER contains helpful articles, plus a special hand-scripted letter for children on various aspects of grief; 11 issues. *($12.00 per year; outside USA, $15.00)*

★ ☆ ★

ORDER FORM

ITEM	HOW MANY?	PRICE EACH	TOTAL
HOPE FOR BEREAVED Handbook *(see shipping charges)*			
LOVE, MARK: A Journey Through Grief *(see shipping charges)*			
LOVE, MARK: Companions On The Journey *(see shipping charges)*			
HOW TO FORM SUPPORT GROUPS *(see shipping charges)*			
HOPEline NEWSLETTER (1 yr. subscription)			
Audiotapes			
CULTURAL CONSTRUCTION OF AIDS - Susan Bordo		$5.00	
UNDERSTANDING ISSUES OF COMPLICATED AIDS GRIEF - Patrick Del Zoppo		$5.00	
GRIEF AFTER AN AIDS DEATH - Bereaved Family Member		$5.00	
RESPONDING TO NEEDS OF THOSE BEREAVED BY AIDS - Patrick Del Zoppo		$5.00	
A TIME TO HEAL ... FOR THOSE BEREAVED BY AIDS - Patrick Del Zoppo		$5.00	

	Total Order
SHIPPING CHARGES	Postage & Handling
$2.50 first book	
$.50 each additional book	
$1.50 per tape	
OUTSIDE USA	Donation
Payment must be made in US Funds	
$3.50 first book	Total of Check or M.O.
$1.00 each additional book	

Payment Must Accompany Order
(allow 4 weeks)

Make check or money order payable to and mail to:

HOPE FOR BEREAVED, INC.
4500 Onondaga Boulevard
Syracuse, New York 13219
(315) 475-HOPE (4673)
(315) 475-9675

Name _____ Phone (_____)

Address _____

City _____ State _____ Zip _____

"HOPE FOR BEREAVED is a wonderfully helpful book for all those who are bereaved, and those who try to help their fellowman work through such a crisis."

— ELISABETH KUBLER-ROSS, M.D.

"HOPE FOR BEREAVED is a magnificent source book of information and inspiration."

— RABBI EARL GROLLMAN

To: **PURCHASERS OF "HOPE FOR BEREAVED"**
From: **Therese S. Schoeneck**
Re: **Publicity of "HOPE FOR BEREAVED" Book**

If appropriate, we would greatly appreciate the following notice being placed in your newsletter, local church/synagogue newspapers, bulletins, or other publications. Please use as much of the following Press Release as space permits. We appreciate your efforts in this matter.

PRESS RELEASE

"HOPE FOR BEREAVED: Understanding, Coping and Growing Through Grief" contains helpful articles for those grieving/those who want to help them. Includes articles on grief, anger, holidays, guilt, depression, murder, suicide, AIDS, plus specific articles regarding the death of family members and friends. *Cost:* $13.50 plus $2.50 postage and handling. Make check payable and mail to: HOPE FOR BEREAVED, INC., 4500 Onondaga Blvd., Syracuse, NY 13219.

- OR -

Are you, or is someone you know, grieving? **"HOPE FOR BEREAVED: Understanding, Coping and Growing Through Grief"** contains realistic, helpful articles for the bereaved, their relatives, friends, and those in the helping professions. The book includes suggestions for coping with grief, anger, holidays, guilt, depression, etc. A unique graph describes the various experiences of grief. Specific articles deal with bereaved parents, grandparents, grieving youth, widows/widowers, death by AIDS, murder, suicide, infant death. *Cost:* $13.50 plus $2.50 postage and handling. Make check payable and mail to: HOPE FOR BEREAVED, INC., 4500 Onondaga Blvd., Syracuse, NY 13219.